UNDERSTANDING MATHEMATICS AND COMPUTERS

A Popular Introduction

K.V. MITAL
M.Sc., Ph.D.

PUBLISHING FOR ONE WORLD

NEW AGE INTERNATIONAL (P) LIMITED, PUBLISHERS
(formerly Wiley Eastern Limited)

New Delhi • Bangalore • Chennai • Cochin • Guwahati • Hyderabad
Jalandhar • Kolkata • Lucknow • Mumbai • Ranchi

Visit us at www.newagepublishers.com

Published by New Age International (P) Ltd., Publishers
First Edition: 1997
Reprint: 2008

ISBN: 81-224-0387-5

Rs. 450.00

C-07-09-2034

3 4 5 6 7 8 9 10

Printed in India at A.H. Print Pack, Delhi.

PUBLISHING FOR ONE WORLD

NEW AGE INTERNATIONAL (P) LIMITED, PUBLISHERS

(formerly Wiley Eastern Limited)

4835/24, Ansari Road, Daryaganj, New Delhi - 110002

Visit us at **www.newagepublishers.com**

UNDERSTANDING MATHEMATICS AND COMPUTERS

"As crest on a peacock, ruby on the head of the king of snakes, so does mathematics stand at the head of all knowledge."

– *Vedang Jyotish*

"Why discourse at length? In the entire universe of the living and the nonliving, there is hardly a thing whose basis is not mathematics."

– *Mahavira*

Introduction

Mathematics: Not a Static Art but a way of Thought

Never before in recorded history had humans acquired so much knowledge of the physical world and succeeded in building a civilization of such amazing technological achievements as the present. Everybody knows that science is at the root of this progress. The pace of development of scientific knowledge and technological innovations is becoming faster and faster everyday, and there seems to be no end to either of these. Most educated people are also aware that mathematics has played an important role in this advancement. Yet, strangely, many people are not even conscious of the fact that alongwith all other sciences mathematics has also been growing, that new mathematics is being created or discovered every day at an increasing pace, that much of the mathematics that is taught in colleges today was unknown two hundred years ago and some of it is as recent as fifty years. To many mathematics is a static art, a body of knowledge consisting of eternal truths handed down to us from ancient times, such as, two plus two is always four and the three angles of a triangle always add up to two right angles. What room is there for research? What new things can be found out?

But mathematics has been growing steadily since the earliest times during all civilizations, in Egypt and Mesopotamia, in India and China, in Greece, in the Arab world, and finally in modern times. The tempo of research and development today is greater than at any time in the past. No mathematician today knows all mathematics. There is practically no branch of science, engineering or technology which does not make extensive use of known mathematics and pose new problems in seeking solutions of which new mathematics is generated. There is no end to discoveries in mathematics just as there is no end to the mystery of the universe. Both are boundless. Hence mathematics is not so much a body of knowledge as a way of thought with inexhaustible possibilities.

New Mathematics

While at the higher level of research and application to technology and natural and social sciences mathematics is making spectacular progress, its nature and role in modern civilization is not commensurately appreciated by common people. The reason partly was that at the school level, courses in arithmetic, algebra and geometry remained unchanged for generations. Of course, much of it has necessarily to remain unchanged, but advances at higher levels do produce significant changes in basic ideas which can be introduced at school level. The experience of introducing changes in school curricula to bring in ideas of what is often referred to as 'new' or 'modern' mathematics has not been without difficulties. Some mathematicians, in their zeal, tried to pump down to the students not only the substance but also, to a certain degree, the form which they had given to mathematics at the higher level. The substance must necessarily percolate down, as it happens in all areas of knowledge, with educational curricula undergoing gradual changes, incorporating new topics and leaving out what may be regarded as dead wood. There is nothing wrong in exerting a little pressure to accelerate the process. But the mathematicians were too eager to initiate the learners, while they were in their teens, into the logical elegance of mathematical abstractions. They overlooked that human mind goes from concrete to abstract, from particular to general, and in the learning process perception of situations based on sense experience and intuition comes first, and logic and abstract generalizations come later.

A Useful Acquisition

Mathematics, despite its modern day penchant for axiomatic structures, is a useful intellectual acquisition solidly based on man's experience of the world around him and his unending quest to unravel its mysteries. In that lies its usefulness. Because of its social worth more and more persons are drawn to it, but perhaps with less and less interest and appreciation. The textbooks often present a body of weird information easier to cram than appreciate. The situation gets worse by the fact that many newer topics were never learned by the teachers themselves. At school level, the teachers are sometimes as much at bay as the parents, and mathematics becomes a dull subject meant only for those 'born with a talent for mathematics'.

Nothing is more detrimental to the study of mathematics than the myth that it requires some special gift. If mathematicians are born, then, well, all great persons in all areas of knowledge and activity are born. But the subject can be learnt intelligently and applied gainfully upto a point by any person intelligent enough to profit from education.

Computer Revolution

When the future generations look back on the history of development of science, technology and civilization, they would, without doubt, regard the computer as the most significant invention of the twentieth century. It has given a new dimension to the capabilities and potentialities of the human race. There is scarcely a field of human endeavour where computers are not aiding or will not aid future growth. Computer literacy, the ability to use computer in one's own area, will in the near future become the basic accomplishment for everybody.

Modern mathematics is at the base of the design and use of the computer. To accomplish any task on the computer, we have to have a 'programme' for that task in a highly formalized language. To be able to write or use a programme, or even to appreciate the concept behind it, a little familiarity with some elementary ideas in modern mathematics is helpful. This puts some new but essentially simple mathematics almost in the same category as the three R's.

What this Book is About?

The present book is a popular introduction to some elementary mathematical ideas including those related to the computer, and is aimed at the general educated public – parents, teachers and the students. It presumes that the reader possesses a knowledge of traditional school mathematics – arithmetic, elementary algebra and elementary plane geometry. It attempts to enlighten the readers about some concepts in modern mathematics which are no more complicated or advanced than the mathematics they already know. It aims to impress that mathematics is a growing subject, and new situations, experiences or requirements lead to invention of new mathematics. It does not aim to be a learned discourse on the nature, history or development of mathematics. Yet, it attempts to give a feel of all aspects of mathematics, its history, its intuitive and common sense basis, the abstraction and logical elegance of the finished product, its usefulness and aesthetic appeal, without unduly emphasizing any one aspect or going beyond the simplest of notions. It is a 'rapid reader' to heighten the reader's appreciation of mathematics, and can be read with profit by students and others merely for cultural enjoyment.

Most chapters can be read independently of others, but a sequential reading would be more rewarding. Exercises at the end of chapters are provided in deference to the admirable belief that mathematics, even as a light reading, is incomplete without sums. However, it is not essential to do them.

Contents

Chapter 1

Numbers, Numerals and Scales of Notation

"Mathematics is nothing more than a game played according to certain rules with meaningless marks on paper."

—David Hilbert, German mathematician (1862—1943)

Like all quotations torn out of context, the above quotation, while expressing a truth, can be misunderstood if the word 'meaningless' is taken too literally. A characteristic feature of all mathematics is the symbols (or marks, of the above quotation) and their manipulation by certain 'rules of the game'. While the symbols are arbitrary, neither they nor the rules by which they are manipulated are exactly meaningless. They represent ideas which, in ultimate analysis, express some truth of human experience. The same truth may be expressed through a variety of symbols.

A human being, inspite of his intellect, is by and large a habit forming animal. With the exception of a gifted few, people think in mental grooves of long habit. For them the symbols become the truth. A remarkable example of this is the way the infinite (or non-ending) set of numbers, namely, one, two, three, four, etc, through which we count have got mixed up in the common mind with the numerals or the symbols we use to denote them. 'One plus one is two' is supposed to be obvious to one with even the meanest intelligence, but only so long as it is written in the familiar notation,

$$1 + 1 = 2.$$

But a different notation, such as,

$$1 + 1 = 10$$

is enough to rattle most people throughout the world.

Every child begins his education by learning to count. Aeons ago, as some anthropoid struggled to become human, one of the first triumphs of his capacity for abstract thinking must have been to identify in a collection of discrete objects a property which we now call number. A collection of students, a collection of desks and a collection of chairs in a classroom may be such that each student has one desk and one chair to himself, and neither a desk nor a chair is in excess. The three collections then have a common property called number. It is this property which a child begins to discern as he learns counting.

Packets of Ten

In the familiar system of writing numbers, we use ten symbols: 0, 1, 2, 3, 4, 5, 6, 7, 8, 9; and with these we can write any number however large. We need ten different symbols because we count in packets of ten. We use zero in a very special manner. Its use perhaps dates back to only about fifteen hundred years. The Romans had no such notation. It is now well established that its invention took place in India in the sixth century, and the Europeans received it through the Arabs in the twelfth century of the christian era. As distinct from the notation in which zero plays a vital role, the scale of ten, namely, the system in which

Eleven is ten and one,
Twenty is ten and ten or two tens,
Forty-five is four tens and five,
Hundred is ten tens,
Thousand is ten hundreds,
and so on,

can be traced far into antiquity. In the *Atharvaveda* occurs a hymn which gives distinct names to powers of ten upto what is now called a trillion or a million million. But what habit makes most of us overlook is the fact that the choice of ten is quite arbitrary. It is the result of biological design of our having ten fingers. If we had only eight, we would perhaps be counting in eights. In fact from one point of view ten has not been a very happy choice. Twelve would have been more convenient. Ten is divisible by only two and five, while twelve can be evenly divided by two, three, four and six.

In modern mathematics other scales of notation have assumed significance. The digital computer, which is revolutionising civilization in the present era as no machine had ever done before, is a prodigy in speed but woefully primitive in many other respects. It has, to speak figuratively, only two fingers, or, in more matter of fact language, two distinctly recognisable states, and so can count only in two's. The scale of two thus becomes important.

Symbols for Numbers

Before considering how any number can be represented by only two symbols, let us have a close look at the way natural numbers (that is, numbers used in counting) can be at all represented. The most elementary procedure would be to make a mark for each item counted, the same mark being used repeatedly. The totality of marks would stand for the corresponding number. The drawback becomes obvious when the number becomes large. One must still count to know the number, and for each collection there has to be a separate name. An infinity of names for an infinity of collections! Even with this serious limitation it is perhaps the only way to make a child understand counting.

An obvious improvement would be to introduce additional symbols for standard collections of marks. The ancient Egyptians had hieroglyphics (picture symbols) for ten, hundred, thousand, etc, upto ten-million. In the Roman system of writing numbers which is still sometimes used, though for limited purposes, V, X, L, C, M stand for symbols for collections of five, ten, fifty, hundred and thousand, respectively. Aryabhat I (born 476 A.D.) described a method of writing numbers through Sanskrit words using thirty-three consonants and nine vowels of the Sanskrit alphabet, and used it to write very concisely very large numbers occurring in his astronomical calculations. Whatever be the symbols – they have a long history of evolution and change – the denary scale, as the scale of ten is called, has been widely prevalent for counting since very ancient times. But the alternatives did exist. For example, as early as 1700 B.C. the ancient Mesopotamians are believed to have evolved a system of counting in groups of sixty, known as the sexagesimal system. It was used for scientific and astronomical work for centuries. The motivation came from the fact that the two natural units of time, the year and the day, were connected through this number, the year being believed to consist of 360 days. Although not very convenient because of the large number of symbols required, ancient records show that as late as 300 B.C. astronomers were carrying out calculations upto seventeen digits in the sexagesimal system which is equivalent to twenty-nine digits on the denary scale. We still have the remnants of this old system in our measurement of time – sixty seconds making a minute and sixty minutes an hour – and also in the division of four right angles into 360 degrees.

Fruitless Diversity

For counting in an abstract sense the denary scale came to be used extensively, but there was no such uniformity in applying the same principle to devise suitable multiples and submultiples of units of measurements for various things. Wide diversity exists in this respect all over the world even to this day. For example, in India, till a few decades ago, the rupee was divided into sixteen annas, and an anna into four pice or twelve pies; the maund was divided into forty seers, the seer into sixteen chhataks; and so on. A mile consists of eight furlongs, and a furlong of two hundred twenty yards, and a yard of three feet. Such examples can be given from all countries and almost all units of weight, measure, money, length, area, etc. A whole lot of units of measurements with multiples or submultiples of sixty, twenty, twelve, eight, six, four and three exist. This leads to complicated conversion factors. Till not long ago much of the arithmetic in lower school classes consisted of problems arising out of these complications. The French or the metric system in which all multiples and submultiples of a unit follow the scale of ten does away with this fruitless exercise. That is why the wind in favour of the decimal system of units has started blowing strongly and more and more countries are progressively adopting this system.

Invention of Zero

The exact history of the invention of zero is still obscure. The attempts to give place value to a symbol can be traced back to much earlier times. The abacus, a mechanical device consisting of counters (nowadays usually in the form of beads) sliding along rods or in grooves, is a familiar aid to teach counting to children. It is very ancient. It is the earliest calculating machine, and represents an attempt at positional notation. One can make an abacus on a paper or a slate by drawing columns and record a number in it by showing the number of counters in each column by some symbol, say x (Fig. 1.1). Starting from right, in the first column each counter means one, in the second column each counter indicates ten, in the third it signifies one hundred, and so on. A blank column indicates absence of any number in it. The number written in Fig. 1.1 is thus three ten-thousand plus two thousand plus four ten plus one. Assuming symbols for one, two, three and four as they are now, one could write this number as in Fig. 1.2 which is also an abacus. Erase the lines indicating the columns and one is left with a blank space between 2 and 4.

3 2   4 1

This was the sort of attempt made prior to the invention of zero not only for the denary but also for the sexagesimal system of the Mesopotamians. But leaving a blank was hardly satisfactory as in hand writing the length of intervening space could not be standardised and one could not unambiguously show the blank spaces without drawing compartments or columns. The next step was to show the blank by a dot which finally came to be recognised as a necessary symbol now called zero. It is significant that *shunya* in Sanskrit means empty, its Arabic equivalent being *sifr* from which are derived both *cipher* and *zero*.

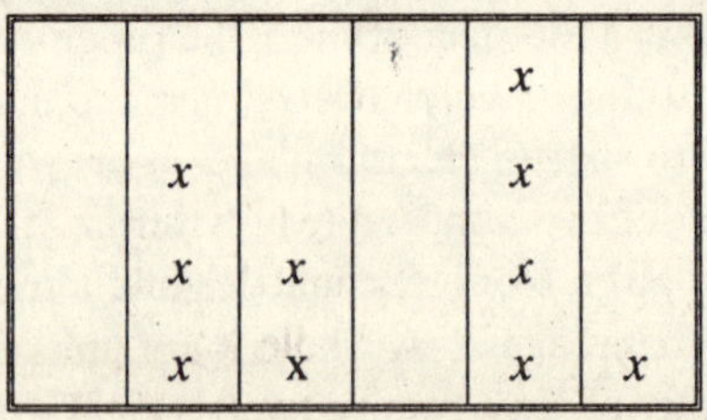

Fig. 1.1

	3	2		4	1

Fig. 1.2

The introduction of zero and the positional system of notation for the denary scale took place in India in the sixth century and gradually travelled to Europe through the Arabs. Around 825 A.D. an Arab mathematician, Al-Khwarizmi, wrote a book on Indian numerals and commended the new technique from the East to the merchants and mathematicians of the West. They were however slow to adopt it and it took almost 600 years for the system to finally supersede the other systems.

Base of Eight

Let us now see how we can write a number to some base other than ten. Suppose we have only eight symbols, 0, 1, 2, 3, 4, 5, 6, 7. Then using the same principle as in denary notation we write the sequence of natural numbers to the base eight, or in the octal system (as it is called), as follows:

1	11	21	..	..	71
2	12	22	..	..	72
3	13	23	..	..	73
4	14	24	..	..	74
5	15	25	..	..	75
6	16	26	..	..	76
7	17	27	..	..	77
10	20	30	..	..	100

Here 7 denotes seven, but 10 denotes eight, 11 denotes eight and one, 12 denotes eight and two, 20 two eights, 77 seven eights and seven (or sixty-three as we call it ordinarily), and finally 100 denotes eight eights (or 8^2 or sixty-four in denary). A shift of a digit by one place to the left implies that its value becomes eight times its previous value. Thus, 10000 represents the number with which we are familiar as 8^4 or 4096 in denary, and 2364 in octal denotes the number which in denary is $2 \times 8^3 + 3 \times 8^2 + 6 \times 8 + 4 = 1268$. It should be noticed that the symbols 8 and 9 do not exist in the octal scale, and the only way to interpret 2364 in the octal without falling back on the denary scale is to write $2364 = 2 \times 10^3 + 3 \times 10^2 + 6 \times 10 + 4$ with 10 standing for eight. It is customary to indicate the base of a notation as a subscript after the numeral. For example, the above number in octal would be written as $(2364)_8$ and its equivalent in denary as $(1268)_{10}$. For convenience the subscripts are always written in the familiar denary notation.

Binary System

In the binary system there are only two symbols, conventionally taken as 0 and 1. Using 0 in the same way as before, we can write the natural numbers to the base two as follows:

Binary		Denary
1	one	$1 = 1$
10	two	$1 \times 2^1 + 0 = 2$
11	three	$1 \times 2^1 + 1 = 3$
100	four	$1 \times 2^2 + 0 \times 2^1 + 0 = 4$
101	five	$1 \times 2^2 + 0 \times 2^1 + 1 = 5$
110	six	$1 \times 2^2 + 1 \times 2^1 + 0 = 6$
111	seven	$1 \times 2^2 + 1 \times 2^1 + 1 = 7$
1000	eight	$1 \times 2^3 + 0 \times 2^2 + 0 \times 2^1 + 0 = 8$

and so on. Since we have only two symbols, all numbers in the binary are written as strings of 0's and 1's. For example,

$$\begin{aligned}(1101011)_2 &= 1 \times 2^6 + 1 \times 2^5 + 0 \times 2^4 + 1 \times 2^3 + 0 \times 2^2 + 1 \times 2 + 1 \\ &= (107)_{10}\end{aligned}$$

The inverse operation of writing a given denary number in binary is a little more complicated. It is accomplished by expressing the number as a polynomial in powers of 2, the coefficient of each term being 0 or 1. Thus

$$\begin{aligned}(243)_{10} &= 1 \times 2^7 + 1 \times 2^6 + 1 \times 2^5 + 1 \times 2^4 + 0 \times 2^3 + 0 \times 2^2 + 1 \times 2^1 + 1 \\ &= (11110011)_2\end{aligned}$$

A simple rule for doing this is the following. Successively divide the given denary number (here 243) by 2, each time writing down the remainder which will be either 1 or 0.

Successive division by 2	$\frac{243}{2}$	$\frac{121}{2}$	$\frac{60}{2}$	$\frac{30}{2}$	$\frac{15}{2}$	$\frac{7}{2}$	$\frac{3}{2}$	$\frac{1}{2}$
Quotient	121	60	30	15	7	3	1	0
Remainder	1	1	0	0	1	1	1	1

Writing the string of remainders, starting from the last, we get the binary equivalent 11110011.

It is paradoxical indeed that since the days of ancient Mesopotamians over three thousand five hundred years ago, humans have moved from the sexagesimal system with its extraordinarily large number of different symbols to the binary system with only two, the minimum possible. The human race left to itself had almost settled for the convenient base ten, but for the creature of its own genius, the digital computer, more than two symbols are far too many to be distinctly recognisable. The more the computer with its amazing speed accomplishes for humankind, the more it will have to rely on the two-based number system for its work, at least till the recognition powers of the computer improve.

Radix Point

So far we have seen how natural numbers can be written in different scales of notation. But all the numbers are not natural numbers. We shall discuss the evolution of different types of numbers in a later chapter. But we all know from elementary arithmetic that there are fractions like 2/3, 192/60, in general like p/q, where p and q are whole numbers. The fractions reduce to whole numbers when $q = 1$ or p is completely divisible by q. (The number p/q is not defined for $q = 0$, but this and other such matters we shall discuss later). A fraction can be written in decimals by performing the operation of division on p by q. Thus

$$2/3 = 0.6666666...$$

$$192/60 = 3.2$$

Some fractions can be expressed in terms of a finite number of digits, like 192/60, while others need an infinity of digits (or a nonending string of digits), like 2/3. The latter type cannot be exactly expressed in terms of decimals because it is not physically possible to write *all* the digits. By making the string sufficiently long we may write a number close enough to the fraction but never equal to it. There is another type of number also, like $\sqrt{2}$, which cannot be expressed in the form p/q but can be written as a nonending string of digits in decimal notation (for example, $\sqrt{2} = 1.414.....$).

The introduction of decimal point extends the principle of positional notation to the right of the unit position. The first place to the right of the decimal point gives to the numeral one-tenth its normal value, the second place one-hundredth its value, and so on. Thus, to take some examples,

$$3.2 = 3 + \frac{2}{10}$$

$$1.414 = 1 + \frac{4}{10} + \frac{1}{100} + \frac{4}{1000}$$

$$53.69 = 5 \times 10 + 3 + \frac{6}{10} + \frac{9}{100}$$

To bring about uniformity of notation, it is possible to write

$$1 \text{ as } 10^0, \frac{1}{10} \text{ as } 10^{-1}, \frac{1}{100} \text{ as } 10^{-2}, \text{ and so on.}$$

Then $\quad 53.69 = 5 \times 10^1 + 3 \times 10^0 + 6 \times 10^{-1} + 9 \times 10^{-2}$

On the same principle, the positional notation can be extended to other base systems also. But the decimal point in the other scales should be given some other name as the word 'decimal' is etymologically related to ten. A general name has been coined to cover all cases – the *radix point*. In the octal system the numerals to the right of the radix point have positional values $8^{-1}, 8^{-2}, 8^{-3}, ...$ times their normal values. Accordingly

$$(6.25)_8 = 6 + 2 \times 8^{-1} + 5 \times 8^{-2} = (6.328125)_{10}$$

Similarly, in the binary notation the positional values of the numerals to the right of the radix point are successively $2^{-1}, 2^{-2}, 2^{-3}, ...$ times their normal values, so that

$$(10.11)_2 = 1 \times 2^1 + 0 \times 2^0 + 1 \times 2^{-1} + 1 \times 2^{-2} = (2.75)_{10}$$

Four Simple Operations

The operations of addition, subtraction, multiplication and division among numbers written to bases other than ten present no new problems. The procedures remain the same as in the denary system. They may look complicated due to non-familiarity. To take examples of the octal scale,

$$\begin{array}{r} (3214)_8 \\ +\,(1256)_8 \\ \hline (4472)_8 \end{array} \qquad \text{because } (4)_8 + (6)_8 = (12)_8$$

$$\begin{array}{r} (3214)_8 \\ -\,(1256)_8 \\ \hline (1736)_8 \end{array} \qquad \begin{array}{l} \text{because } (14)_8 - (6)_8 = (6)_8 \\ (10)_8 - (5)_8 = (3)_8 \\ (11)_8 - (2)_8 = (7)_8 \end{array}$$

$$\begin{array}{r} (24)_8 \\ \times\,(6)_8 \\ \hline (170)_8 \end{array} \qquad \begin{array}{l} \text{because } (6)_8 \times (4)_8 = (30)_8 \\ (6)_8 \times (2)_8 = (14)_8 \end{array}$$

$$(4)_8 \,\big)\, (36)_8 \,\big(\, (7.4)_8 \quad \text{because} \quad (4)_8 \times (7)_8 = (34)_8$$

$$\begin{array}{r} 34 \\ \hline 20 \\ 20 \\ \hline 0 \end{array} \qquad (4)_8 \times (4)_8 = (20)_8$$

In the binary system the apparent complexity of the above examples disappears. Since there are only two symbols, either a position is occupied by 0 or by 1. The procedures for the four elementary arithmetical operations turn out to be simple enough to be reduced to 'mechanical' rules. Indeed therein lies the secret of a machine being able to do them easily.

With two symbols only the following four cases of addition and four of multiplication arise.

Addition

0 + 0 = 0
0 + 1 = 1
1 + 0 = 1
1 + 1 = 10

+	0	1
0	0	1
1	1	0 with 1 to 'carry over'

Multiplication

0 × 0 = 0
0 × 1 = 0
1 × 0 = 0
1 × 1 = 1

×	0	1
0	0	0
1	0	1

The tables given on the right side above indicate a concise way of writing the addition and multiplication rules. With no preconceived notions, it would be far easier to do the sums in binary than in denary. Here are a few examples:

```
  101101        101101
+ 110110        -10110
 1100011         10111

  101101     11) 1001 (11
×    101          11
  101101           11
 000000            11
101101              0
11100001
```

The reader may find it interesting to write the above problems in denary and verify.

There is a rule of doing subtraction which may appear somewhat round about but which is particularly convenient for binary numbers. It essentially reduces subtraction to addition, and is therefore especially suited for machine calculation so that the machine can handle both addition and subtraction by the same mechanism.

To describe this method we first define the complement of a binary number. The complement of 0 is 1 and of 1 is 0 in the binary system. The complement of a binary number is obtained by replacing every digit in that number by its complement. It is obvious that the sum of a number and its complement is a number in which all the digits are 1. Also the number of digits in a number, in its complement, and in the sum of the two are equal. For example, for a six-digit number 101110,

$$\begin{array}{rl} 101110 & \text{original number} \\ +\ 010001 & \text{complement} \\ \hline 111111 & \\ \hline \end{array}$$

or, which means the same thing,

$$\begin{array}{rl} 111111 & \\ -\ 101110 & \text{original number} \\ \hline 010001 & \text{complement} \\ \hline \end{array}$$

We are now in a position to understand the rule for subtraction. Suppose we have to subtract y (= 101110) from x (= 111001), $y \leq x$. It is easy to follow the following steps.

$$\begin{aligned} x - y &= 111001 - 101110 \\ &= 111001 - (111111 - 010001) \\ &= 111001 + 010001 - 111111 \\ &= 111001 + 010001 - (1000000 - 1) \\ &= 111001 + 010001 + 1 - 1000000 \\ &= x + \text{complement of } y + 1 - 1000000 \end{aligned}$$

This means we can do subtraction as follows.

$$\begin{array}{rl} 111001 & x \\ +\ 010001 & \text{complement of } y \\ \hline 1001010 & \\ -\ 1000000 & \\ \hline 001010 & \\ +\ \quad\ \ 1 & \\ \hline 001011 & x - y \end{array}$$

or more simply as

$$\begin{array}{rl} 111001 & x \\ +\ 010001 & \text{complement of } y \\ \hline 1001010 & \text{remove 1 from extreme left and add} \\ & \text{to extreme right} \\ 001011 & \end{array}$$

As we shall see later (chapter 5), these steps can be taken more conveniently by the computer than those involved in direct subtraction.

We conclude this section by an example to illustrate how a number in the denary scale can be transcribed in the binary. We shall write .2 of the ordinary decimal notation in binary.

$$(.2)_{10} = \left(\frac{1}{5}\right)_{10} = \left(\frac{1}{101}\right)_{2}$$

Let us divide $(1)_2$ by $(101)_2$

```
          .0011001.....
    101 | 1.0000000.....
            101
          ---------
            110
            101
          ---------
             1000
              101
          ---------
              ...
```

The above division operation will never terminate. Thus

$$(.2)_{10} = (.001100110011.......)_2$$

It is an example of recurring 'decimal' in the binary. This brings out a fact of great significance in numerical mathematics. A number expressible in finite number of digits in one scale of notation may not be expressed in finite terms in another scale. Since in practical numerical work numbers have to be rounded off to some finite number of digits, those which are supposed to be exact in the denary system may involve some error in conversion to binary, and vice versa.

Via Media

The inordinate length of a number in binary is rather discouraging to us, though it is no problem to the computer. The human programmers, not only from habit but also for conciseness, think in denary but have to communicate with the computer in binary. The conversion is hardly convenient. As a compromise they find the base eight more suitable. It is only a little less concise than the base ten, but its conversion to binary and vice versa can be done just by inspection. A close look at the following table suggests how this can be done.

Denary	Octal	Binary	Denary	Octal	Binary
0	0	000	9	11	1,001
1	1	001	10	12	1,010
2	2	010	11	13	1,011
3	3	011	12	14	1,100
4	4	100	13	15	1,101
5	5	101	14	16	1,110
6	6	110	15	17	1,111
7	7	111	16	20	10,000
8	10	1,000	17	21	10,001

We need three positions of the binary to write one digit of the octal. Therefore, reading the binary numerals from the right in groups of three, each group can be replaced by the corresponding octal digit. Thus the binary number $(101, 110, 001, 101, 010, 001)_2$ is $(561521)_8$, because $(101)_2$ is $(5)_8$, $(110)_2$ is $(6)_8$, and so on.

Lately the hexadecimal base (that is, counting in packets of sixteen) which is still more concise has come into use for interpreting and handling large binary numbers. The hexadecimal notation requires sixteen different symbols to denote numbers from 0 to 15. We already have ten (0 to 9). The letters A, B, C, D, E, F have been adopted as the next six. The following table gives the hexadecimal and binary equivalents of numbers.

Denary	Hexa-decimal	Binary	Denary	Hexa-decimal	Binary
0	0	0000	16	10	1,0000
1	1	0001	17	11	1,0001
2	2	0010	18	12	1,0010
3	3	0011	19	13	1,0011
4	4	0100	20	14	1,0100
5	5	0101	21	15	1,0101
6	6	0110	22	16	1,0110
7	7	0111	23	17	1,0111
8	8	1000	24	18	1,1000
9	9	1001	25	19	1,1001
10	A	1010	26	1A	1,1010
11	B	1011	27	1B	1,1011
12	C	1100	28	1C	1,1100
13	D	1101	29	1D	1,1101
14	E	1110	30	1E	1,1110
15	F	1111	31	1F	1,1111

It will be noticed that one hexadecimal symbol takes the place of four binary digits. To convert a binary number into hexadecimal we simply divide the string of 0's and 1's into groups of four digits counting from right (just as we formed groups of three to convert it into octal), and replace each group by its hexadecimal symbol. For example, the binary number

$$(111110011011010011)_2$$

$$= 0011, 1110, 0110, 1101, 0011$$

$$= 3\,E\,6\,D\,3 \text{ in hexadecimal}$$

Conclusion

The great variety in symbols and systems used for writing numbers since ancient times points to a simple truth about the nature of mathematics. An immutable, abstract but highly useful concept (that of numbers) intuitively derived from the concrete realities of the physical world (the need for counting) can be expressed through arbitrarily chosen symbols connected and manipulated through prescribed rules. The symbols, being arbitrary, are meaningless in any absolute sense. The rules which lay down some formal relationships among symbols (for example, $1 + 1 = 10$) and possible formal operations on them (for example, addition or multiplication) give a structure to the collection of symbols, providing a framework of thought and logical reasoning.

Such is human nature and the mystery of the universe that superstition, magic and miracle have existed side by side with logical reasoning. In various societies and at various times numbers too have figured in charms, rituals and magic. Their forms and relationships have been attributed weird significance and mystic powers. But all that has nothing to do with mathematics. Mathematics is neither magic nor mystery. It is cold logic with down to earth usefulness.

OF HISTORICAL INTEREST

Aryabhat's system of writing large numbers

Aryabhat (5th century A.D) described and used a system of writing large numbers encountered in astronomy in the form of very concise Sanskrit words. The letters of the Sanskrit alphabet were used as symbols for numbers according to the following scheme:

Consonants

क	(k)	1	च	(c)	6	ट	(ṭ)	11	त	(t)	16	प	(p)	21
ख	(kh)	2	छ	(ch)	7	ठ	(ṭh)	12	थ	(th)	17	फ	(ph)	22
ग	(g)	3	ज	(j)	8	ड	(ḍ)	13	द	(d)	18	ब	(b)	23
घ	(gh)	4	झ	(jh)	9	ढ	(ḍh)	14	ध	(dh)	19	भ	(bh)	24
ङ	(ṅ)	5	ञ	(ñ)	10	ण	(ṇ)	15	न	(n)	20	म	(m)	25

य	(y)	30	श	(ś)	70
र	(r)	40	ष	(ṣ)	80
ल	(l)	50	स	(s)	90
व	(v)	60	ह	(h)	100

Vowels

अ	(a)	1	one
इ	(i)	100	hundred
उ	(u)	100^2	ten thousand
ऋ	(ṛ)	100^3	million
ऌ	(ḷ)	100^4	hundred million
ए	(e)	100^5	ten thousand million
ऐ	(ai)	100^6	
ओ	(o)	100^7	
औ	(au)	100^8	

A consonant in conjunction with a vowel denoted the number obtained by multiplying the value of the consonant with that of the vowel. For example, टे (te) denoted 11×100^5 (= 110,000,000,000). Two consonants denoted the sum of two numbers. In this notation Aryabhat defined a 'mahayug' (a period of time) as ख्युघृ (khyughṛ) years which interpreted according to the above code is

$$(2 + 30) \times 100^2 + 4 \times 100^3 = 4{,}320{,}000 \text{ years.}$$

It is interesting to note that the method essentially uses the scale of ten, the conciseness arising from the large number of symbols used (33 consonants and 9 vowels). In an age when knowledge was still mainly transmitted through memorizing, this system had some merit for recording large numbers arising in astronomy. It was obviously unsuitable for any mathematical operations. Moreover, a slight error in pronunciation or writing could lead to serious mistake.

Al-Khwarizmi, Mohammad Ibn Musa

Most famous among Arab mathematicians, Mohammad Ibn Musa (780–850 A.D.), born at Khwarizm, modern Khiva in Uzbekistan, U.S.S.R., was the author of *Ilm al-jabr* (Book of Algebra). It was through his book that the Indian numerals (called *Hindsa*, from *Hind*, the Arab term for India) went to the Arab world and then on to Europe.

Al-Khwarizmi has been, in a way, immortalised by the word 'algorithm', a distortion of '*al-khwarizm*', very popular in modern mathematics, meaning 'a series of mathematical or logical steps constituting a rule'.

Bhaskaracharya

The Indian mathematician, Bhaskara (1114–1185), wrote two books, Bijaganita (meaning Algebra) and Lilawati. The latter was named after his daughter. The method of subtraction described earlier in this chapter for binary numbers is similar to the one suggested by Bhaskara for numbers in the usual scale of ten. Bhaskara's method essentially avoided subtraction from numbers higher than ten by replacing the number to be subtracted by its complement (obtained by subtracting from ten) and then adding. Thus, for instance, 13 – 8 was replaced by $3 + (10 - 8) = 3 + 2$. A problem like

$$\begin{array}{r} 8274 \\ -\ 1429 \\ \hline \end{array}$$

would, by Bhaskara's method, be done step by step as follows:

Replace 9 by its complement 1, add to 4, get 5;
Subtract 2 from 6, get 4;
Replace 4 by its complement 6, add to 2, get 8;
Subtract 1 from 7, get 6.

Thus the answer is 6845.

Bhaskaracharya also came close to ideas which gave birth to calculus six centuries later (see chapter 9). A nonzero number divided by zero was clearly understood by him as an infinite quantity. Also he had some notion of small quantities, called infinitesimals in calculus, which he called *tatkaalgati* which literally means instantaneous motion.

Leonardo Fibonacci de Pisa

This most accomplished mathematician of Europe (Leonardo, son of Bonacci, of Pisa, 1170–1230) of the middle ages gets the credit for introducing and popularizing the Indian numerals in Europe through his book Liber Abaci (Book of Abacus), published in 1202, so-called because the positional notation was implicit in abacus, the earliest computing device invented by man.

Binary Notation

The use of only two symbols for writing numbers can be traced to some primitive tribes and is therefore very old. In modern times Leibniz (1646–1716) worked out the system. He was immensely gratified as to him 1, the symbol of one-ness, represented God, and 0 was the symbol of nothingness or void, and out of the two came the whole universe.

Evolution of Numerals

Indian (Brahmi),
300 B.C

Indian (Devanagari),
11th century, also modern.

Arabic, 16th century
also modern.

European/International
modern.

International, modern.
Used in frequently changing signs. Each numeral is made by lighting required number of lines out of the three horizontal and four vertical lines.

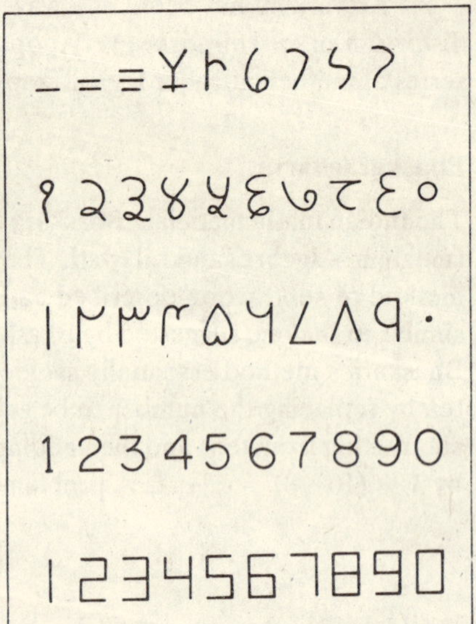

EXERCISES

1. Assuming that in the octal scale there are eight digits, 0, 1, 2, ... 7, and $(10)_8$ denotes eight, the numeral $(316)_8$ denotes the number which on the denary scale is

$$3 \times 8^2 + 1 \times 8 + 6 = (206)_{10}$$

In the same way write the numbers in denary corresponding to the following numbers in octal.

(i) $(20)_8$ (ii) $(67)_8$ (iii) $(112)_8$

2. If one-fourth of 20 is four, what is one-fifth of 36?
(Hint: 20 is written in octal, because then only it indicates sixteen whose one-fourth is four.)

3. Write in ordinary denary notation the following binary numbers.

(i) 10111 (ii) 110.1 (iii) 111.01

4. Do the following sums in binary. Also write their denary equivalents and verify that your answers are correct.

(i)
```
  100011
+ 1001001
```

(ii)
```
  1001001
-  100011
```

(iii)
```
  1000110
×   10101
```

(iv) $101\overline{)1111}$

5. Write the complement of $(11000)_2$ and use it to do the following subtraction.

$$\begin{array}{r} 100000 \\ -\ 11000 \\ \hline \end{array}$$

Verify your answer by writing the problem in denary.

6. Write $(35)_{10}$ in binary notation.

7. Devise a scheme by which a row of electric lamps, each of which can glow or not glow, can be made to signal all the twenty-six letters of the English alphabet, one at a time. What is the minimum number of lamps required? How many more symbols can be signalled without increasing the number of lamps?

8. Using the tables on page 12, write the following binary number in octal and hexadecimal notations.

110110001001111001011100111110111

(Hint: Groupings for octal are ......, 011, 110, 111; and for hexadecimal ......, 1100, 1111, 0111).

ANSWERS

1. (i) $(16)_{10}$ (ii) $(55)_{10}$ (iii) $(74)_{10}$
2. 6
3. (i) $(23)_{10}$ (ii) $(6.5)_{10}$ (iii) $(7.25)_{10}$
4. (i) 1101100, $35 + 73 = 108$
   (ii) 100110, $73 - 35 = 38$
   (iii) 10110111110, $70 \times 21 = 1470$
   (iv) 11, $15 \div 5 = 3$
5.
$$\begin{array}{r} 100000 \\ +\ 00111 \\ \hline 100111 \end{array} \qquad \begin{array}{r} 32 \\ -\ 24 \\ \hline 8 \end{array}$$

   1000

6. 100011
7. 5 lamps; 5 more symbols; each lamp indicating 1 if glowing and 0 if not glowing. Proposed scheme:

A: 00001	E: 00101	I: 01001
B: 00010	F: 00110	J: 01010
C: 00011	G: 00111	K: 01011
D: 00100	H: 01000	L: 01100

M: 01101	Q: 10001	U: 10101
N: 01110	R: 10010	V: 10110
O: 01111	S: 10011	W: 10111
P: 10000	T: 10100	X: 11000
Y: 11001	Z: 11010	

8. 33047456367; D89E5CF7

Chapter 2

Sets and Relations

"One of the chief triumphs of modern mathematics consists in having discovered what mathematics really is."
—Bertrand Russell, British mathematician and philosopher, (1872-1970)

Most people regard mathematics as 'the science of numbers', or, if they can generalise a little more, 'the science of quantitative description of things'. Over a century ago this definition would have been more or less acceptable, though mathematicians were aware of its inadequacy. Number is the first thing taught in mathematics; it is still one of the last things holding the attention of the most gifted of mathematicians. But it is no longer the starting point of all mathematics. The stuff modern mathematics is made of is of a finer, more fundamental variety.

Search for Unity

The growth of mathematics has been in two directions, like that of a tree. The superstructure, with its increasingly numerous branches, thick foliage, and a bewildering variety of flowers and fruits, has assumed a size no longer comprehensible to a single individual. Each new branch, indeed each new little offshoot, reaches out into areas of knowledge which earlier were least suspected to be within the reach of mathematics. Some other offshoot sprouting from some other branch may also hang out in the same area, establishing not only its kinship with the first but also revealing a different approach.

With only this external growth, the mathematicians sitting on distant branches would have long become strangers to each other. Fortunately, they have laboured at the roots also and contemplated on the nature and aim of ultimate mathematical abstractions. The basic concepts have been examined more and more closely in search of fundamental unity. Ideas from which mathematical entities like numbers, spaces, operations, functions etc. emerge as deductions in a single framework of logic have been formulated, establishing not only a basic unity in all the apparently diverse branches of mathematics but also giving rise to common terminology which helps in discovering essential similarities.

The concept of *set* is one such fundamental idea. The various branches of mathematics, such as algebra, geometry, calculus, with all their developments, subdivisions and offshoots, rest securely on it. The terminology of the theory of sets is the current fashion among mathematicians. It enables them to compare the tools of different branches of mathematics and to make them as freely interchangeable as possible.

The notion of sets was introduced explicitly by the German mathematician George Cantor (1845-1918) for a better understanding of infinite sequences, which, ever since the birth of calculus at the hands of Newton (1704) and Leibniz (1684), provided the most vulnerable ground for attack on the logicality of this new mathematical development. Eventually, however, set theory was invented to provide not only a logical foundation to infinite processes but also to finite processes throughout the entire domain of mathematics.

Simple but Useful

Set in mathematics means exactly what it means in ordinary language, namely, a collection of objects. A *battalion* of soldiers, a *swarm* of bees, a *ream* of paper, the *alphabet*, Newton's *three laws* of motion, all are examples of sets. The idea looks trivial with nothing more in it than the obvious, but in the hands of mathematicians it turned out to be of tremendous use.

Let us start with the formal definition of a set. *A set is a collection of definite and distinguishable objects of our perception, intuition or intellect to be conceived as a whole.* The objects contained in the set are called its *members* or *elements*. The essential point is that the collection is to be regarded as a single entity. No restrictions are imposed on the nature of the objects except that they be recognisable by the human mind as separate. The objects themselves may be collective, for example, Indian universities is a set every element of which is a university which is itself collective. Nor is there any restriction on the number of elements in a set. There may be a few, many, a very large number, an infinity of them, or by logical extension, none at all. To take a few examples:

(i) Ram, Sita and Lakshman	(three elements)
(ii) The Ten Commandments	(ten elements)
(iii) Natural numbers, 1, 2, 3, 4, ...	(an infinity of them)
(iv) Points within a circle	(an infinity of elements)
(v) Families with more than three children	(a large number)
(vi) Men living on moon	(no element)

There is nothing mathematicians love more than concise and precise symbolism. Since a set is to be regarded as a single entity, we may denote it with a single symbol. For example, we may denote by S the set of all students of the

University of Roorkee. If we want to know whether x is an element of the set S or not, we have only to check if x is a student of the University of Roorkee or not. The standard symbolic abbreviation of 'x is an element of S' is $x \in S$. If x is not an element of S, we write $x \notin S$.

What is crucial to the definition of a set is that it should be possible to decide unambiguously if a particular element belongs to it or not. This can be done in two ways. Either all the members of the set are enumerated, or a test is prescribed to decide whether an element belongs to the set or not. In the foregoing example the set S may be defined either by a complete list of the students of the University of Roorkee, or by the statement that a person is a member of the set S if he has paid fees as prescribed. If somebody wants to check whether a particular person is a member of the set S, he has, in the first case, to check if his name appears in the complete list, or, in the second case, to verify from the university office if he has paid his fees. The test is objective and does not depend on the subjective judgement of the investigator.

Depending upon convenience, a set may be defined in either way. When the number of elements in a set is small, the enumerative method is quite convenient, but when the number is large the set-builder method (as the second method is called) is preferred. In the notation of the set-builder method, the set S of the foregoing example will be denoted as

$$S = \{ x : x \text{ has paid fees as prescribed} \}$$

which is read as: 'S is the set of all x's such that each x has paid fees as prescribed'.

To have another example, the set A consisting of elements 2, 4, 6, 8, 10 may be denoted as either

$$A = <2, 4, 6, 8, 10>$$

or

$$A = \{x : x = 2n,\ 1 \leq n \leq 5,\ n \text{ an integer}\}.$$

The latter prescribes a test of membership of the set A which is that x is a member of A if it is twice any integer lying between and including 1 and 5.

Sets within Sets

Two sets A and B are said to be equal if they contain the same elements. In other words, if every element of A is also in B, and every element of B is also in A, then we say that $A = B$. As an example, if $A = <1, 2, 3>$ and $B = <1, 3, 2>$, then $A = B$. The point is that, by definition of a set, the order in which the elements in a set occur is immaterial. So long as the elements are the same the sets are equal.

We can easily imagine a set within a set. The contained set is called a subset of the containing set. Population of Delhi is a subset of the population of India, children in a family constitute a subset of the family, organic compounds are a subset of chemical compounds, benevolent thoughts are a subset of thoughts. In each of the above examples every element of the subset is an element of the larger set also. But the reverse is not true. Every person living in Delhi lives in India, but every person living in India does not live in Delhi. The precise mathematical definition of a subset, however, includes the possiblity, though not the necessity, of the reverse also. The definition goes as follows.

> *If every element of the set A is also an element of the set B, then A is said to be a subset of B, symbolically written as $A \subseteq B$. It may also be said that B contains A or $B \supseteq A$.*

In the above definition we have said nothing about B having members which are not in A. There may or may not be any such members in the set B. It is equivalent to saying that if B has in it all the members of A, and may or may not have more, then A is a subset of B. Therefore, if $A = B$ then also $A \subseteq B$. If B has additional elements in it, we say A is a proper subset of B, and write as $A \subset B$. A little reflection will show that if $A \subseteq B$ and $B \subseteq A$ then $A = B$. As examples, if $A = <1, 2, 3>$, $B = <1, 3, 2>$, $C = <1, 2, 3, 4>$, then $A \subseteq B$, $A \subseteq C, B \subseteq C, B \subseteq A, A \subset C, B \subset C, A = B$.

There can be sets containing a single element and sets containing no element at all. The set of 'moons of the earth' has a single element in it, whereas the set of 'men living on the moon' has no element. A set with no element is called an *empty* or *null* set and is generally denoted by ϕ. It is interesting and of considerable mathematical significance to realise that the empty set is a subset of all sets. Every non-empty set contains 'nothing' and something more. The seemingly trivial concept of an empty set is as important in set theory as zero is in number theory.

Union and Intersection

Two binary operations, (that is, operations between a pair of objects), called union and intersection, are defined between any two sets as follows. The union of A and B, written as $A \cup B$, is the set C which contains every element of A and every element of B. To illustrate, if A is the set of all Ph.D's in a university and B is the set of all professors in it, then $C = A \cup B$ is the set which has as its elements all Ph.D.'s and all professors.

The intersection of A and B, written as $A \cap B$, is the set D which contains every element which is in A and also in B. In the above example $D = A \cap B$ is the set of all those persons in the university who are Ph.D.'s as well as professors. Non-Ph.D. professors and non-professor Ph.D.'s are excluded from the set D.

As a further example, if $A = <0, 1, 2>$, $B = <0, -1, -2>$, then $A \cup B = <-2, -1, 0, 1, 2>$, $A \cap B = <0>$.

The term intersection here has really the same meaning as in elèmentary geometry. The intersection of two curves are the points common to both of them. The term union can also be given a geometrical interpretation. The two curves taken together as a single entity may be regarded as the union of the two curves.

Two sets may not have any common element. They are then said to be *disjoint*. The intersection of two disjoint sets is the empty set ϕ. If A is the set of all girls in a class, and B is the set of all boys, then A and B are disjoint sets and their intersection is ϕ.

In a particular context one may define a universal set. If we are talking of persons associated with a university, we may call the set of all such persons as a universal set W, and then the students of a class, the teachers of a department, the watch and ward personnel, the students studying mathematics, etc. are all subsets of the universal set W.

If S is a subset of a universal set W, we may define a set $\bar{S}$ such that it includes all those elements of W which are not in S. The set $\bar{S}$ is said to be the *complement* of S with respect to W. From definition it is obvious that $S \cup \bar{S} = W$ and $S \cap \bar{S} = \phi$.

Venn Diagrams

The operations of union and intersection can be very simply and elegantly represented through what are known as Venn diagrams. These are pictorial representations of sets and their inter-relations, and often some basic results in set theory become obvious or can be easily proved through these diagrams.

Any closed curve enclosing an area may be supposed to represent a set in the sense that all its elements lie within the enclosed area. Thus let the circles A and B (Fig. 2.1) represent the sets A and B respectively. In Fig. (a), the two circles are apart; nothing that lies within A lies within B, and vice versa. The two sets are disjoint, that is, $A \cap B = \phi$. In Fig. (b), the circle B lies within the circle A, and so all the elements of B lie in A also. Thus $B \subset A$, $A \cap B = B$, $A \cup B = A$. In Fig. (c), A and B partly overlap. The portion common to two

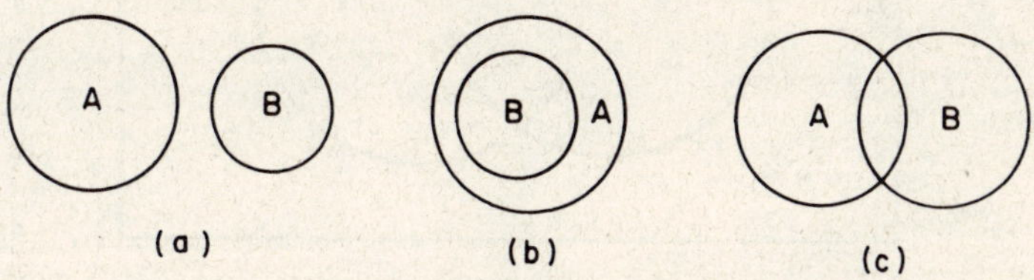

Fig. 2.1

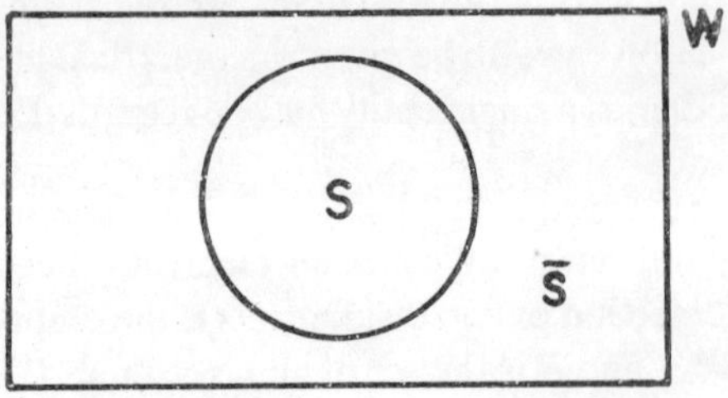

Fig. 2.2

circles represents $A \cap B$, while $A \cup B$ is represented by the total area covered by the two circles together.

Suppose we represent the universal set W by the rectangle in Fig. 2.2 and a subset S of W by the circle within it. The complement of S with respect to W, denoted by $\overline{S}$, is then represented by the area outside the circle but within the rectangle.

Here is an example to illustrate the use of Venn diagram. Anand (A), Bishan (B), Chander (C) and Daud (D) are good speakers, while Chander, Daud, Edward (E) and Ghani (G) are good writers. Fateh (F) and Hari (H) have neither of these qualities. If X denotes the set of good speakers, and Y the set of good writers, what are the elements of the sets $X \cup Y, X \cap Y, \overline{X} \cup \overline{Y}$, $\overline{X} \cap \overline{Y}$, $\overline{X \cup Y}, \overline{X \cap Y}$?

Fig. 2.3 is the Venn diagram for the problem. The rectangle W denotes the universal set consisting of A, B, C, D, E, F, G, H; the circle X denotes the set of good speakers and so contains A, B, C, D; the circle Y is the set of good writers

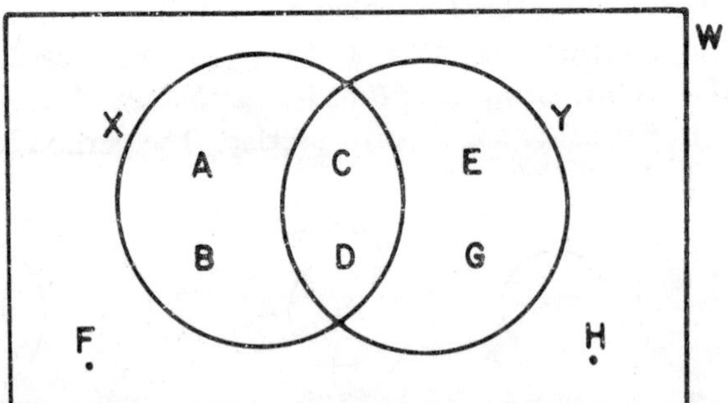

Fig. 2.3

and contains *C*, *D*, *E*, *G*; *F* and *H* are neither in *X* nor in *Y* but are in *W*. Obviously now,

$X \cup Y = < A, B, C, D, E, G >$	(Speakers or writers or both)
$X \cap Y = < C, D >$	(Speakers and also writers)
$\overline{X} = < E, G, F, H >$	(not speakers)
$\overline{Y} = < A, B, F, H >$	(not writers)
$\overline{X} \cup \overline{Y} = < A, B, E, G, F, H >$	(not speakers or not writers)
$\overline{X} \cap \overline{Y} = < F, H >$	(neither speakers nor writers)
$\overline{X \cup Y} = <F, H>$	(complement of $X \cup Y$)
$\overline{X \cap Y} = < A, B, E, G, F, H >$	(complement of $X \cap Y$)

The binary operations of union and intersection of sets give rise to what is called the algebra of sets, like the algebra of numbers based on the binary operations of addition and multiplication. How different rules for manipulating expressions involving symbols give rise to different algebras will be discussed in later chapters. For the present we only observe that, as in ordinary algebra symbols stand for numbers and algebraic expressions consist of symbols connected by signs of addition and multiplication, so in the algebra of sets symbols stand for sets, and set-algebraic expressions consist of symbols connected with signs of union and intersection. There are rules to manipulate these expressions. The basic rules are axioms; they are not, in the strict logical sense, provable, but their truth can be verified through Venn diagrams. We take just one example by way of illustration. A rule in set algebra is that if *A*, *B*, *C* are three sets, then

$$A \cap (B \cup C) = (A \cap B) \cup (A \cap C)$$

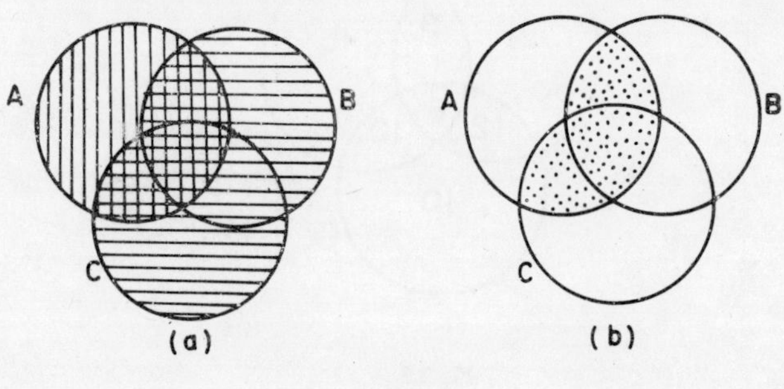

Fig. 2.4

Fig. 2.4 is the Venn diagram to illustrate the truth of this statement. In Fig. (a) $B \cup C$ is shaded by horizontal lines and A by vertical lines. The intersection of the two, namely $A \cap (B \cup C)$, is thus automatically shaded by squares. In Figure (b), $A \cap B$ and $A \cap C$ are shown dotted and the total dotted area indicates $(A \cap B) \cup (A \cap C)$. The dotted area in (b) is the same as the square shaded area in (a). This justifies the rule.

Venn diagrams can also help in visualising some types of problems. Consider the following.

In a children's party 10 children are above the age of eight years and 15 are below the age of twelve. How many children are there in all? Obviously the question cannot be answered unless we know how many of them are between eight and twelve. In adding the two numbers, 10 and 15, we add such children twice, and therefore their number must be subtracted from $10 + 15$ to get the answer. If there are 4 children between eight and twelve, the total number of children is $10 + 15 - 4 = 21$. The Venn diagram for this problem would be two intersecting circles with 10 elements in one and 15 in the other and 4 in the common area.

Consider another problem. A teacher assigned three problems, A, B, C, to a class of 100 students. A was solved by 46 students, B by 40, C by 38, A and B both by 15, B and C both by 16, A, B and C, all the three, by 6, 12 students solved A and C but not B. How many students did not solve any problem?

Fig. 2.5 shows the Venn diagram for this problem. The numbers written in various areas may be easily calculated from the given data. The total number of students who solved problems is the number in the union of the three circles, which is 81. Therefore 19 students solved no problem.

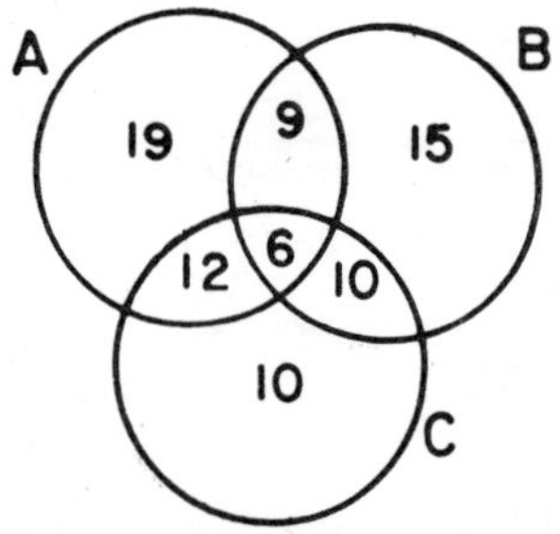

Fig 2.5

Relation

The concept of *relation* between different elements of the same set is another fundamental notion of great significance arising out of everyday experience. Here the word 'relation' is used in the sense of 'relationship', and is concerned with the existence of some type of bond between two elements of a set taken in a particular order.

In a set <Alok, Anil, Ajaya> of three brothers, each is related to either of the other two by the relation of brotherhood. For brevity let us denote their names by a_1, a_2, a_3, and denote 'is the brother of' by **B**. Then we may write the statement 'Alok is the brother of Anil' as $a_1\ \mathbf{B}\ a_2$. All such statements that are possible about the three members of the set are:

$$a_1\,\mathbf{B}\,a_2 \qquad a_2\,\mathbf{B}\,a_3 \qquad a_3\,\mathbf{B}\,a_1$$
$$a_2\,\mathbf{B}\,a_1 \qquad a_3\,\mathbf{B}\,a_2 \qquad a_1\,\mathbf{B}\,a_3$$

We may say that if x and y are any two elements of the set of brothers, then x **B** y.

If x **B** y, then y **B** x (if x is the brother of y, then surely y is the brother of x). Such a relation is called *symmetric*. Not that all relations are symmetric. For example, in the set <Amla, Batuk>, if Batuk is the brother of Amla, then Amla is not the brother of Batuk, she is the sister. Denoting the sister and the brother by a, b, we may say b **B** a but not a **B** b. The **B** relation is not symmetric between a and b.

Also if x **B** y and y **B** z, then x **B** z (if x is the brother of y and y is the brother of z, then surely x is the brother of z). Such a relation is called *transitive*. The **B** relation is transitive in a set of brothers. Not all relations are transitive. Let <a, b, c> be the set of three persons, son, father and grandfather, and let **S** denote the relation 'is the son of'. Then a **S** b and b **S** c but not a **S** c.

Let us consider a set of boys, and let **H** stand for 'is of the same height as'. If x and y are two boys of the same height, then x **H** y. Also obviously y **H** x. Further if z is another boy of the set such that y **H** z, the x **H** z. The **H** relation is thus symmetric and transitive. It has yet another interesting property, namely x **H** x (since obviously x is the same height as x). This property is called *reflexive*. Not all relations are reflexive. Neither **B** nor **S** of the preceding examples are reflexive. We do not say b is the brother of b, and even if, by a generalised definition of **B**, we accept it to be so, by no stretch of imagination can we say that a is the son of a.

A relation like **H**, namely one which is reflexive, symmetric and transitive, is called an *equivalence* relation. Another example of it is the relation 'lives in the same house as ' in the set of all persons living in houses. It is reflexive since x certainly lives in the same house as x; it is symmetric since, if x lives in the same house as y, then y lives in the same house as x; it is transitive since, if x lives in the same house as y and y in the same house as z, then x lives in the same house as z. This example brings out a simple but highly significant property of equivalence relations. All persons living in houses are divided by this relation into smaller collections, each collection consisting of persons living in the same house. No one person can live in two houses. So these collections do not overlap. They are disjoint subsets. An equivalence relation partitions a set into disjoint subsets. This idea has found wide applications in providing a logical base to mathematics. It has, for instance, its use in logically deducing negative numbers, fractions, complex numbers, etc. from the almost intuitive concept of positive integers.

Simple and Partial Ordering

A relation plays a somewhat bourgeois role in an otherwise classless set. It provides a criterion for arranging the members in a certain order introducing precedence, seniority and such other notions. Suppose L is the set of all teachers in a college, and suppose the symbol

$=$ stands for 'gets the same salary as',
$<$ stands for 'gets salary less than',
$\leq$ stands for 'gets salary less than or equal to'.

Then if x and y are any two members of L, either $x \leq y$ or $y \leq x$. The teachers thus get arranged in order of their salaries, no teacher being left out of this arrangement. The set is said to be simply or linearly ordered. The relation $\leq$ is obviously reflexive and transitive. It is not symmetric, since if $x \leq y$ then not necessarily is $y \leq x$. But if it does happen that x gets less than or the same as y and y gets less than or the same as x, then the only conclusion is that x and y get the same amount. In symbols, if $x \leq y$ and $y \leq x$, then $x = y$. This property is called *antisymmetric*. A relation which is reflexive, antisymmetric and transitive and relates every pair of members of a set produces *simple ordering* in the set.

If in the above example the set of teachers is such that no two teachers receive equal salary, then for no x and y is $x = y$. For each pair x, y either $x \leq y$ or $y \leq x$. The teachers can then be arranged strictly and uniquely in a certain order with no two teachers claiming equality. The set is then said to be *well-ordered*. To take another example, the set of children of the same mother is a well-ordered set under the relation 'was born earlier than '. The set of integers under the relation 'less than' is another example of a well-ordered set.

It may happen that all pairs of members of a set may not be related through a given relation. A relation which is reflexive, antisymmetric and transitive but does not necessarily relate every pair of members of the set is said to produce *partial ordering*. As the name implies, partial ordering means an ordering from which some members are left out. As an example of partial ordering, consider the set of numbers $< 1, 2, 3, 5, 6, 10, 15, 30 >$, and the relation 'is multiple of'.

The relation is reflexive because x is a multiple of x; it is antisymmetric because if x is a multiple of y and y is a multiple of x, then necessarily $x = y$; it is transitive because if x is a multiple of y and y is a multiple of z, then x is a multiple of z. It produces partial ordering in the set in the sense that we can choose a subset of this set and arrange its members in order such that each member, starting from the second, is a multiple of all preceding members. For example, $< 1, 2, 6, 30 >$ is such a subset. All the partial orderings possible in this set can be graphically represented as in Fig. 2.6. The vertices in the figure represent the numbers in the set. Each directed line ends at a number which is a multiple of the number

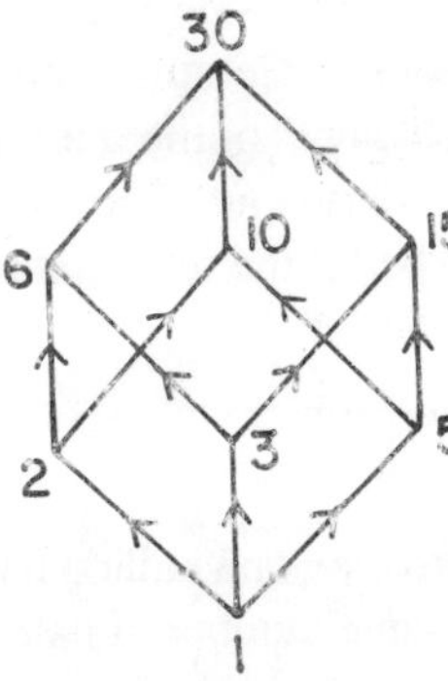

Fig. 2.6

from where it begins. A directed path consisting of a sequence of directed lines starting from some number, going through others, and finally ending at another number gives a sequence of numbers each of which is a multiple of the preceding numbers. Each directed path from vertex 1 to vertex 30 represents such a partial ordering.

Cardinal Number

Though set as a useful concept entered in mathematics only about a hundred years ago, it is not difficult to appreciate that it is a more primitive concept than number. We shall see how intuitively as well as formally number can be defined as a property of a set.

Let the set of students and the set of chairs in a class room be such that no student is without a chair and no chair is without a student. The set of chairs is thus paired off with the set of students. There exists a one-one correspondence between the two sets. Such sets are called *equinumorous* or *similar*. Similar sets have a common property. Without bringing in the word 'number' in our discussion yet, this provides the starting point of the concept of number. That is what must have dawned on the mind of the earliest man who started counting.

That is what the child unconsciously realises through constant repetition of counting. That is what the mathematician takes as the definition of *cardinal number*. Two sets, if they are similar, are said to have the same cardinal number. It is a measure of the size of the set. The common property of all empty sets is given the name zero, of all sets with single element the name one, and so on.

By pairing elements of a set with those of another we can decide which set has a larger cardinal number. For example, on associating one student with one chair in a class room, if we run out of chairs first and some students remain without chairs, the cardinal number of the set of students is larger. It might seem a very round about way of saying that there are more students than chairs in the room, but what we are trying to do is to understand the operation of counting in its fundamental sense. Counting the elements of a set involves pairing its elements with the elements of the unending set of natural numbers $<1, 2, 3, 4, \ldots>$. The moment we run out of elements of the given set, we have finished the count, the last number of the set of natural numbers used in pairing giving the cardinal number of the set.

Here is an amusingly simple problem whose solution becomes trivial once our thinking becomes set-oriented.

Show that if no man has more than one million hair on his head, then at least two persons in Delhi have the same number of hair on their heads.

The solution goes like this. Pair off each individual in Delhi with that number in the set of numbers 0, 1, 2, 3, ... 1000000, which corresponds to the number of hair on his head. As the number of inhabitants of Delhi is more than one million and one, we shall run out of numbers before we run out of people, so that at least two shall be paired with the same number.

Ordinal Numbers

But why is the number used in counting introduced in the last section called cardinal? It was realised that the same names, one, two, three, four, etc are used to indicate ordering in a well-ordered set. In a family if the children are arranged in the order in which they were born, the eldest occupies position one, the next two, and so on. Here one, two, three, etc are not measures of the size of any sets but an indication of the seniority or precedence of elements with respect to each other in a well-ordered set. This is basically a different notion and is called an *ordinal number*. The ordinal numbers, in language, are sometimes referred as first, second, third, etc but in mathematics are denoted by the same symbols as the cardinal numbers, namely 1, 2, 3, 4, ...

Paradoxical Sets

Logic can play strange tricks, and clear cut definitions can lead to awkward situations. The apparently satisfactory definition of a set as a collection of discrete objects of our intuition or thought was shown to have its pitfalls by

Bertrand Russell. The following are two examples of what has become famous as the Russell paradox.

There is a barber who, being the only barber in his village, claims that he shaves all those male adult villagers, and those only, who do not shave themselves. The male adult population of the village has thus been divided into two disjoint sets, the set of those who shave themselves and the set of those who are shaved by the barber. To which set does the barber belong? If he shaves himself, then the barber, that is he himself, should not shave him; if the barber does not shave him, then he, that is the barber, should shave him. Thus if he belongs to one set, he should not belong to it. The barber is in a dilemma, and the definition of set has broken down.

To take another example, suppose in India all libraries maintain a bound volume called catalogue in which all the books in the library are listed. Some libraries classify this catalogue also as one of its books and list it in the catalogue itself, others do not. The catalogues are thus divided into two disjoint sets, one, the set A, containing catalogues which list themselves, and the other, the set B, which consists of catalogues which do not list themselves. Now suppose there is a national library which prepares a master catalogue of all the catalogues of set B. To which set, A or B, does the master catalogue belong? If it belongs to A, then it should list itself, but since the entries in this catalogue are only of the members of the set B, it can list itself only if it belongs to set B. Similarly it can be argued that if it belongs to B, then it should belong to A. But A and B are disjoint sets. Hence there is a contradiction.

Russell's paradox put the intuitive concept of a set in jeopardy. Inspite of these difficulties, and inspite of the fact that when Cantor introduced the notion of set as a useful concept in mathematics, it was received with suspicion and distrust by many mathematicians, set has come to be accepted as a fundamental concept in mathematics providing logical foundations and a unifying base to all its branches.

FROM THE GALLERY OF MATHEMATICIANS

George Cantor

In deference to his father's wishes, Cantor (German, 1845 – 1918) studied engineering and started to follow a down-to-earth career, but ended with epoch making research in abstract mathematics. He propounded that just as finite sets can be compared to decide about their relative size, so could infinite sets be compared, and that all infinite sets were not of the same size. He invented the idea of transfinite numbers to denote the sizes of infinite sets. His work was received by distinguished mathematicians of his time with suspicion, neglect and ridicule. So severe were the attacks on him that he suffered depression and mental breakdowns. Finally, however, towards the end of his life the importance of his work came to be recognised. David Hilbert, one of the greatest mathematicians of this century, paid a rich tribute to him with the words 'No one shall expel us from the paradise which Cantor has created for us'.

Bertrand Russell

Bertrand Russell (1872–1970), British mathematician and philosopher, an unconventional and bold social thinker and writer, a pacifist and a crusader for many humanitarian causes, was an outstanding intellectual of this century. Losing his parents in early childhood, he was brought up by his grandmother. His grandfather had been Prime Minister of England, and was an earl. Bertrand, much later, inherited this earldom from his brother, but preferred not to use the title. For his pacifist opinions and opposition to all wars, he lost his college post in 1918, spent some time in jail, had his appointment in an American college cancelled in 1940 and was again briefly jailed in 1961. He was awarded Nobel Prize for literature in 1950.

Russell was one of the foremost exponents of modern mathematical logic. After a decade of very hard labour, and in collaboration with A.N. Whitehead, another outstanding intellectual, he wrote Principia Mathematica, 1910-13. This was the most ambitious and nearly successful effort to make all mathematics completely rigorous deductive logic, but as Gödel was to show twenty years later, all such efforts were intrinsically doomed to failure. Russell took logic out of the traditional Aristotelian rut of a closed and completed body of doctrine. To the students of logic he had this advice to give; 'If you wish to become a logician, do not learn the traditional logic. In Aristotle's days it was a creditable effort, but so was Ptolemaic astronomy'.

EXERCISES

1. Verify that the following two sets, one written in enumerative form and the other in set-builder form, are the same.

   $$< 1, 3, 5, 7, \ldots >, \ \{x : x = 2n - 1, n \text{ a positive integer}\}$$

   Complete the set-builder form in the following examples.

   (i) $< \frac{1}{2}, \frac{1}{3}, \frac{1}{4}, \cdots \frac{1}{10} > = \left\{x : x = \frac{1}{n}, n = \qquad \right\}$

   (ii) $< 1^2, 3^2, 5^2, \ldots > = \{y : y = \qquad \}$

   Write the membership list in the following sets:

   (iii) $< \qquad\qquad > = \{x : x = n^3, n \text{ is a positive integer less than } 3\}$

   (iv) $< \qquad\qquad > = \{x : x = z^2 < 17, z \text{ an integer}\}$

2. All the subsets of the set $<1, 2, 3>$ are:
   $<1>, <2>, <3>, <1, 2>, <1, 3>, <2, 3>, <1, 2, 3>, \phi$.

   In the same way write all the subsets of the following sets.

   (i) $<$ Sun, Earth, Moon $>$
   (ii) $\{x : x^2 = 4\}$

3. Given the sets S_1 and S_2, their union $(S_1 \cup S_2)$ and intersection $(S_1 \cap S_2)$ are found as illustrated in the following example. Find them in other examples.

   (i) $S_1 = <x, y, z, t>, S_2 = <t, w, x, u, v>;$
   $S_1 \cup S_2 = <x, y, z, t, w, u, v>, S_1 \cap S_2 = <x, t>.$

   (ii) $S_1 = \{x : x \text{ an integer greater than } 100\},$
   $S_2 = \{y : y \text{ an integer less than } 150\}.$

   (iii) $S_1 = <\text{George, Dick, Harry}>,$
   $S_2 = <\text{Susan, Lucy}>.$

   (iv) $S_1 = <\text{All flowers}>$
   $S_2 = <\text{All roses}>$

4. Given $A = <0, 1, 2>, B = <0, 2, 4, 6>, C = <1, 4, 6, 8>$, we can verify that

   $$(A \cap C) \cup (B \cap C) = (A \cup B) \cap C$$

   as follows:

   $A \cup B = <0, 1, 2, 4, 6>$
   $A \cap C = <1>, B \cap C = <4, 6>,$
   $(A \cup B) \cap C = <1, 4, 6>,$
   $(A \cap C) \cup (B \cap C) = <1, 4, 6>.$

   Thus the formula is verified.

   Similarly verify the following formulae:

   (i) $(A \cup B) \cup C = (B \cup C)$
   (ii) $(A \cap B) \cap C = A \cap (B \cap C)$
   (iii) $A \cup (B \cap C) = (A \cup B) \cap (A \cup C)$

5. Let S be a set of variously coloured balls, and **r** the relation 'is the same colour as'. Let x, y, z be three balls of the set. Then obviously x **r** x, so the relation is reflexive. If x **r** y, then y **r** x, so the relation is symmetric. If x **r** y and y **r** z, then x **r** z, so the relation is transitive. Hence **r** is an equivalence relation.

   On the same lines answer the questions in the following problems.

(i) Let S = <0, 1, 2, ..., 99, 100>, and let **r** be the relation 'ends in the same digit as'. Thus 0 **r** 10 as 0 ends in the same digit as 10. Also, as another example, 27 **r** 67 as 27 ends in the same digit as 67.

Is **r** reflexive? Yes/No
Is **r** symmetric? Yes/No
Is **r** transitive? Yes/No
Is **r** an equivalence relation? Yes/No

(ii) Let S be a set of persons and **r** be the relation 'has weight within four kg of weight of'.

Is **r** reflexive? Yes/No
Is **r** symmetric? Yes/No
Is **r** transitive? Yes/No
Is **r** an equivalence relation? Yes/No

6. A study to find the relative popularity of three weeklies was made among a sample of 250 students. It was found that 158 read the Weekly News, 139 read the Sunday, 53 read the Weekend, 100 read both the Sunday and the Weekly News, 25 read both the Sunday and the Weekend, but none read both the Weekly News and the Weekend. How many students read none of the weeklies?

ANSWERS

1. (i) $n = 2, 3, 4, ..., 10$ (ii) $y = (2n + 1)^2, n = 0, 1, 2, 3, ...$
(iii) <$1^3, 2^3$> (iv) <0, 1, 4, 9, 16>.

2. (i) <sun>, <earth>, <moon>, <sun, earth>, <earth, moon>, <sun, moon>, <sun, earth, moon>, ϕ.

(ii) <2, –2>, <2>, <–2>, ϕ.

3. (ii) $S_1 \cup S_2$ = <all integers>.
$S_1 \cap S_2$ = <all integers greater than 100 and less than 150>.

(iii) $S_1 \cup S_2$ = <George, Dick, Harry, Susan, Lucy>.
$S_1 \cap S_2 = \phi$.

(iv) $S_1 \cup S_2$ = <all flowers>.
$S_1 \cap S_2$ = <all roses>.

5. (i) yes, yes, yes, yes.

(ii) yes, yes, no, no.

6. 25.

Chapter 3

Evolution of Numbers

"God made the whole numbers, all the rest is the work of man"
—L. Kronecker, German mathematician, (1823-1891)

As every school boy or girl knows, there are numbers other than those used in counting. Beginning with the natural numbers 1, 2, 3, 4, ..., the child soon learns to work with fractions, and later, in algebra, is introduced to negative numbers. On learning to extract square roots he begins to recognise $\sqrt{2}$, $\sqrt{3}$, etc also as numbers. In geometry he comes across the ratio of the circumference to the diameter of a circle which for some reason not clear to him is denoted by Greek letter π. Whenever in calculations it is taken as $\frac{22}{7}$ or 3.1416, it is understood that these are approximations and not exactly equal to the number π. By the time he leaves school his mental bag is further stuffed with imaginary numbers like $\sqrt{-2}$ and complex numbers like $2 + \sqrt{-3}$. With each new kind of number that is thrown before the student like a rabbit out of a magician's hat he is also told certain rules of operation which enable him to manipulate mathematical expressions involving them. All these various types of numbers and operating rules form a sizable part of the mathematical knowledge of the student as he leaves school. Most of it consists of thumb rules which by constant use become habit. In this chapter we propose to illumine blind habit by some light of understanding.

We shall see how each new kind of number grows out of the older kind as a logical necessity serving practical ends. The history of its development spans the entire history of human civilization. At different times, in India, in China, in Greece, in the Arab world, and finally in Europe, ideas grew and concepts were accepted, rejected, accepted again, formally practised but logically denounced, till the final picture as it stands today emerged by the middle of the nineteenth century. There are at present three schools of philosophy of mathematics, the intuitionist, the logist and the formalist, and the entire number system can be built up rigorously from any one of the three standpoints. We shall, however, neither make a historical survey nor any learned attempt from any particular philosophical viewpoint. Our approach will not be rigorous, logically or historically, but it would provide the reader with a general appreciation of the motivation and logic of the growth of numbers, sometimes seeking justification from intuition, sometimes from logic and sometimes from merely formal rules agreed upon by common consent.

Natural Numbers

The infinite set of natural numbers, $N = <1, 2, 3, 4, 5, \ldots\ldots>$, satisfies our need to compare the sizes of various collections of objects by providing a standard scale. It is a well-ordered set which means that its elements can be arranged in a strict order. Between any two members x, y of the set, it can be decided which comes first. If x comes first and y comes later, x is said to be less than y ($x < y$) or y is said to be greater than x ($y > x$). A child begins to appreciate this property of the set gradually as he gains experience of the physical world and makes use of the set in counting. Without going into what exactly the psychologists mean by intuition, let us agree to call this mysterious process of understanding as intuitive. A learned and logically more precise way of defining natural numbers in terms of the notion of the cardinal number of a set has been described in Chapter 2.

If we have three apples and get five more, we shall in all have eight apples. The result is the same if we had five first and then got three. The truth of this experience we express as

$$3 + 5 = 5 + 3 = 8.$$

In general terms, for any two natural numbers a and b, a third natural number c exists such that

$$a + b = b + a = c.$$

The operation between a and b is called *addition* and c is said to be the *sum* of a and b. We can experimentally verify the truth of this statement for any two particular natural numbers (or elements of N), but the general statement is not logically deducible from particular cases. It is not proved. What we do is to assume its truth, or, in other words, to *define* that '+' is a *binary operation* between any two elements a, b of N which results in another element c of N. It is called binary because it is between two elements.

Let us introduce another symbol '–' (minus sign) by agreeing that $3 + 5 = 8$ can also be written as $3 = 8 - 5$. The symbol '–' can be given a meaning. From eight apples if we take away five, we are left with three. We define '–' as an operation, called *subtraction*, between two elements 8 and 5 of N such that the result 3 is also in N. The question arises: Can we perform this operation between any two elements of N? Is it possible that for any a and b in N there is an element x in N such that

$$a - b = x?$$

The answer is no. If $a > b$ then such an x can be found. But if $a < b$ or $a = b$, it is not possible. You cannot subtract a larger or equal natural number from a natural number to get another natural number. This failure leads to the invention of zero and negative numbers which we shall discuss a little later. Just now let us define another binary operation on N.

We define the binary operation '×', called *multiplication*, between any two elements a, b of N such that

$$a \times b = b \times a = c$$

where c is also in N. The justification for the definition is easily found in particular cases. If we take three collections of four apples each, we have in all twelve apples. We get the same number if we take four collections of three apples each. In abstract terms, three (collections) of four (apples) is twelve (apples), or three times four is twelve. This truth we may denote as $3 \times 4 = 12$. Also $4 \times 3 = 12$.

Let us agree that an alternative way of writing $3 \times 4 = 12$ is $4 = \frac{12}{3}$. This may also be interpreted to mean that if twelve apples are divided into three equal collections, each collection contains four apples. This is termed the operation of *division*. The question now arises, can we always divide one natural number by another to get a natural number. In other words, is there always an x in N for any a, b in N such that $x = \frac{a}{b}$? The answer is no, not always. If $a = 12$ and $b = 3$, there is an x in N, which is 4. But if $a = 11$, $b = 3$, then there is no such x in N.

We see that the definitions of subtraction and division introduced as inverses of addition and multiplication respectively both lead to a breakdown of these operations if we confine ourselves to the set of natural numbers. If we were confronted with only indivisible units of objects in the physical world, there would have been no practical need to understand how much is each part when a collection of four things is divided into three equal collections. But life is more varied. If there are apples, there is milk too. We can devise an arbitrary unit of milk, say one litre, and then in terms of the set of natural numbers we can have 2, 3, 4, ... litres of milk. We may have to divide four litres of milk equally among three children, and it is natural to ask how much each child gets. This provides a motivation to overcome the breakdown in the definition of division.

Fractions

The way out is to recognise that if 4 is divided into 3 equal parts, each part is of a definite size which we agree to call 'four by three' and write as $\frac{4}{3}$. This is only a notation, and it could have been different. There is nothing to prevent us from denoting this new 'animal' as 3_4, (3, 4), 4^3 or any other way. But a notation and a name have to be universally accepted and we have accepted $\frac{4}{3}$ or 4/3.

Thus a new kind of number is born. It is called *fraction*. It is denoted as $\frac{a}{b}$ or a/b, where a and b are natural numbers. a is called the *numerator* and b the *denominator*. For any particular a and b, $\frac{a}{b}$ can be understood as one of the b equal subdivisions into which a is divided. Accordingly, $\frac{4}{1}$ means one of the one subdivision into which 4 is divided, which obviously means 4 itself. It would be, therefore, reasonable to assume that $\frac{4}{1}$ and 4 denote the same idea. We, therefore, assume that for every a in N, $\frac{a}{1} = a$, which means that a natural number can also be regarded as a fraction. The set of natural numbers is thus a subset of the set of fractions. All fractions are not natural numbers, but all natural numbers are fractions too.

If we divide 2 units into 4 equal parts, the size of each part is $\frac{2}{4}$. By a simple diagram (Fig. 3.1) it is obvious that we get the same size if we divide 1 into 2 equal parts. Thus $\frac{2}{4}$ and $\frac{1}{2}$ represent identical notions. It is, therefore, necessary to ascribe a property to fractions which will take care of the type of relations,

$$\frac{1}{2} = \frac{2}{4} = \frac{3}{6} = \frac{4}{8} = \ldots.$$

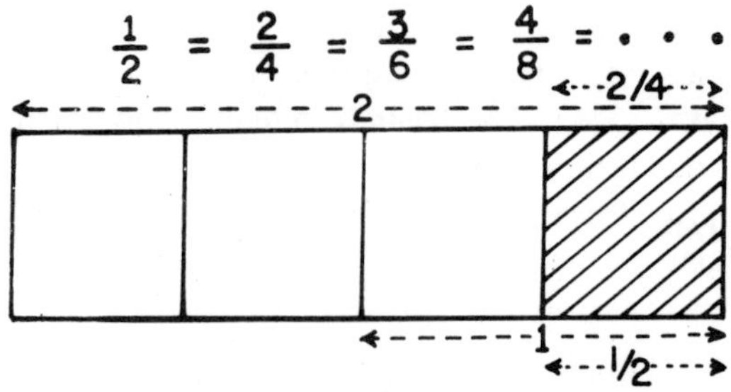

Fig. 3.1

This is done by postulating that if $a = m \times p$ and $b = m \times q$, where a, b, m, p, q are natural numbers, then $\frac{a}{b}$ and $\frac{p}{q}$ are equivalent. An alternative way is to postulate that fractions $\frac{a}{b}$ and $\frac{c}{d}$ are equivalent if $a \times d = c \times b$.

The binary operations of addition and multiplication when extended to fractions must satisfy two requirements, one intuitive and the other logical. To take the intuitive consideration first, we have defined 2/3 litres of milk as the quantity in each part obtained by dividing 2 litres in 3 equal parts. If we regard 2 litres in two parts of 1 litre each, divide each litre into 3 equal parts thus getting each part as 1/3 litre, and take two of such parts, we shall still get the same quantity as before. Therefore our rule of addition should be such that

$$\frac{2}{3} = \frac{1}{3} + \frac{1}{3} = 2 \text{ of } \frac{1}{3}.$$

Consistently with the above rule and the property of equivalence, the quantity of milk obtained by adding 2/3 litres to 4/5 litres may be reasonably calculated as follows. By equivalence relation we may make the denominators of the two fractions the same. Thus

$$\frac{2}{3} = \frac{10}{15}, \ \frac{4}{5} = \frac{12}{15}.$$

But 10/15 may be interpreted as 10 of 1/15 and 12/15 as 12 of 1/15. So on addition there would be in all 22 of 1/15 or 22/15. Thus we see the relevance of the following procedure.

$$\frac{2}{3} + \frac{4}{5} = \frac{10}{15} + \frac{12}{15} = \frac{10 + 12}{15} = \frac{22}{15}.$$

This leads to the idea that the sum of two fractions a/b and c/d may be defined as

$$\frac{a}{b} + \frac{c}{d} = \frac{(a \times d) + (b \times c)}{b \times d}$$

We again emphasize that this is no proof. What we have shown is that such a rule makes sense in practical cases and serves a useful purpose.

The logical requirement of this rule is that, since natural numbers are also included in the set of fractions, the rule should be in conformity with the rule of addition for natural numbers. It is so, as is clear from the following:

$$a + b = \frac{a}{1} + \frac{b}{1} = \frac{(a \times 1) + (b \times 1)}{1 \times 1} = \frac{a + b}{1} = a + b$$

To extend the rule of multiplication to fractions, we recall that for natural numbers, 4×3 corresponded with the practical need to find 4 of 3 (four of three units each). Hence, the practical use or meaning of $\frac{2}{3} \times \frac{4}{5}$ may be sought in $\frac{2}{3}$ of $\frac{4}{5}$. Fig. 3.2 illustrates how $\frac{2}{3}$ of $\frac{4}{5}$ is the same as $\frac{8}{15}$.

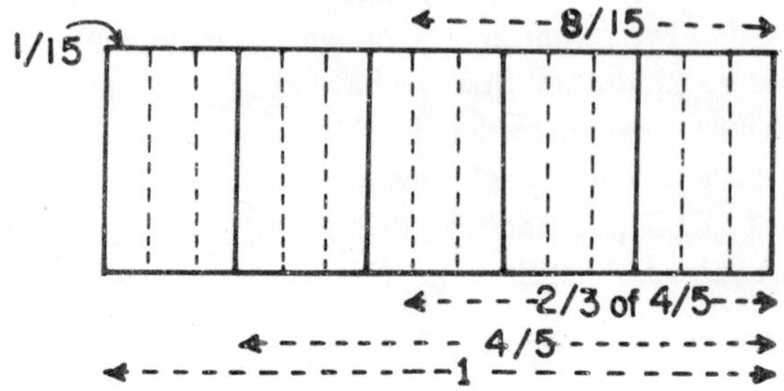

Fig. 3.2

Hence, with practical justification, we postulate the rule of multiplication as

$$\frac{a}{b} \times \frac{c}{d} = \frac{a \times c}{b \times d}.$$

It is consistent with the rule for natural numbers because

$$a \times b = \frac{a}{1} \times \frac{b}{1} = \frac{a \times b}{1 \times 1} = \frac{a \times b}{1} = a \times b.$$

The fractions form an ordered set. We can define the rule of ordering them as follows. Let a/b and c/d be two fractions. Then by equivalence relation

$$\frac{a}{b} = \frac{a \times d}{b \times d}, \ \frac{c}{d} = \frac{b \times c}{b \times d}$$

$a \times d$ and $b \times c$ are natural numbers. We have already defined that if $a \times d = b \times c$ the two fractions are equivalent (or equal). We now further say that $\frac{a}{b} >$ or $< \frac{c}{d}$ according as $a \times d >$ or $< b \times c$. This enables us to decide whether the two fractions are equal, and if not, which is greater.

Further, the operation of subtraction of a smaller fraction from a larger fraction can now be defined as follows:

$$\frac{a}{b} - \frac{c}{d} = \frac{(a \times d) - (b \times c)}{b \times d}$$

If $\frac{a}{b} > \frac{c}{d}$, then $a \times d > b \times c$, and so the numerator is a natural number. Also the denominator $b \times d$ is a natural number. The result of subtraction is therefore another fraction.

Zero and Negative Numbers

Let us extend the operation of subtraction further. As we have seen, for any two natural numbers or fractions, a, b if $a > b$, then there is a number x such that

$$x = a - b.$$

which is only an alternative way of writing

$$x + b = a.$$

But if $a = b$ or $a < b$, then there is no such number x in the set of natural numbers or fractions.

Let us extend our notion of number and say that there is a number x in every case. If $a > b$, the number x already exists in the set of fractions. But if $a = b$, let us give x a special name zero (symbol 0). Zero is thus defined as that number which has the special property that the sum of zero and any other number is equal to the latter number itself:

$$0 + a = a.$$

To come back to the equation

$$x + b = a,$$

if $a < b$, let x be a new kind of number. Since $a < b$ means the same thing as $b > a$, there is a number y such that

$$y + a = b.$$

Adding the two numbers $x + b$ and $y + a$ on the left and a and b on the right of the above two equations, we get

$$(x + y) + (a + b) = a + b,$$

from which, by definition of zero, it follows that

$$x + y = 0.$$

Thus we find that to every new kind of number x there is a number y such that the sum of the two is zero. This is equivalent to saying that there is a one-one correspondence between the new kind of numbers and the old ones. To every natural number or fraction there is a unique new kind of number. How best to denote it? We may use this correspondence to devise a suitable notation. In a monogamous society of married men and women with a one-one correspondence between the set of men and the set of women, it is possible to designate a woman unambiguously with the prefix Mrs before her husband's name. A similar procedure is followed for the new numbers. The new number corresponding to the old number a is denoted by $-a$ (called minus a). Thus corresponding to numbers 5 and 10/3, the new numbers are -5 and $-10/3$ respectively. The new numbers are said to be *negative*, and, in contrast, the old are called *positive*.

We have now arrived at an extended set of numbers. It consists of positive and negative fractions (including natural numbers) and zero. To further appreciate the motivation behind the invention of negative numbers, let us turn to some examples of everyday life where negative numbers can be used to satisfy practical needs.

Starting from a fixed point on a road, a person goes 5 km along the road. Is this information enough to find his position after he has moved the specified distance? A road has two directions, and one should also know in what direction the person has moved. If he moves 5 km first and then moves 3 km further in the same direction, he is $5 + 3 = 8$ km from the place of start. But in the second lap of his journey, if he moves 3 km back, he is $5 - 3 = 2$ km from the starting point. If he had moved back 7 km, he would still be 2 km from the start but on the opposite side. It would surely be convenient if a method of associating direction with numbers describing distances along a road could be devised.

To every distance x that can be travelled in one direction, there is a corresponding equal distance y that can be travelled in the opposite direction. If one were to go through distance x first and subsequently were to go back through the equal distance y, he would finally be where he started from. This fact may be stated as $x + y = 0$. This brings us to the definition of the negative number y if x is the originally defined number (which in contrast we call positive). As mentioned before, y is customarily denoted as $-x$. Thus a meaningful interpretation is given to negative numbers. This is only one example. Numerous other instances from everyday life can be cited where negative numbers can be put to use. The prescribed level of water in a water supply reservoir could be marked as zero and higher and lower levels marked with positive and negative numbers respectively. A certain point in a thermometer is marked zero, and higher and lower temperatures are recorded by positive and negative numbers.

The credit and debit sides of a person's bank account could also be recorded as positive and negative numbers. But the banks do not follow this method. They prefer to make entries in two separate columns. If the totals of the credit and the debit columns of an account on a particular date are c and d respectively, then the number $c - d$ indicates the position of the person *vis-a-vis* the bank on that date. Instead of calculating $c - d$, using negative numbers if necessary, the bank merely records the pair of numbers (c, d) to express the state of affairs between the bank and the depositor. To the bank this is a more convenient way of expressing $c - d$. This is also the underlying idea of the theory which obtains the set of positive and negative numbers, including zero, from the set of positive numbers by regarding an ordered pair of elements of the latter as an element of the former. By this procedure (5, 3) denotes $5 - 3$ (which we know to be 2) and (3, 5) denotes $3 - 5$ (which we have denoted by -2). Also (5, 5) denotes

5 – 5, that is zero. But this notation is not unique because in this sense (5, 3), (6, 4), (8, 6), (22, 20), etc all denote the same number. Therefore, in this notation we have to accept the following equivalence relation as a rule:

$$(a, b) = (a + x, b + x).$$

The binary operations of addition and multiplication already defined between two fractions can be formally extended to the entire set of numbers, positive, negative and zero, defined so far. In fact the rules of addition of a negative and positive, and of two negatives, are easy to justify by referring to any of the physical situations in which negative numbers are meaningfully used. For example, the rules

$$a + (-b) = a - b,$$

$$(-a) + (-b) = -(a + b),$$

can be justified by interpreting positive numbers as distances measured in one direction along a line and negative numbers as distances on the same line but in the opposite direction, and the sum of two numbers as the net result of covering distances successively. The rule that the multiplication of a positive number with a negative number results in a negative number, that is,

$$a \times (-b) = -(\mathrm{a} \times \mathrm{b}),$$

is also easy to comprehend. For, 3 × (–2) can be understood as 3 of –2 or (–2) + (–2) + (–2) = – 6.

The multiplication of two negatives resulting in a positive number is not so easy to interpret in physical terms. What does (–1) × (–1) mean, and how does it equal 1? The justification of the rule that two negatives multiplied together, give a positive number, comes not from intuitive understanding or common experience but from logical extension, which we proceed to explain.

We have defined the set of positive and negative numbers as the set of ordered pairs of positive numbers. The rules for addition and multiplication of such ordered pairs are taken as

$$(a, b) + (c, d) = (a + c, b + d),$$

and $$(a, b) \times (c, d) = (ac + bd, ad + bc),$$

where a, b, c, d are positive numbers. (We omit the multiplication sign, ×, between two symbols as by well-known convention $a \times c$ is also written as ac). These rules, when applied to positive numbers, are essentially the old well-known rules; they look strange as they are put in an unfamiliar form. The merit of this form is that the rules can be extended to negative numbers in terms of operations defined earlier only for positive numbers. That the rules coincide with the familiar rules for positive numbers can be easily verified as follows.

For example, let $a = 6, b = 4, c = 8, d = 3$.
Then $(a, b) = (6, 4) = 2, \quad (c, d) = (8, 3) = 5.$

Applying the rule for addition,

$$(6, 4) + (8, 3) = (14, 7) = 7$$

which is correct, for $2 + 5 = 7$.

Also by the rule of multiplication,

$$(6, 4) \times (8, 3) = (6\times 8 + 4 \times 3, 6 \times 3 + 4 \times 8) = (60, 50) = 10$$

which also is correct, because $2 \times 5 = 10$.

(Once again we emphasize that verification is no proof. The essential point is that the rules of operation cannot be proved. They are axioms).

The rules also give the familiar results when one number is positive and the other negative. For instance, let $a = 6, b = 4, c = 3, d = 8$. Then,

$$(a, b) = (6, 4) = 2, (c, d) = (3, 8) = -5.$$

Adding them, $(6, 4) + (3, 8) = (9, 12) = -3$,

and multiplying them,

$$(6, 4) \times (3, 8) = (6 \times 3 + 4 \times 8, 6 \times 8 + 4 \times 3) = (50, 60) = -10,$$

both of which are correct as $2 - 5 = -3$ and $2 \times (-5) = -10$.

Let us see what happens when we apply the rules to two negative numbers. Let $a = 4, b = 6, c = 3, d = 8$. Then

$$(a, b) = (4, 6) = -2, (c, d) = (3, 8) = -5.$$

By the addition rule,

$$(4, 6) + (3, 8) = (7, 14) = -7.$$

any by the multiplication rule,

$$(4, 6) \times (3, 8) = (4 \times 3 + 6 \times 8, 4 \times 8 + 6 \times 3) = (60, 50) = 10.$$

Thus we find that $(-2) \times (-5) = 10$.

The rule that two negative numbers multiplied together result in a positive number is thus consistent with the general rule for multiplication.

Integers and Rational Numbers

Having defined zero and negative numbers, we may now introduce the term integer. The set

$$< \ldots -4, -3, -2, -1, 0, 1, 2, 3, 4 \ldots >$$

is called the set of integers. The positive integers are the natural numbers.

The integers, as we have seen, are a subset of fractions. In modern mathematics the term rational number is preferred to fraction. A rational number is defined as an ordered pair p, q, generally written as p/q, where p and q are any integers *except that q cannot be zero*. We had not mentioned this restriction earlier as we had defined fraction in terms of natural numbers, and zero till then had not bothered us. The restriction is very important. A concept like 2/0 or –8/0 is not defined at all. Division of a number by zero is not accepted as a meaningful or valid operation. (The more knowledgeable reader should not hasten to assert that 2/0 is infinity. He should have patience till we come to the discussion of infinity later).

The term 'rational' in this connection (and 'irrational' in connection with another type of number to which we shall come later) should not be taken to reflect some attribute akin to the dictionary meaning of the word. Perhaps the term is derived from 'ratio' in which case it becomes meaningful.

The set of rational numbers is an ordered set. Between two numbers a and b, if $a - b$ is a positive number, a is said to be greater than b, and if $a - b$ is negative, a is less than b. $a - b$ can be zero only if a and b are the same number. The set of integers is also an ordered set, and the test whether one number is greater or less than the other is also the same. But there is a very interesting difference between the two. Integers can be arranged consecutively such that each succeeding number is greater than the preceding, and between two consecutive integers there is no third integer. For example, 21 is followed by 22 and preceded by 20, and there is no integer between 20 and 21 or 21 and 22. This cannot be said about rational numbers. Between two rational numbers, however close, there can always be found a third rational number which is greater than one and smaller than the other. For example, between 4/1 and 5/1 is 9/2, and between 4/1 and 9/2 is 17/4, and between 17/4 and 9/2 is 35/8, and so on. This means that between any two rational numbers there are infinity of other rational numbers. They are all closely packed together, and there is no limit to their closeness.

Rational Numbers in Decimal Notation

An alternative way of writing a rational number is the decimal notation. The conversion from fraction to decimal can be done by the method of long division known to every school boy. For example, 35/8 = 4.375. It is not necessary that the division of the numerator by the denominator should terminate in the sense that the remainder should become zero at some stage. For example, 5/11 = .4545454545.... The digits 45 go on repeating endlessly. This is an example of a nonterminating recurring decimal. To take another example, 1/7 = .142857142857142857..... Here the digits 142857 go on repeating in this very order.

A characteristic property of a rational number is that it can always be expressed in terms of a recurring decimal. The terminating decimal may also be regarded as a recurring one if we suppose that the recurring digit is zero. Thus we may regard 4.375 as 4.3750000... The reason why in the decimal representation of a fraction, some packet of ordered digits must repeat itself is not difficult to understand. Let the fraction be a/b where a and b are natural numbers. When we start dividing a by b, the remainder at each step is some positive integer less than b. Since the number of such integers is finite, there is bound to come a stage when the remainder is some integer which has already occurred before. From then on all the digits in the quotient (the result of the division) will repeat themselves in the same order as they have after the earlier occurrence of the same remainder.

If every fraction can be put as a recurring decimal, it is also true that every recurring decimal representation of a number represents a fraction. The method of this conversion is well-known.

Irrational Numbers

Integers and rational numbers satisfy the need of measuring sizes of things. The rational numbers are ordered but closely packed and extend unendingly on the positive as well as the negative side of the number line. A straight line, unending on either side, can be intuitively imagined as a series of infinitely many points, all closely packed so that between any two points, however close, one can imagine an infinity of other points, but all strictly ordered in the sense that one can decide which point comes first and which later as one moves along the line in a particular direction. An infinite straight line thus provides a geometrical representation of the entire set of rational numbers. We may mark 0 and 1 at any two points arbitrarily. Conventionally, the point chosen to represent 1 is marked to the right of 0. Then all the other rational numbers (including integers) can be marked on this line, negative on the left and positive on the right of zero. We can always express a rational number as the difference between two rational numbers, and so it can be represented by the distance between two points on the line. Thus all rational numbers can be represented by distances along a line.

Is the converse also true? Do all distances measured along lines represent rational numbers? Since the rational numbers are all very closely packed along a line, one may be tempted to believe that they do not leave any space between them for any other 'animal' to stand. But number is an idea, not a thing, and ideas do not occupy physical space. Even then the discovery that the rational numbers do not exhaust all points along a line came somewhat as a shock.

The theorem of Pythagoras in plane geometry is well-known. If there is a right-angled triangle with two smaller sides each of unit length, and if the length of the hypotenuse is denoted by x, then

$$x^2 = 1^2 + 1^2 = 2.$$

What number is x? Obviously it is a number which when multiplied by itself gives 2. We may state the fact symbolically as

$$x = \sqrt{2}.$$

Is $\sqrt{2}$ a rational number? By a simple argument given in every school arithmetic now-a-days, it can be shown that $\sqrt{2}$ cannot be expressed as p/q where p and q are integers. The proof goes as follows.

Let, if possible, $\sqrt{2} = p/q$ where p and q are positive integers with no common factor between them (except of course 1). It is always possible to select p and q like this because, by equivalence relation, the common factor, if any, can be cancelled out.

Since, $\frac{p}{q} = \sqrt{2}$, by squaring both sides,

$$\frac{p \times p}{q \times q} = 2$$

or $$p \times p = 2 \times q \times q$$

$2 \times q \times q$ has a factor 2 in it, and so $p \times p$ should also have a factor 2. But every factor in $p \times p$ is repeated. If it occurs in one p, then it occurs in the other p also. No factor which does not occur in p can occur in $p \times p$. Hence 2 must be a factor in p. Putting $p = 2 \times r$, we get

$$2 \times r \times 2 \times r = 2 \times q \times q$$

or $$2 \times r \times r = q \times q$$

Repeating the above argument we now find that q must have a factor 2. Thus both p and q have a common factor 2. But we started with the assumption that p and q have no common factor. We are thus up against a contradiction. Our assumption that $\sqrt{2}$ can be put as p/q is self-contradictory and so not valid. So $\sqrt{2}$ is not a rational number.

But we need this concept. We have a line whose length is $\sqrt{2}$. Let us therefore give it a name and recognise it as a new type of number. In contrast to the rational, we call it *irrational*. The name is unfortunate in view of the dictionary meaning of the word. There is nothing unreasonable or nonsensical about this new concept. It is the product of as much good sense as any other. 'Irrational' in the present context should better mean 'unrational' or 'that which cannot be put as a ratio'.

Like $\sqrt{2}$ many other numbers like $\sqrt{3}, \sqrt{5}, \sqrt{8}$, etc can be proved to be irrational. There are negative irrationals like $-\sqrt{2}, -\sqrt{3}, -\sqrt{5}$, etc. Not only square roots but other roots of positive rational numbers can also be irrational. For instance, the fourth root of 5 (the number which when multiplied by itself three times gives 5) is also irrational. One can easily recognise any number of such roots of rational numbers as irrationals.

One may look at the way these numbers arise from another angle. $\sqrt{2}$ is a solution or root of the equation $x^2 = 2$. A large variety of equations occur in mathematics. This one belongs to the type known as algebraic equations. An algebraic equation is, in general, of the form or can be put in the form

$$x^n + a_1x^{n-1} + a_2x^{n-2} + ... + a_{n-1}x + a_n = 0,$$

where $a_1, a_2 ... a_n$ are integers and n is a positive integer. Numbers which can be roots of algebraic equations are called *algebraic* numbers.

Integers and rational numbers are algebraic, so are some irrational numbers, but not all. The examples of irrational numbers cited above are algebraic. A different type is presented by the well-known number universally denoted by π. It is the measure of the length of the circumference of a circle of diameter 1. It has been proved by methods not easy enough to be presented here that π is an irrational number in the sense that it cannot be expressed as a ratio of two integers. Also it has been proved to be nonalgebraic in the sense that there is no algebraic equation of which π is a solution. Nonalgebraic numbers are called *transcendental*.

The irrational numbers have been a hard nut to crack. Popping up before mathematicians ever since the beginning of algebra and geometry, they defied a systematic understanding till almost the end of the nineteenth century. What ultimately proved satisfactory is too abstract to be brought down to the level of this book.

One characteristic of the irrational number is that it cannot be exactly written in terms of a recurring or terminating decimal notation. One may write it upto five, ten, hundred, million or a billion decimal places, but the representation would still be incomplete. If we proceed to extract the square root of 2 by the method taught in schools, the process will neither come to an end nor will any arrangement of digits repeat itself *ad infinitum*. By working out the result to more and more decimal places we get numbers closer and closer to $\sqrt{2}$ but never exactly equal to it. We can prescribe exact limits between which $\sqrt{2}$ lies, and these limits can be narrowed down as much as we please. For instance, calculated upto ten places of decimal,

$$\sqrt{2} = 1.4142135623....$$

We can say that $\sqrt{2}$ lies between 1.41 and 1.42, or between 1.4142 and 1.4143, or between 1.4142135623 and 1.4142135624. Thus, it is possible to specify two rational numbers between which an irrational number lies, and that is the best that can be done in terms of decimal notation. The only way to describe an irrational number exactly is to give it a special symbol as we do when we write $\sqrt{2}$ or π.

The value of π calculated upto ten decimal places is 3.1415926535. When we take π = 22/7 = 3.1428..., we are taking a value which is correct only upto two decimal places. A more correct value is 355/113 = 3.1415929... which is correct upto six places. Adventurous people who do things for no other purpose except the thrill of it are found among mathematicians too. π had been calculated upto 707 decimal places by 1873. In our times the computers have joined the game and the value had been pushed to 10,017 places by 1955.

Irrational numbers are elusive but not rare. Not many have been given names or special symbols, but there is reason to believe that their population far exceeds the population of rational numbers (if infinity can exceed infinity!). An interesting argument in support of this belief is based upon what is known as the Monte Carlo method. Monte Carlo in France is the Mecca of gamblers. The games of chance played in the casinos there bring fortune to few and ruin to many. The place has lent its name to a class of methods in mathematics based upon considerations of chance.

Suppose we have three identical counters marked a, b, c in a bag, and a child takes out blindly the three counters one after another. What is the probability that he would draw the letters in an order which would make a meaningful word of the English language? Very little, for the simple reason that for one meaningful arrangement *cab* (meaning a vehicle) there are five meaningless arrangements *abc*, *acb*, *bca*, *bac*, *cba*. Suppose there are 26 counters in the bag, each marked with one letter of the English alphabet, and a counter is drawn out blindly, the letter on it noted, and the counter put back in the bag. Suppose four counters are drawn out successively like this and the word formed by them noted. The act is repeated a hundred times. If we find that most of the time we are drawing out meaningless words, we shall be justified in concluding that meaningless four letter arrangements far exceed the meaningful arrangements in the English language.

To follow the same method, let there be ten identical counters marked 0, 1, 2, 3, ..., 9 in a box, and we draw out a counter blindly, note it and replace it in the bag. We go on doing it for all time (it is not possible, of course, but we can imagine). What is the chance that we would draw out numerals which from a certain stage onwards would be repeated in exactly the same order for all time to come? Commonsense says the chances are nil. Looked at differently it means that if through some miracle which only God himself could perform, all the numbers, rational and irrational, were to be thoroughly mixed up in a bag and a celestial child were asked to pick up any one number, the likelihood of his picking up a rational number is almost nil. The rational numbers are completely lost in the crowd of irrationals.

Real Numbers

The rational and irrational numbers together are called *real* numbers. A real number is either rational or irrational. No effort to discover in these numbers any attribute akin to reality need be made. The name only separates them from other types of 'creatures' to which we shall come in our exploration of the world of numbers.

The two binary operations of addition and multiplication are defined on real numbers, the result of either operation being a real number. The inverse operations of subtraction and division (except by zero) are also defined. The real number set is well ordered; given any two different numbers, one is greater than the other. Also between any two different numbers, rational or irrational, however close they may be to each other, an infinity of other real numbers, rational as well as irrational, occur. These two properties lead to the graphical representation of real numbers on an infinitely long line. Choosing 0 and 1 as any two points on a straight line, (conventionally 1 is chosen to the right of 0), all other numbers find their proper positions on the line. Every point on the line corresponds uniquely to a real number, and every real number has a unique representative point. For this reason the set of real numbers is often referred to as the *real line* (Fig. 3.3).

Fig. 3.3

We shall discover yet other kinds of numbers in the universe of mathematics, but in one way the search has come to an end. The numbers discussed so far, the positive and negative integers, the rationals, the irrationals all are inhabitants of the real line. Further examination of the real line reveals no new type of numbers. Between the integers were discovered the rationals, between the rationals, even though they apparently left no room between them, were found the irrationals. But now, however minutely and by whatever apparatus of logic we dissect the real line, we do not discover any 'new object' lying on it.

How large is Infinity?

Starting from the natural numbers 1, 2, 3, 4, ... we have step by step defined larger and larger classes of objects such that each class includes all the preceding classes as subsets. Each set is infinite in the sense that its members are countless. The set of rational numbers and the set of integers both are infinite, but the latter is a subset of the former. One is tempted to conclude that the rational numbers are far more numerous than the integers. Similarly there seems to be reason to believe, as we have seen in the last section, that the real numbers far exceed the rational numbers in their numerical strength. It means that infinity can be of different degrees of largeness. Does it make sense?

Infinity is not a definite number or quantity and so in the domain of exact knowledge, as mathematics had come to be looked upon, it created conceptual and logical difficulties. For centuries infinity was an apparition for mathematicians which they could neither face nor dispel. It disturbed the orderly world of mathematics, as, for instance, in the following manner.

Consider the set of natural numbers and the set of positive even numbers:

(i) < 1, 2, 3, 4, 5, ... >
(ii) < 2, 4, 6, 8, 10 ... >

Obviously, set (i) contains all the members of set (ii), and many more besides. It would be right to say that for every one member in (ii) there are two members in (i). Shall we say then that there are twice as many members in (i) as in (ii)? The answer in the affirmative looks reasonable, but, far from getting us out of the difficulty, it leads us deeper into a dilemma. It is like holding two ropes in our hands, both hanging side by side endlessly into a bottomless pit, and we asserting that one is twice as long as the other. How can we compare the sizes of two infinitely large bodies?

In mathematics, when common sense and intuition fail, arbitrary definitions, provided they lead to consistently logical extension of accepted ideas, are often admitted as the basis for such extensions. In the present case we have first to agree to a definition of when two infinite sets are equal (or rather of equal degree of infiniteness) before we can decide if one is larger than the other.

Transfinite Numbers

Let us recall how we measure the size of a finite set. We place the objects in the set in one-one correspondence with the set of natural numbers. The natural number against which the last object appears measures the size of the set.

Let us do the same with infinite sets. To measure the size of the set of even positive numbers, let us place them in one-one correspondence with the natural numbers:

1	2	3	4	5	6	7	8	...
|	|	|	|	|	|	|	|	
2	4	6	8	10	12	14	16	...

No matter how far we go, this correspondence continues. So we agree to say that the two sets are equal in size. What is that size? Well, it is a particular size of infinity. It will have to be given a name. Cantor, the mathematician, who was the originator of the idea, gave it the symbol, $\aleph_0$ (Aleph zero, Aleph being the first letter of the Hebrew alphabet). We thus reject the view that one of these sets is twice as large as the other. The definition now is: Any infinite set which can be placed in one-one correspondence with the set of natural numbers is of the size $\aleph_0$.

The definition leads to some surprising results. For example, if we take away, say, the first five numbers from the set of natural numbers, the remaining set is of the same size as the original set, because it can still be placed in one-one correspondence with the natural numbers:

1	2	3	4	5	6	7	8 . . .
|	|	|	|	|	|	|	|
6	7	8	9	10	11	12	13 . . .

What is still more surprising is that the set of rational numbers, which as we have seen are packed closely between integers, is also of the same size. It is possible to write down positive rational numbers in a sequence (as shown below by arrows) such that no rational number will be missed and all of them will eventually find a place:

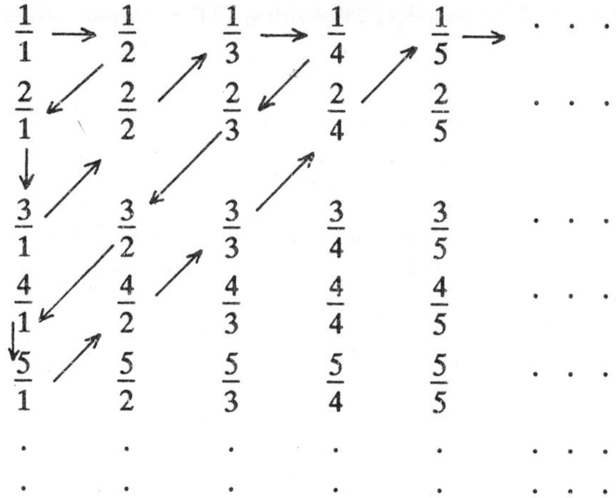

They can therefore be arranged in one-one correspondence with the natural numbers:

1	2	3	4	5	6	7	8	9	10
|	|	|	|	|	|	|	|	|	|
$\frac{1}{1}$	$\frac{1}{2}$	$\frac{2}{1}$	$\frac{1}{3}$	$\frac{2}{2}$	$\frac{3}{1}$	$\frac{1}{4}$	$\frac{2}{3}$	$\frac{3}{2}$	$\frac{4}{1}$

It looks hard to swallow, but only if we cannot get over our notions of finite objects.

The question arises: are there infinite sets which cannot be placed in one-one correspondence with the natural numbers. It has been proved that the set of real numbers is one such set. There is no way to arrange all real numbers so that none will be left out. The set of real numbers is therefore of a higher order of infinity. Its size is denoted by $\aleph_1$ (Aleph one). Points along any finite segment of a line, real numbers between 0 and 1 (or between any two numbers), points on any finite or infinite area of a plane, points in any volume of space, are also examples of sets of the same size. We leave out the proof as it is beyond our scope.

These are the two lowest known levels of infinity. It has been proved that there are not only higher levels of infinity but also an infinite number of them. The various levels or degrees of infinity have been called transfinite numbers.

Imaginary Numbers

By the rule of multiplication of real numbers the result of multiplying a real number (positive or negative) by itself is a positive number. The question arises -- what is that which when multiplied by itself gives a negative real number? The practical need of such a concept becomes apparent when we look for the solution of, say, the equation $x^2 + 2 = 0$. There is no such real number. We meet the situation with the usual response. If you have a new baby, give it a name first, then nurture it and let it grow to its full potentialities.

The new idea is given the name *imaginary number*. The name does indicate the initial conceptual difficulties the mathematicians faced, but now it is only a name with no insinuation of literal meaning. For the mathematician all numbers, real or imaginary, rational or irrational, positive or negative, are just pure ideas and stand on equal footing.

The imaginary number which when multiplied by itself gives -2 is denoted as $\sqrt{-2}$. Accordingly, in general, if a is a positive real number, $\sqrt{-a}$ is an imaginary number. By a formal extension of the rules

$$-a = (-1) \times a, \sqrt{a \times b} = \sqrt{a} \times \sqrt{b}$$

which hold for real numbers, we may write

$$\sqrt{-a} = \sqrt{-1} \times \sqrt{a},$$

where $\sqrt{a}$ is the square root of a positive real number and is therefore real (positive or negative). Thus all imaginary numbers can be formally written as real numbers multiplied by $\sqrt{-1}$.

It is customary to denote $\sqrt{-1}$ by the symbol i, and the imaginary number $\sqrt{-a}$ as $i\sqrt{a}$ or $\sqrt{a}\, i$. Since $\sqrt{a}$ is a real number, we may denote an imaginary number simply as bi or ib where b is a real number. Thus $2i$, $-3i$, $\frac{3}{4}i$, $1.45i$, πi are examples of imaginary numbers. The symbol i is such that

$$i \times i = i^2 = -1.$$

Therefore a formal definition of multiplication between two imaginary numbers may be taken as

$$ai \times bi = a \times b \times i^2 = -(a \times b)$$

which implies that the product of two imaginaries is real. Similarly the product of an imaginary and a real may be formally defined as an imaginary number as follows:

$$a \times bi = a \times b \times i = (a \times b)i$$

Thre rule for the addition of two imaginary numbers is taken as

$$ai + bi = (a + b)i$$

which may be regarded as a formal extension of the rule

$$ac + bc = (a + b)c.$$

Addition between a real and an imaginary is not defined. We may say that they are two different 'animals'. Three cows and four cows are seven cows but three cows and four horses are just three cows and four horses. Similarly, $3i + 4i = 7i$ but $3i$ and 4 are just $3i$ and 4. The analogy, of course, is hardly convincing, for if extended to multiplication, the product of 3 cows and 4 horses should also be meaningless.

By the notation that we have introduced for imaginary numbers it is obvious that there is a unique imaginary number corresponding to each real number. There is a one-one correspondence between the set of real numbers and the set of imaginary numbers. We may therefore represent all imaginary numbers also along an infinite straight line. But it will have to be different from the one on which the real numbers are represented, if the two sets are sought to be simultaneously shown on the graph.

Zero continues to occupy a special position. In conformity with the multiplication rule $0 \times a = 0$, we take

$$0i = 0 \times i = 0$$

which means that we shall be justified in treating the zero of the imaginary set as coincident with the zero of the real set. This sort of justification may look arbitrary, but definitions are always arbitrary in a strictly logical sense and their justification is to be sought in their being consistent with what has been accepted before.

Complex Numbers

As mentioned before, addition between a real and an imaginary number is not defined, and a real number a and an imaginary number bi (or ib) are just a pair (a, bi). It is customary to write this pair as $a + bi$, but with the clear understanding that it does not in any way represent the sum of a and bi. With this understanding the pairs $(3, 4i)$, $(-3, 6i)$, $(-2, -i)$ are respectively written as $3 + 4i, -3 + 6i, -2 - i$.

The next step in the evolution of numbers is to regard the pair (a, bi) as a new type of number with the real and imaginary numbers being only subsets of this more comprehensive class. It may look odd to regard a pair of numbers as one number, but let us recall that we are not doing it for the first time. The fraction a/b is also a pair of numbers (a, b). The negative numbers too could be logically defined as a pair of two numbers. In both these cases the two members of the pair belonged to the same set. The only new thing we are doing in defining a complex number is that the two members of the pair are from two different sets, one from the real and the other from the imaginary. Even this difference is only superficial. As we shall see presently, we can look upon a complex number as an ordered pair of real numbers.

To establish the real and imaginary numbers as special cases of complex numbers, we postulate that

$$a + 0i = a, 0 + bi = bi$$

The rules of addition and multiplication of two complex numbers are assumed as follows:

$$(a + ib) + (c + id) = (a + c) + i(b + d)$$

$$(a + ib) \times (c + id) = (ac - bd) + i(ad + bc)$$

The justification of these rules lies in their being consistent with the already accepted rules for real and imaginary numbers. If b and d are zero, the complex numbers above reduce to real numbers, and if a and c are zero, they reduce to imaginary numbers. In either case the rules reduce to the ones already accepted.

As an extension of the idea of representing real numbers along an infinite line, the complex numbers are, as a rule, represented on a plane determined by two perpendicular infinite straight lines (Fig. 3.4). The horizontal line OR represents the real numbers and the vertical line OI the imaginary numbers.

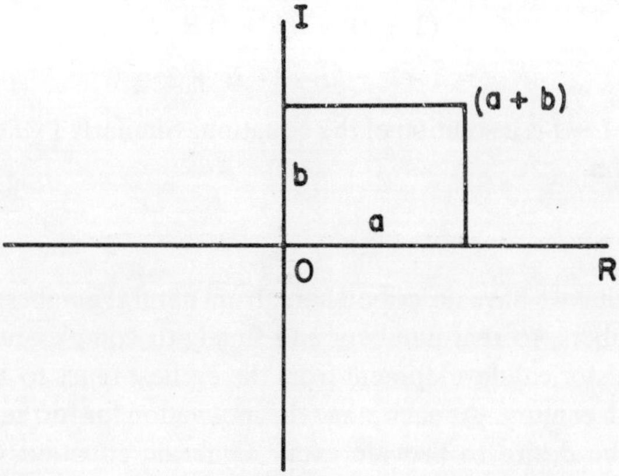

Fig. 3.4

The point of intersection O of the two lines represents zero. The complex number $a + ib$ is represented by the point whose distance from O parallel to the real axis is a and parallel to the imaginary axis is b. Readers familiar with coordinate geometry would recognise that the point $a + ib$ is identical with the point whose coordinates are (a, b) with respect to the coordinate axes OR and OI. Every complex number is represented by some point in this plane, and every point in the plane has a complex number corresponding to it. The plane representing the complex numbers is generally called *complex plane*.

It should be clear now that it should be possible to define the complex number as an ordered pair (a, b) of real numbers instead of a real and an imaginary. We can drop the symbol i but with the clear understanding that the order of numbers in the pair is crucial. (a, b) is different from (b, a), the former being $a + ib$ and the latter $b + ia$. Also the following binary operations are obeyed. These are the same as the earlier ones but in the new notation.

$$(a, b) + (c, d) = (a + c, b + d)$$

$$(a, b) \times (c, d) = (ac - bd, ad + bc)$$

In practice the symbol i is generally retained while working with complex numbers.

What is the need to invent complex numbers? As in earlier stages of the development of the number system, the motivation for complex number also comes from the solution of algebraic equations. Consider, for example, the equation

$$x^2 - 2x + 2 = 0$$

The problem is to find a number, if any, which when put in place of x makes the left side expression zero. It is not possible to find any such real or imaginary number, but the complex numbers $1 + i$ and $1 - i$ meet the requirement. Putting $1 + i$ in the left side of the above equation,

$$(1 + i)^2 - 2(1 + i) + 2$$

$$= 1 - 1 + 2i - 2 - 2i + 2 = 0$$

which means $1 + i$ is a solution of the equation. Similarly $1 - i$ can also be seen to be a solution.

Conclusion

The process that we have described here, from natural numbers to fractions, to negative numbers, to real numbers and finally to complex numbers, follows roughly the historical development from the earliest times to about the end of the nineteenth century. At each stage the motivation for further generalization came from the desire to provide every algebraic equation with a solution, though in the process numbers which were not solutions of algebraic equations were also discovered. This end was finally achieved with the invention of complex numbers. No further generalization is called for, because a famous theorem, known as the fundamental theorem of algebra was proved. According to it an algebraic equation of the nth degree of the general type

$$x^n + a_1x^{n-1} + a_2x^{n-2} + ... + a_{n-1}x + a_n = 0$$

where, a_1, a_2, ... a_n are integers and n is a positive integer, has n roots, real, imaginary or complex. So there is no need to postulate any other object in connection with this equation.

Does it mean the end of the road? Mathematicians are for ever looking for generalizations. Nothing is more satisfying to them than to postulate an idea, prove a theorem or discover a method which includes an already existing idea or theorem or method as a special case. Starting from notions directly suggested by the impact of environment on our senses, they proceed to construct structures of thought progressively more and more abstract but not necessarily, for that reason, less and less useful.

The natural question is – why stop at ordered pairs of numbers to define new numbers? Why not consider ordered triplets, quadruplets, and so on. This was exactly the attempt made. A collection of four ordered real numbers, called a quaternion was defined such that the complex numbers were a subset of quaternions. A perfectly general attempt was made to work out a theory for ordered sets of n (that is any number of) real numbers. These efforts resulted in a new insight into the nature of binary operations serving as fundamental postulates. For example, one could define a non-commutative binary operation according to which $a \times b$ and $b \times a$ will not be the same thing. The attention was subsequently diverted to a closer scrutiny of postulates or axioms of ordinary algebra and to the study of systems with slightly different postulates. The surprising thing was that the new systems, seemingly abstract and useless, made mathematics even more useful in its applications to science, technology and human affairs. Subsequent chapters provide a glimpse into such developments.

OF HISTORICAL INTEREST

The discovery or invention of natural numbers and the elementary operations on them belong to prehistoric times. Fractions were known to Egyptians and Babylonians four thousand years ago.

Pythagoras

Known to every school boy through the famous theorem about the right-angled triangle, Pythagoras (Greek, 580-500 B.C) travelled to Egypt, Babylon and possibly to India during Buddha's lifetime to learn mathematics and astronomy. He, and after him, the Pythagorean school gave to natural numbers a divine status and believed in mystical properties associated with them. Number mysticism is still prevalent in many societies as a pseudo-science of numerology which from the scientific viewpoint is pure superstition. "All is number', declared the Pythagoreans.

Aryabhat I

There have been two mathematicians by the name Aryabhat. The second one lived in the 10th century. It is the first one who is more important in the history of ancient mathematics and astronomy. Aryabhat I (Indian, born 476 A.D) was the author of two books, one of which is lost, but later mathematicians, Varahmihira and Bhaskara I, have referred to it, and Brahmagupta based his book on the astronomical constants given in it. Aryabhat's other book, *Aryabhatiyam*, is still extant.

Aryabhat's contributions to astronomy were remarkable. One thousand years before the idea was introduced by Copernicus in Europe, Aryabhat propounded the heliocentric theory of the solar system. He discarded the traditional priestly astronomy and ushered in a mathematics-based astronomy. He rejected the Puranic view that the eclipses were caused by the demon Rahu and propounded the modern scientific view.

Aryabhatiyam gives many rules in arithmetic, algebra and geometry, many of them having been known and practised by earlier mathematicians. The method of extracting the cube root of a number and formulae for determining the sum of the squares and cubes of natural numbers were given in the book for the first time.

By Aryabhat's time fractions and irrational square roots of numbers were unhesitatingly accepted by mathematicians. The value of π is given in Aryabhatiyam by the following formula. 'Add 4 to 100, multiply by 8, and add 62000; the result is approximately the circumference of the circle of diameter 20,000.' By this formula the value of π turns out to be 3.1416, a remarkably accurate value even from modern standards. Aryabhat also frequently used $\sqrt{10}$ for π.

Brahmagupta

Brahmagupta (Indian, about 598-660 A.D) worked at Ujjain, the centre of learning in India for many centuries. His work in astronomy was summarised in a book written about 628, the most notable feature of which was the application of algebraic methods to astronomy. He is also credited with the first known use of negative numbers and for stating the four simple rules of operation applying to them. The systematized arithmetic of negative numbers and zero is for the first time found in his work. He stated clearly that the product of two negative numbers is positive and the product of a positive and a negative is negative.

Mahavira

The rules of adding and multiplying numbers, positive and negative, became common in India after their restatement by Mahavira (Indian, 9th century A.D). Negative numbers appearing in problems concerning money came to be interpreted as debts, positive numbers being understood as assets. Mahavira's remark that in the nature of things a negative number has no square root, is regarded as very intelligent for his times, as a thousand years later, Cauchy (1789-1857), one of the greatest French mathematicians, did something similar by discarding $\sqrt{-1}$ as meaningless.

Development of Number System in Europe

Fibonacci (1170-1230) introduced the Indian ideas to Europe, but little progress was made for the next four hundred years. Cardan, in 1545, restated Mahavira's rules but still called the negative numbers fictitious. He also used imaginary numbers formally but failed to incorporate them in the number system. Leibniz (1646-1716) in the 17th century had progressed no further.

The geometrical representation of complex numbers and their consistent interpretation was given by C. Wessel (Norewegian, 1745-1818) in 1797. A similar interpretation was given by Argand (French, 1768-1822) nine years later. It needed the great authority of Gauss (1777-1855) to get complex numbers accepted as respectable members of the number family. The interpretation of complex numbers as pairs of real numbers is due to Gauss (1831) and also independently to Hamilton (1805-1865).

The irrational numbers presented the most difficult step in completing the set of numbers. A rational understanding of the irrationals came only with J.W.R. Dedekind (German, 1831-1916) and Cantor (1845-1918).

Chapter 4

From Algebra to Algebras

"Mathematicians do not study objects, but the relations between them."
—H. Poincare, French mathematician (1854—1912)

School algebra, commonly understood as generalised arithmetic, deals with the manipulation of expressions involving operations of addition, subtraction, multiplication and division and their variations like powers and roots on symbols which stand for numbers. The rules of manipulation have to be the same as are applicable to numbers. 2, $\sqrt{3}$, 5⁄4, 1.76, etc are also symbols for numbers, but the algebraic symbols *a, b, c, x, y, z,* etc stand generally not for one particular number but for any one of a set of numbers.

A Matter of Rules

In the last chapter we saw how practical needs and demands of consistency led to more and more comprehensive concept of a number till finally, by the middle of the nineteenth century, the quest culminated in the invention and acceptance of complex numbers which included, as special cases, all other types of numbers. The mathematician's passion for generalisation knows no bounds. When further extension of the number concept was attempted by considering more than two ordered real numbers as a single entity, strange things happened. The commutativity of the law of multiplication (that is, $a \times b = b \times a$) which was hitherto regarded as too obvious to be questioned broke down. A quaternion was conceived as an ordered collection of four real numbers such that a complex number, which is an ordered collection of two real numbers, turned out to be a special case of a quaternion. For this purpose the binary operations on quaternions had to be so defined that they were consistent with the corresponding rules for complex numbers. This consistency could be achieved only when the multiplication of two quaternions was defined in a way that made the operation non-commutative.

This and similar other observations confronted during other attempts at further generalization of the number system brought in question the very basis of the rules of algebraic manipulation. Were they assumed or were they logically provable? Which of them, if any, had to be accepted as axioms, and which could be derived from them? Could we discard or modify a rule, and invent a new algebra based on modified rules? After all, algebra looks like formal manipulation of expressions of symbols according to prescribed rules. Problems which students are taught to solve by mechanical application of rules such as changing an expression from one form to another or solving an equation are like games. One could play the game under different rules. The surprise was that not only new algebras could be created but they could be useful too. Abstraction in mathematics has not always led towards uselessness. More often natural phenomena as well as human activities have nicely fitted into abstract patterns of the mathematician.

Axioms of Algebra

A close scrutiny of algebra revealed that a minimum number of rules have to be accepted as axioms or postulates. They have to be such that they cannot be proved from each other and all the other rules can be derived from them. We again emphasize that usefulness or meaningfulness of a rule from a practical viewpoint is no proof of its truth. It still remains an assumption, a useful assumption. We give below the currently accepted postulates of the algebra of real numbers which is what we all know as the common algebra.

The set of real numbers is a set R with two binary operations '+' and '×' defined on it such that, if a, b, c are any three elements of R, then the following rules apply.

1a *Addition*
$a + b$ is in R (i.e. R is closed with respect to +)

1b *Multiplication*
$a \times b$ is in R (i.e. R is closed with respect to ×)

2a $a + b = b + a$, (+ is a commutative operation)

2b $a \times b = b \times a$, (× is a commutative operation)

3a $a + (b + c) = (a + b) + c$, (+ is associative)

3b $a \times (b \times c) = (a \times b) \times c$ (× is associative)

4a *Special property of 0*
There is an element 0 in R such that $a + 0 = a$. (0 is called the identity element with respect to +)

4b *Special property of 1*
There is an element 1 in R such that $a \times 1 = a$. (1 is called the identity element with respect to ×)

5a *Existence of negatives*
For every a in R there exists $-a$ in R such that $a + (-a) = 0$.

5b *Existence of inverses*
For every a in R, ($a \neq 0$), there exists $1/a$ in R such that $a \times (1/a) = 1$.

6. *Distributive Law*

$$a \times (b + c) = (a \times b) + (a \times c)$$

These eleven postulates are independent of each other and from them all the other rules of manipulation can be derived. It is possible to state these axioms in some alternative forms. If two statements are equivalent in the sense that each can be derived from the other, then it is immaterial which of them is taken as basic and which is treated as derived.

It is interesting to note that the distributive law 6 is an axiom. In fact one may wonder why $a, b, c, +, \times$ should be such that

$$a \times (b + c) = (a \times b) + (a \times c)$$

and not

$$a + (b \times c) = (a + b) \times (a + c)$$

One could substitute some particular numbers for a, b, c and verify that the first rule is true and the second is not, but in logic verification is not proof. Later we shall come across systems in which both the above types of distributive laws hold.

It can be easily verified that the above eleven postulates equally well apply to the set of rational numbers. The complex numbers also obey all the postulates. But not the integers or the natural numbers. The integers (positive and negative whole numbers and zero) satisfy all of them except 5b, because there are no numbers like 1/2, 1/3, 1/4, .. among integers. The natural numbers 1, 2, 3, 4, etc do not satisfy 4a, 5a and 5b because the set neither contains zero nor inverses like 1/2.

The fact that rational numbers, real numbers and complex numbers, all satisfy the eleven axioms listed above shows that a set of postulates does not define a unique system. Many systems may obey the same axioms. A set of postulates therefore defines a certain basic quality of a system which has been called *structure*. The real, the rational and the complex numbers have the same algebraic structure in so far as they obey the same postulates. As it happens, both the real and the rational numbers are ordered sets, but there is no such ordering in the complex numbers. An additional postulate imposing ordering on the set may be included as an axiom. Then with respect to this augmented set of postulates the real and the rational numbers have the same structure but the complex numbers are different.

The interest thus shifts to fundamental postulates and the study of algebraic structure. The set with two binary operations and the eleven postulates listed above is called a *field*. There is a field of real numbers, a field of complex numbers, etc. We have noticed that the set of integers does not satisfy the eleven postulates, it satisfies only ten. Therefore, it is not a field. The natural numbers satisfy only eight of the postulates. The question is, can we have systems with still less number of axioms? The lesser the number of axioms, the simpler may be the algebraic system, and so, hopefully, more useful in understanding and building more complicated algebraic systems. We start with a very simple algebraic structure called group. It is now regarded as a basic concept of fundamental importance and occupies a central position not in algebra alone but in all mathematics.

Hour Marks on a Clock

Consider the twelve markings or symbols on a clock, *I, II, III, IV, V, VI, VII, VIII, IX, X, XI, XII*. Let us call them the set A. Let us not, with our preconceived notions, regard them as the first twelve numbers used in counting about which we may feel we know everything. To guard against this we are using the Roman symbols. We take them to be twelve and just twelve symbols. In this connection we know neither zero nor *XIII* nor any other symbol. Based on the knowledge of what these symbols signify on a clock, we assume that they denote two ideas: (i) marks on the clock (ii) intervals of time. For example, *III* is a mark such that if the hour hand is on it, then a certain fixed interval of time has elapsed since it was last on the mark *XII*, and that this interval is also denoted by *III*. If the same time has elapsed after the hour hand was last on *II*, the new position of the hour hand would be *V*. We may state this fact symbolically as

$$II * III = V$$

The symbol * indicates a binary operation between the elements of the set A. We purposely refrain from using the symbol + as it would again bring in our minds a preconceived notion, addition between numbers, which we want to keep out because we have neither defined numbers nor addition. The symbol '=' indicates that the operation indicated by the left side expression results in the situation expressed by the symbol on the right side.

We may write similar other statements also concerning the symbol *III*, such as

$$III * III = VI, VIII * III = XI, X * III = I, XII * III = III.$$

Similarly for other intervals of time, for example,

$$VIII * II = X, X * V = III.$$

As a general rule, given any two elements a and b of the set A, we can always find an element c in the set such that $a * b = c$. This property is called closure. We say that the set A is closed with respect to the operation *. Table 4.1 is a ready reckoner giving a complete list of c for every pair a, b in A. The extreme left column lists a, the top row lists b, and the corresponding c is entered against a and below b.

Table 4.1

	I	*II*	*III*	*IV*	*V*	*VI*	*VII*	*VIII*	*IX*	*X*	*XI*	*XII*
I	*II*	*III*	*IV*	*V*	*VI*	*VII*	*VIII*	*IX*	*X*	*XI*	*XII*	*I*
II	*III*	*IV*	*V*	*VI*	*VII*	*VIII*	*IX*	*X*	*XI*	*XII*	*I*	*II*
III	*IV*	*V*	*VI*	*VII*	*VIII*	*IX*	*X*	*XI*	*XII*	*I*	*II*	*III*
IV	*V*	*VI*	*VII*	*VIII*	*IX*	*X*	*XI*	*XII*	*I*	*II*	*III*	*IV*
V	*VI*	*VII*	*VIII*	*IX*	*X*	*XI*	*XII*	*I*	*II*	*III*	*IV*	*V*
VI	*VII*	*VIII*	*IX*	*X*	*XI*	*XII*	*I*	*II*	*III*	*IV*	*V*	*VI*
VII	*VIII*	*IX*	*X*	*XI*	*XII*	*I*	*II*	*III*	*IV*	*V*	*VI*	*VII*
VIII	*IX*	*X*	*XI*	*XII*	*I*	*II*	*III*	*IV*	*V*	*VI*	*VII*	*VIII*
IX	*X*	*XI*	*XII*	*I*	*II*	*III*	*IV*	*V*	*VI*	*VII*	*VIII*	*IX*
X	*XI*	*XII*	*I*	*II*	*III*	*IV*	*V*	*VI*	*VII*	*VIII*	*IX*	*X*
XI	*XII*	*I*	*II*	*III*	*IV*	*V*	*VI*	*VII*	*VIII*	*IX*	*X*	*XI*
XII	*I*	*II*	*III*	*IV*	*V*	*VI*	*VII*	*VIII*	*IX*	*X*	*XI*	*XII*

A property of the element *XII* is at once noticeable. The binary operation of *XII* with any element leaves the latter unchanged. Thus

$$XII * VIII = VIII, IV * XII = IV.$$

In general, if *a* is any element of *A*,

$$XII * a = a * XII = a.$$

Such an element in a set is given a special name. It is called the identity element. *XII* is the identity element of *A*.

Another property of the set can also be observed. For every element *a* of *A*, there exists an element *x* in *A* such that

$$x * a = XII.$$

For example, if *a* is *VIII*, *x* is *IV*. *x* is said to be the inverse of *a*.

Yet another property of the set *A* is the following. Given three elements *a*, *b*, *c*,

$$a * (b * c) = (a * b) * c$$

where the binary operation between elements enclosed in the parentheses is to be performed first. This is called the associative property. It implies that if the binary operation is to be performed between three elements in succession, it is immaterial in what order the operation is performed. We may verify the above property as follows.

$$IV * (VI * IX) = IV * III = VII.$$

Also

$$(IV * VI) * IX = X * IX = VII$$

Hence

$$IV * (VI * IX) = (IV * VI) * IX.$$

Group

Collecting the properties enumerated above, we find that the set A with the binary operation '*' defined on it satisfies the following properties.

(G1) The set is closed with respect to the binary operation '*', that is, if a and b are elements of the set, $a * b$ is also an element of the set.

(G2) The binary operation '*' is associative, that is, if a, b, c are elements of the set, then

$$a * (b * c) = (a * b) * c$$

(G3) There exists an element in the set called the identity element (denoted here by e) such that

$$a * e = a$$

(G4) For every element a in the set, there is an element in the set called the inverse of a (denoted as a^{-1}) such that

$$a * a^{-1} = e$$

A set with the above four axioms (G1, 2, 3, 4) is called a group. The set consisting of the hour marks on the clock as discussed above is an example of a group.

Notice that the four properties have not been proved. They have been accepted because in a particular physical situation they make sense. Forget the physical situation and treat the elements of the set and the binary operation as abstract concepts, and we have a purely mathematical structure with the above four properties as axioms. The marks on a clock presented a system which had this structure. There can be other situations too which have the same structure. For example, the following.

Pack of Three Cards

Take a pack of three cards, say, King (K), Queen (Q) and Jack (J). We could take more cards but three are enough to illustrate the principle. Let us suppose, to start with, K is the top card in the pack, then Q and then J. We denote this arrangement as KQJ. Let us shuffle the pack. How many different arrangements can result after a shuffle? A little reflection will show that only the following six arrangements, including the one we started with, are possible.

1 KQJ 2 KJQ 3 JQK

4 QKJ 5 JKQ 6 QJK

The shuffle leading from arrangement 1 to arrangement 2 involves K retaining its position and Q and J interchanging. We may denote this shuffle by S_2, defining it as

$$S_2\colon K \to K, Q \to J, J \to Q$$

Similarly, we define the other possible shuffles as

$$S_3: K \to J, Q \to Q, J \to K$$

$$S_4: K \to Q, Q \to K, J \to J$$

$$S_5: K \to J, Q \to K, J \to Q$$

$$S_6: K \to Q, Q \to J, J \to K$$

To this set of shuffles we also add the shuffle from 1 to 1, namely,

$$S_1: K \to K, Q \to Q, J \to J$$

Thus we have defined a set of six shuffles, $S_1, S_2, S_3, S_4, S_5, S_6$. Let us denote this set of six elements by B.

Let us shuffle the pack once, and then shuffle again. Suppose the first shuffle happens to be S_2, and the second S_5. Let the two consecutive operations be denoted as $S_2 * S_5$. Since S_2 means the change $K \to K, Q \to J, J \to Q$, and S_5 means $K \to J, Q \to K, J \to Q$, the two shuffles performed one after the other would mean

$$K \to K \to J, Q \to J \to Q, J \to Q \to K$$

which is equivalent to the single shuffle

$$S_3: K \to J, Q \to Q, J \to K$$

Hence we may say that

$$S_2 * S_5 = S_3$$

In fact the result of any two consecutive shuffles would be the same as of some single shuffle. Defining the binary operation '*' in the above sense, we may say that if a and b are any two elements of B, then

$$a * b = c$$

where c is also some element of B. Thus the set B is closed with respect to the operation '*', which is property (G1).

This binary operation is also associative, that is,

$$a * (b * c) = (a * b) * c$$

To verify this, let $a = S_2, b = S_3, c = S_4,$

Now,

$$S_3 * S_4: = K \to J \to J, Q \to Q \to K, J \to K \to Q$$
$$= K \to J, Q \to K, J \to Q = S_5$$

and so

$$S_2 * (S_3 * S_4) = S_2 * S_5$$
$$= K \to K \to J, Q \to J \to Q, J \to Q \to K$$
$$= K \to J, Q \to Q, J \to K = S_3$$

Also,

$$S_2 * S_3 = K \to K \to J, Q \to J \to K, J \to Q \to Q$$
$$= K \to J, Q \to K, J \to Q = S_5$$

and so $(S_2 * S_3) * S_4 = S_5 * S_4$

$$= K \to J \to J, Q \to K \to Q, J \to Q \to K$$
$$= K \to J, Q \to Q, J \to K = S_3$$

Thus $$S_2 * (S_3 * S_4) = (S_2 * S_3) * S_4$$

which verifies the associative property (G2).

The shuffle S_1 has the obvious property of leaving an arrangement unchanged. We may say that

$$a * S_1 = a$$

where a is any element of B. S_1 is thus an identity element of B which means B satisfies property (G3) also.

Further, corresponding to any shuffle, there is a shuffle which will restore the original arrangement. For example,

$$S_5 * S_6 = K \to J \to K, Q \to K \to Q, J \to Q \to J$$
$$= K \to K, Q \to Q, J \to J = S_1$$

S_6 is therefore the inverse of S_5. It can be verified that S_5 is the inverse of S_6. It is interesting to see that S_1, S_2, S_3 and S_4 are their own inverses. Every element of B has an inverse which is also in B. Thus B satisfies property (G4) also. The set B is therefore a group. Table 4.2 is a ready recokner for the binary operations for B, similar to Table 4.1 for the set A.

Table 4.2

*	S_1	S_2	S_3	S_4	S_5	S_6
S_1	S_1	S_2	S_3	S_4	S_5	S_6
S_2	S_2	S_1	S_5	S_6	S_3	S_4
S_3	S_3	S_6	S_1	S_5	S_4	S_2
S_4	S_4	S_5	S_6	S_1	S_2	S_3
S_5	S_5	S_4	S_2	S_3	S_6	S_1
S_6	S_6	S_3	S_4	S_2	S_1	S_5

Sets A and B described above are both groups. There are some obvious differences between them. The set A has twelve elements, B has six. There is no restriction on the number of elements a group can have. There are groups with infinitely many elements, and groups only with one element. The number of elements in a group is called its order.

Another difference between the groups A and B is that in A the binary operation is commutative, while in B it is not so. For every pair of elements of A, $a * b = b * a$, as can be seen in Table 4.1. But it is not so for all pairs of elements of B. For example, in Table 4.2, $S_3 * S_2 = S_6$, but $S_2 * S_3 = S_5$. The binary operation in a group may or may not be commutative.

Rotations of a Triangle

It would be instructive to consider yet another example of a group. Consider a plane sheet, say of cardboard, in the shape of an equilateral triangle (Fig. 4.1). Let it be divided into three parts, each in the shape of a quadrilateral, by three lines drawn perpendicular from the centre to the sides. To distinguish between them, let each part be coloured differently, one red (R), the other yellow (Y) and the third green (G), on both sides of the cardboard. It is possible to rotate

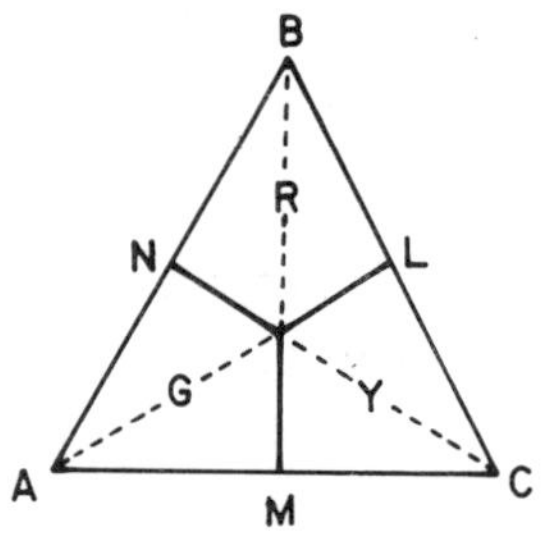

Fig. 4.1

the triangle about any of its three medians AL, BM, CN, and also about an axis through the centre O perpendicular to the plane of the triangle, the final position after each rotation being still the same as the initial position except that the positions of the coloured portions get interchanged. For example, a rotation about BM through 180° can bring vertex C in the position of vertex A and vertex A in the position of vertex C, thus interchanging the positions of colours G and Y. Also a rotation through 120° about the perpendicular axis through O (which we shall henceforth call rotation about O) can bring B in the position of A, A in C, and C in B, thus bringing R in place of G, G in place of Y and Y in place of R. The following different rotations of the triangle resulting in the interchange of positions of colours are possible. We denote the rotations by $R_1, R_2, \ldots R_6$.

$R_1: R \to R, Y \to Y, G \to G$ (about O through 360°)

$R_2: R \to R, Y \to G, G \to Y$ (about BM through 180°)

$R_3: R \to G, Y \to Y, G \to R$ (about CN through 180°)

$R_4: R \to Y, Y \to R, G \to G$ (about AL through 180°)

$R_5: R \to G, Y \to R, G \to Y$ (about O, anticlockwise, through 120°)

$R_6: R \to Y, Y \to G, G \to R$ (about O, clockwise, through 120°)

R_1 is the rotation which keeps the order of colours unchanged.

Let us define the binary operation '*' between any two rotations, say $R_2 * R_3$, as 'the rotation R_2 followed by the rotation R_3'. Accordingly,

$$R_2 * R_3 = R \to R \to G, Y \to G \to R, G \to Y \to Y$$
$$= R \to G, Y \to R, G \to Y = R_5.$$

Similarly, we can interpret other possible binary operations. Table 4.3 gives the result of all such operations. We leave it to the reader to satisfy himself that the set of six rotations is a group by verifying step by step all the four properties (G1, 2, 3, 4) required of a group. The identity element is R_1. A comparison of Tables 4.2 and 4.3 reveals that they are identical except for the symbols R and S. It means the algebraic structure of the set of card shuffles and the set of rotations is exactly the same.

Table 4.3

*	R_1	R_2	R_3	R_4	R_5	R_6
R_1	R_1	R_2	R_3	R_4	R_5	R_6
R_2	R_2	R_1	R_5	R_6	R_3	R_4
R_3	R_3	R_6	R_1	R_5	R_4	R_2
R_4	R_4	R_5	R_6	R_1	R_2	R_3
R_5	R_5	R_4	R_2	R_3	R_6	R_1
R_6	R_6	R_3	R_4	R_2	R_1	R_5

Abstract Structure

The three examples discussed above to explain the idea of a group also illustrate an important aspect of modern mathematics. None of the three examples are about numbers. The marks on the clock, the card shuffles and the rotations of a triangle, all these are ideas or things which are not numbers. (The dial of a clock or a watch is often marked in numbers, but as often it is not, making it obvious that the use of numbers is not essential). In each case operations were defined which established relationships between 'things'. The relationship gave a structure to the set of things. This structure, in the three examples, was similar and was given the name group. The physical nature of the things and of the operations between them could be widely different, yet their basic structure, in an abstract sense, was the same. Modern mathematics deals with such abstract structures, and these are not necessarily always in terms of numbers. Undoubtedly, however, because mathematics originally started as a tool for the study of quantitative relationships, numbers still continue to be one of its major concerns. But in case of numbers too, mathematics generally investigates the nature of relationships and structure among them.

Examples of groups can be given from numbers also. The set of integers

$$< 0, 1, 2, 3, 4, \ldots -1, -2, -3, -4, \ldots >$$

with the binary operation '+' (addition) can be seen to form a group, as it satisfies all the four properties of the group:

It is closed; any two numbers in the set added together give a number which is also in the set; (G1).

The operation of addition is associative; (G2).

There is an element 0, such that $x + 0 = x$ for every element x in the set; (G3).

For every element x, there is an element $-x$ in the set, such that $x + (-x) = 0$; (G4).

The elements in this group are infinitely many.

A finite number of numbers can also form a group. Here is an example of just three numbers, 1, $-(1 + \sqrt{3}i)/2$, $-(1-\sqrt{3}i)/2$, forming a group. These are three cube roots of 1. It can be verified by actual multiplication that the cube of each of these numbers is 1. These three numbers form a group with respect to multiplication, as is clear from the following properties.

The product of the two complex numbers, $-(1 + \sqrt{3}i)/2$ and $-(1 - \sqrt{3}i)/2$, is 1. Also multiplication by 1 leaves a number unchanged. Thus it turns out that the product of any two numbers of the set is a number in the set. Further, the product is associative. The identity element is 1. The inverse of 1 is 1, while the inverse of each of the complex numbers is the other complex number. Table 4.4 shows these properties in a tabular form.

Table 4.4

$\times$	1	$-(1 + \sqrt{3}i)/2$	$-(1-\sqrt{3}i)/2$
1	1	$-(1 + \sqrt{3}i)/2$	$-(1-\sqrt{3}i)/2$
$-(1 + \sqrt{3}i)/2$	$-(1 + \sqrt{3}i)/2$	$-(1-\sqrt{3}i)/2$	1
$-(1 - \sqrt{3}i)/2$	$-(1 - \sqrt{3}i)/2$	1	$-(1 + \sqrt{3}i)/2$

Other Algebraic Structures

The elements in a group obey four axioms. There could be still simpler structures with lesser number of axioms. For example, consider the set of natural numbers, $<1, 2, 3, 4, \ldots>$, and the binary operation of addition. The set is closed with respect to this operation because the sum of any two elements of this set is also an element of the set. Also the operation is associative, as for any elements a, b c of the set, $a + (b + c) = (a + b) + c$. But there is no identity element because there is no element in the set which when added to any number in the set leaves the number unchanged. (Note that 0 is not included in the set). Also, consequently, there is no inverse. Such a set is called a *semigroup*. If the set of natural numbers 1, 2, 3, 4, ... with the binary operation of multiplication is considered, it is found to be closed and associative and to have an identity element 1, (since $a \times 1 = a$). But there is no inverse, because there is no element x in this set such that $a \times x = 1$. Such a set is given the name *monoid*. The set of natural numbers including zero with the operation of addition is also a monoid.

One could look on the other side of the group to discover sets which obey more than four axioms. Between the field with eleven postulates, defined earlier, and the group with four postulates, a number of other algebraic structure have been recognised and defined.

The point is that the rules of ordinary algebra are not applicable to all systems. So long as we are dealing with the whole set of rational, real or complex numbers, ordinary algebra is valid. But if our symbols stand for elements of some subsets of these, some of the rules of operation may become meaningless. For instance, if our symbols denote only integers, an expression like a/b is ruled out. If we restrict ourselves to numbers 1, 2, 3, 4, ...10, 11, 12, as they are used in a clock, the rules of addition of ordinary arithmetic do not hold. Special rules have to be devised which would justify statements like $3 + 12 = 3$ and $11 + 10 = 9$. When our symbols do not represent numbers but some other objects or ideas, the situation may be still more different. The operation of addition or multiplication or division may lose its meaning completely, but some other operations may be meaningful and useful. It may be possible to codify the rules of operation and invent a new algebra applicable to the objects the symbols represent. There are many such algebras in modern mathematics. The next three chapters provide a glimpse at some of them.

FROM THE GALLERY OF MATHEMATICIANS

Augustin – Louis Cauchy

A brilliant mathematician and a bigoted catholic, Cauchy (French, 1789–1857) combined in himself supreme mathematical ability with utterly blind religious faith. His early promise as a mathematician came to the notice of the great French mathematicians, Lagrange (1736–1813) and Laplace (1749–1827), the former prophetically telling the latter and some other notable mathematicians, 'this boy will one day surpass all of us in mathematics'.

After a brilliant school career in which he won many national prizes instituted by Napolean to discover talent, Cauchy went to Ecole Polytechnique and then to Ecole de Ponts et Chaussees (School of Bridges and Roads) to become a military engineer.

By the age of twenty-six Cauchy had reached the level of front rank mathematicians and took up professorial appointments. He was a prolific writer of lengthy research memoirs and mathematical texts.

In a sense Cauchy may be called the father of modern mathematics with its emphasis on abstractions and logical rigour. Till then, except for the theory of numbers, most mathematics grew out of applications. Cauchy started the tradition of developing a subject as an abstract system on its own merits without enquiring whether it had any applications. Looking deeper into the laws of algebraic operations beneath formal manipulations, he was led to the theory of groups.

Cauchy's fundamental ideas about limits, continuity and convergence pulled calculus out of some initial logical difficulties (see chapter 9) and put it on a sound basis. His definitions of these concepts are still standard material for any introductory course to higher mathematics.

Evariste Galois

Evariste Galois (French, 1811 – 1832) was a mathematical genius who died at the age of twenty in a senseless duel over a disreputable woman. He was the first to give a clear cut definition of group as it is understood now, though many others before him made their contributions to the development of the idea. Galois' short life was as tragic as his death. Nobody in his lifetime, except he himself, knew that he was a mathematical genius. In school he was a mediocre; because of lack of systematic training he could not be admitted to Ecole Polytechnique, the nursery of famous mathematicians. At the age of seventeen he submitted a paper of fundamental importance to the famous mathematician Cauchy which was misplaced and lost. Another submitted for the Academy prize was also lost. A third submitted through Poisson, another famous mathematician, was returned with the remark that it was unintelligible. With premonition of his death, the night before the fateful duel, he in a letter to his friend jotted down short notes on his fundamental discoveries. On that basis alone he is recognised as one of the greatest mathematicians of all time.

EXERCISES

1. The eleven axioms (1a to 5a, 1b to 5b, 6) given on page 61 govern the operations of addition and multiplication on the set of real numbers. Test which of the axioms hold and which do not for the following sets.

   (i) Set of natural numbers: < 1, 2, 3, 4, 5,... >

   (ii) Set of integers: < 0, 1, 2, 3, 4,...; –1, –2, –3, –4,... >

   (iii) Set of even integers: < 1, 2, 4, 6,...; –2, –4, –6,... >

   (iv) Set of odd integers: < 1, 3, 5, 7,...; –1, –3, –5, –7,... >

2. Which of the following sets are groups with respect to the given operation? Indicate which of the axioms (G1 to G4 given on page 65) do not hold in cases when the set is not a group.

   (i) Set of integers <0, 1, 2, 3, 4,... > with respect to addition.

   (ii) Set of rational numbers with respect to addition.

   (iii) Set of rational numbers with respect to multiplication.

3. We define four rotations, R_0, R_1, R_2, R_3 of a square about its centre as indicated in the following diagram.

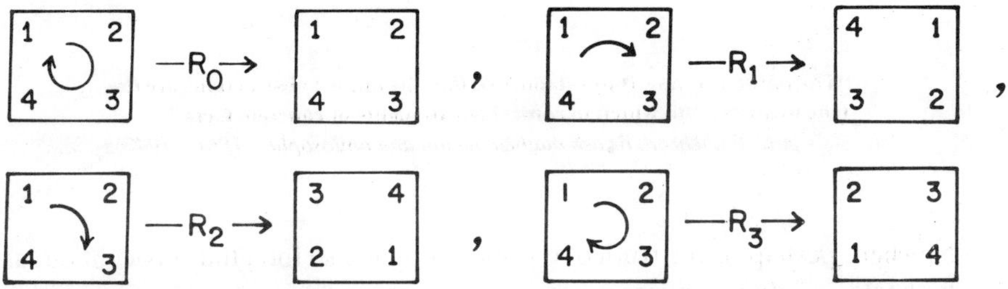

Make a table of the type 4.3 (page 69) and show that the four operations form a group. Identify the identity element and the inverse of each element.

ANSWERS

1. (i) 41, 5a, 5b do not hold.
   (ii) 5b does not hold.
   (iii) 4b, 5b do not hold.
   (iv) 1a-5a, 5b, 6 do not hold.

2. (i) G4 does not hold; the set is not a group.
   (ii) It is a group.
   (iii) It is a group.

3. R_0 is the identity element; R_1, R_3 are the inverse of each other; R_2 is its own inverse.

Chapter 5

Algebra for Computers

"The paradox is now fully established that the utmost abstractions are the true weapons with which to control our thoughts of concrete facts."
—*A.N. Whitehead, British mathematician and philosopher (1861—1947).*

Nowhere perhaps is the truth of the above opinion so forcefully brought out as in the design of the modern computer. The computer is a machine in as much as it is a substitute for human labour doing far more quickly what a large number of persons could do in a much longer time. But it is a machine with a big difference. Its advent heralded the advance of technology from mechanical contrivances to decision making devices. So far machines aided human hands and feet, now with the coming of the computer they were aiding the human brain. So far machines utilised, for their design, principles of the movement of matter; they had moving parts which through material connections translated different types of motion into each other. Now the computers were designed on the principles of thought; they sat at a place and processed information; the little mechanical movements they did were no more than like the hand holding the pencil while the brain did the thinking.

A Mathematician's Machine

Mathematics played an indirect though significant role throughout the development of mechanistic technology. It provided language to the physical sciences and reliable analytical procedures to the rational understanding of mechanisms. But mathematics was not directly and explicitly involved in the invention, construction and development of machines. Mathematicians did not design machines; that was the work of scientists, engineers and artificers guided more by practical insight and experience than mathematical knowledge.

With the computer the story is different. It is a mathematician's machine. Its design is primarily and basically mathematical. The function of its components and the effect of interconnections are first described and understood in terms of abstract mathematics. Over the last four decades of its development, the physical components of the computer have changed from electronic valves to transistors and then to chips, as researches in physics produced more and more compact and sophisticated devices, but the essential design stays in the area of abstract mathematics.

Logic and Mathematics

The logical design of the computer, as the design in terms of abstract mathematics is called, utilises an algebra different from the ordinary algebra of numbers. It is an algebra of logic, an algebra applicable to the science of reasoning.

Logic and mathematics are intimately connected. In fact logic is the very fabric of mathematical thought. It is the breath of mathematics without which it will be reduced to a decaying and disintegrating jumble of meaningless symbols. This intimate relation between mathematics and logic has brought logic itself within the purview of mathematics. The last hundred and fifty years have witnessed the development of mathematical or symbolic logic, which is a fundamental area in mathematics linking it with and profoundly influencing the more classical subjects of logic and philosophy. The subject has two aspects. Firstly, its aim is to analyse, systematize and codify the principles of valid reasoning. In this respect it merely takes over the field of classical logic and introduces in it symbolic language with all its brevity, unambiguity and abstraction. Thus logic is freed from the common language which is developed more for the purposes of the literary artist than the cold logician, with words and phrases designed not to express truth or untruth but a thousand shades of meanings often purposely conveying different things to different people. Released from the limitations of such a language logic is able to probe more deeply in its own domain.

The other aspect of modern symbolic logic is concerned with the reduction of basic mathematical concepts to a system of pure logic. The idea of regarding mathematics as a logical system originated with the German mathematician G. Frege (1848 – 1925), and was carried forward by the Britishers, A.N. Whitehead and Bertrand Russell, through their monumental work, the Principia Mathematica (1910-13), which is regarded as a landmark in the history of mathematics. The attempt led to the study of fundamental problems about the nature of mathematics, and has laid bare not only the beauty but also the weaknesses and inconsistencies inherent in such an attempt. This, however, is too abstruse a subject to receive any but a passing mention here.

Truth and Validity

We shall introduce some simple and elementary concepts of the first aspect of symbolic logic, namely its application to the science of reasoning. It gives logic an abstraction which makes it a powerful tool to judge the correctness of a chain of reasoning. It is important to understand that logic concerns itself only with the validity of a deduction and not whether the deduction is true or not. Truth and validity of a conclusion are two different things. A statement may be logically valid but not true or vice versa.

The question of truth is generally outside the scope of mathematics. In his famous and oft-quoted three 'boasts' of a mathematician, one of which is that a mathematician does not know whether what he says is true or not, Bertrand Russell was not indulging in mere rhetoric. In fact the mathematician does not care much about truth. His main concern is validity. For example, whether it is true that the three angles of a triangle add upto two right angles is beside the point for a mathematician. Even if all the surveyors and all the draftsmen were unable to draw triangles with this property, the mathematician's deduction of this property of the triangle would still remain valid. His proof is based on certain definitions and axioms about points and lines and is logically sound so long as one accepts those definitions and axioms. Their rejection on philosophical, scientific or practical grounds will affect the truth of the conclusion but not its logical validity.

This distinction between truth and validity must be fully appreciated to understand the basic nature of mathematics and its close affinity with logic. It need not land us, however, into the difficult question of what is truth. We shall be concerned with situations where truth can be recognised without getting involved into metaphysical discussions about its nature.

Statements and Connectives

In mathematical discourse and elsewhere we constantly come across declarative sentences. A declarative sentence is either true or false. Such a sentence, in mathematical logic, is called a *statement*. A statement can only be either true or false. There is no other possibility. The following are a few examples of statements.

This book is written in English.
There are exactly 2178 stars in the universe.
Logic is not a branch of mathematics.
2 is an odd number.

It should be understood that the definition of statement given above is quite independent of an individual's knowledge or belief about its truth or otherwise. One may not know anything about this book, one may have no idea of the number of stars in the universe, one may know neither logic nor mathematics, one may be ignorant of what an odd number is, and yet it cannot be denied that each of the above statements is either true or false. A sentence which is neither true nor false is by definition not a statement in mathematical logic. The following sentences, for example, are not statements.

Go away.
Why don't you stand up?
Hip hip hurrah.
May God bless you.

Compound or complex sentences can generally be broken into simple ones, called *prime components*. A number of simple sentences may be connected together to form a single compound statement. The most obvious and common connective is 'and'. Its symbol in mathematics is $\wedge$. 'I am hungry and cannot sleep' can be symbolised as $P \wedge Q$, if P stands for the statement 'I am hungry' and Q for 'I cannot sleep'. It is worth noting that 'but' of the common language is also $\wedge$ in logic. 'It rained yesterday but it is bright this morning' is logically identical with 'It rained yesterday and it is bright this morning'. The difference in the shades of meaning of 'and' and 'but' expresses not a difference of fact but a difference of the reaction the fact has on the speaker.

Another connective is 'or' whose symbol is $\vee$. If P stands for 'It would rain' and Q for 'It would be cloudy', then $P \vee Q$ means it would either rain or be cloudy or both. The inclusion of 'both' in the definition of 'or' is important. $P \vee Q$ does not indicate P alone or Q alone to the exclusion of the other, but indicates at least one, P or Q, with the possibility of both P and Q not excluded. In language of legal documents this is expressed rather clumsily as P or/and Q.

A statement modified by the addition of 'not' is called the negation of the statement. The negation of 'The sun is shining' is 'The sun is not shining'. Symbolically, the negation of the statement P is denoted as $\overline{P}$ (read as 'not P').

The three symbols, $\wedge$, $\vee$, $\overline{}$, defined above, are the three fundamental operations through which compound statements can be formed out of prime components. The first two of these are connectives which can connect two statements; they are binary operations. The third one is an operation on one statement alone; it is an unary operation. Any compound statement can be written in terms of its prime components joined through these three symbols. Of course, from the literary point of view the construction would be outrageously clumsy, but logically it would be precise.

There are in ordinary language many other connectives joining prime components to produce compound statements. For example, the 'exclusive or', that is, 'one or the other but not both' is very common. 'Either P or Q' generally means 'one of the two but not both', and this connective is different from $\vee$ that we have defined.

Another common connective is 'if'. 'If it rains, I carry an umbrella' is a combination of two sentences, 'It rains' and 'I carry an umbrella'. In customary mathematical terminology the first statement *implies* the second. 'It rains' implies 'I carry an umbrella'. If P stands for the first sentence and Q for the second, then the compound sentence is 'If P then Q' or, symbolically, $P \Rightarrow Q$. It is important to note that rain implies carrying an umbrella, but carrying an umbrella does not imply rain. It is not stated that I carry an umbrella if and only if it rains. I may carry it otherwise too. So $P \Rightarrow Q$ means that if P is true then Q is true, but Q may or may not be true if P is false.

A stonger connective is 'if and only if'. If and only if P, then Q. Symbolically it is written as $P \Leftrightarrow Q$. In words it means: If P then Q, and if Q then P. If it rains I carry an umbrella, and if I carry an umbrella it rains. The umbrella is carried if and only if it rains.

However, these three and several other connectives used in ordinary language are not independent. It has been found possible to express all these in terms of the three* fundamental operations $\wedge$, $\vee$, $\bar{\ }$. The expressions with only these three connectives may be far from elegant, but they indicate that logically only three operations may be admitted axiomatically; others are deducible from them.

Truth Values of Compound Statements

As has already been observed, a statement can either be true or false. These are called *truth values*. In mathematical language it can have only two values, true or false. Let us use the symbols 1 and 0 for true and false, respectively. 1 and 0 here are not to be taken to mean the numbers one and zero. The advantage of using this notation is that it is more abstract and therefore of more general interpretation than the words true and false. It can be applied to other systems also where we deal with entities or variables with only two possible states or values. Such systems are basic to computer design.

Since the choice for the value of each statement is limited to only two, it is easily possible to examine all possible combinations of the values of the prime components involved in a compound statement, particularly if the number of prime components is small. With two prime components, the number of such combinations is four, and with three prime components, it is eight. For each such combination, it is possible to determine whether the compound statement is true or false. We proceed to use this procedure to derive some results which form the basis of the new algebra.

Let us first examine the compound statements $P \wedge Q$, $Q \wedge P$, $P \vee Q$, $Q \vee P$. That $P \wedge Q$ and $Q \wedge P$ are equivalent is obvious. It is just the same whether we say 'the rose is red and the rose is beautiful' or 'the rose is beautiful and the rose is red'. Similarly $P \vee Q$ and $Q \vee P$ are equivalent. In other words, the operations $\wedge$ and $\vee$ are both commutative.

$$P \wedge Q = Q \wedge P, \quad P \vee Q = Q \vee P$$

* In fact only two of them are independent; any one of them can be expressed in terms of the other two. But we shall not go into that refinement.

It is necessary to note this property explicitly even at the risk of appearing to emphasize the obvious, because we have already seen in the last chapter that a binary operation need not always be commutative. Table 5.1 gives the truth values of $P \vee Q$ for all possible combinations of the truth values of P and Q separately, and Table 5.2 gives the same for $P \wedge Q$.

Table 5.1

$P \vee Q$

	∨	P = 1	P = 0
Q	1	1	1
	0	1	0

Table 5.2

$P \wedge Q$

	∧	P = 1	P = 0
Q	1	1	0
	0	0	0

To appreciate these tables, let P stand for 'It rained yesterday' and Q for 'It is bright this morning'. If P and Q are both true (that is each has value 1), or, in other words, it is true that it rained yesterday and also it is true that it is bright this morning, then the compound statement $P \wedge Q$, that is, 'It rained yesterday and is bright this morning' is certainly true. This explains entry 1 against $P = 1, Q = 1$ in Table 5.2. If, however, either $P = 0$, that is, it did not rain yesterday, or $Q = 0$, that is, it is not bright this morning, then the statement $P \wedge Q$, that is, 'It rained yesterday and it is bright this morning' is false or has the value 0. This explains the entries 0 in the other three positions in table 5.2.

As for $P \vee Q$ (Table 5.1), if $P = 1, Q = 1$, that is both the statements are true, then one of them is certainly true, and so $P \vee Q = 1$. For $P = 1, Q = 0$, or $P = 0, Q = 1$, that is, for the cases when one of the statements is true and the other is false, P or Q is again true, that is $P \vee Q = 1$. But for the combination $P = 0, Q = 0$, that is when both the statements are false, P or Q is also false, that is $P \vee Q = 0$.

It can be verified by constructing a table that

$$(P \wedge Q) \wedge R = P \wedge (Q \wedge R)$$

This expresses the associative law for the operation $\wedge$. In Table 5.3 the values of the statements $P \wedge Q$ and $Q \wedge R$ are written in accordance with Table 5.2, and the values of $(P \wedge Q) \wedge R$ and $P \wedge (Q \wedge R)$ are written by regarding $P \wedge Q$ and $Q \wedge R$ as single statements and R and P as the other single statements and then applying Table 5.2 on them. It would be observed that the values of $(P \wedge Q) \wedge R$ and $P \wedge (Q \wedge R)$ are the same for every combination of the values of P, Q, R. Hence the associative law is valid. A similar law can be seen to hold for the operation $\vee$:

$$(P \vee Q) \vee R = P \vee (Q \vee R)$$

Table 5.3

P	Q	R	$P \wedge Q$	$(P \wedge Q) \wedge R$	$Q \wedge R$	$P \wedge (Q \wedge R)$
1	1	1	1	1	1	1
1	1	0	1	0	0	0
1	0	1	0	0	0	0
1	0	0	0	0	0	0
0	1	1	0	0	1	0
0	1	0	0	0	0	0
0	0	1	0	0	0	0
0	0	0	0	0	0	0

The following two distributive laws can also be seen to be true:

$$P \wedge (Q \vee R) = (P \wedge Q) \vee (P \wedge R)$$

$$P \vee (Q \wedge R) = (P \vee Q) \wedge (P \vee R)$$

In Table 5.4 the first of these laws is verified. The columns for $Q \vee R, P \wedge Q$, $P \wedge R$ are written from Tables 5.1 and 5.2, and then regarding these as single statements, columns for $P \wedge (Q \vee R)$ and $(P \wedge Q) \vee (P \wedge R)$ are written again using the same tables. It will be observed that the last two columns are identical which establishes the validity of the first distributive law. The second can also be similarly verified.

Table 5.4

P	Q	R	$Q \vee R$	$P \wedge Q$	$P \wedge R$	$P \wedge (Q \vee R)$	$(P \wedge Q) \vee (P \wedge R)$
1	1	1	1	1	1	1	1
1	1	0	1	1	0	1	1
1	0	1	1	0	1	1	1
0	1	1	1	0	0	0	0
1	0	0	0	0	0	0	0
0	1	0	1	0	0	0	0
0	0	1	1	0	0	0	0
0	0	0	0	0	0	0	0

Given any statement P, we can form its negation $\overline{P}$ by merely adding 'not' to it. For example, the negation of the statement 'My shoe is black' is 'My shoe is not black'. It is obvious that if P is true, $\overline{P}$ is false, and vice versa. Therefore both P and $\overline{P}$ cannot be true at the same time, that is,

$$P \wedge \overline{P} = 0.$$

Also either P or $\overline{P}$ is true, both cannot be false. Therefore

$$P \vee \overline{P} = 1$$

A simple but interesting pair of rules is

$$P \wedge P = P, \quad P \vee P = P.$$

Looked at through an example, the rules are trivial. 'It rains and it rains' is certainly equivalent to 'It rains', so also is 'It rains or it rains'. But as an abstract algebraic rule it is significant.

The following four simple rules also deserve notice.

$$P \wedge 1 = P, \quad P \vee 1 = 1,$$

$$P \wedge 0 = 0, \quad P \vee 0 = P.$$

Keeping in mind that 1 stands for a statement which is always true, and 0 for one which is always false, the validity of the above rules is not difficult to see. For example, if P is true $P \wedge 1$ is true, and if P is false $P \wedge 1$ is false. Thus $P \wedge 1$ has always the same value as P, that is, $P \wedge 1 = P$. Similarly one can see that the other rules also hold.

We add two more results, known as De Morgan's theorems:

$$\overline{P \vee Q} = \overline{P} \wedge \overline{Q}, \quad \overline{P \wedge Q} = \overline{P} \vee \overline{Q}$$

These can be verified easily by constructing the tables for the values of these expressions. Table 5.5 verifies the first theorem because the columns for $\overline{P \vee Q}$ and $\overline{P} \wedge \overline{Q}$ are identical.

Table 5.5

P	Q	$\overline{P}$	$\overline{Q}$	$P \vee Q$	$\overline{P} \wedge \overline{Q}$	$\overline{P \vee Q}$
1	1	0	0	1	0	0
1	0	0	1	1	0	0
0	1	1	0	1	0	0
0	0	1	1	0	1	1

Let us also examine the other connectives mentioned earlier, namely 'if', 'if and only if' and 'exclusive or'. The 'if' connects two statements P and Q thus: 'if P then Q', (in other words, 'P implies Q'), symbolically written as $P \Rightarrow Q$. To recall our old example, 'if it rains then I carry an umbrella'. This statement is true in the following three cases:

It rains (true), I carry an umbrella (true);
It rains (false), I carry an umbrella (true);
It rains (false), I carry an umbrella (false);

but is false in the case:

It rains (true), I carry an umbrella (false).

Thus to work out the truth table for $P \Rightarrow Q$, we note that $P \Rightarrow Q$ is false only for the case when P is true but Q is false; in all other cases it is true, (see Table 5.6).

'If and only if' is a stronger connective. 'If and only if P then Q' is true if P is true, otherwise it is false. If it rains, I carry an umbrella; if it does'nt, then I don't. It is equivalent to saying that 'if P then Q' and 'if Q then P', and so is symbolically written as $P \Leftrightarrow Q$. The truth table for this statement is also given in Table 5.6.

Table 5.6

P	Q	$P \Rightarrow Q$	$P \Leftrightarrow Q$	$\overline{P}$	$\overline{P} \vee Q$
1	1	1	1	0	1
1	0	0	0	0	0
0	1	1	0	1	1
0	0	1	1	1	1

As was stated earlier, $\wedge$, $\vee$, $\_$ are the three connectives in terms of which other connectives can be expressed. It can be verified that $P \Rightarrow Q$ can also be expressed as $\overline{P} \vee Q$. The verification lies in making a truth table for $\overline{P} \vee Q$ (also shown in Table 5.6), and observing that it is identical with the table for $P \Rightarrow Q$. Similarly $P \Leftrightarrow Q$ can also be expressed as $(\overline{P} \vee Q) \wedge (P \vee \overline{Q})$. It is easy to verify this by constructing the truth table for the latter which will turn out to be the same as for the former. One can also prove this as follows.

$$
\begin{aligned}
P \Leftrightarrow Q &= P \Rightarrow Q \text{ and } Q \Rightarrow P \\
&= (\overline{P} \vee Q) \text{ and } (\overline{Q} \vee P) \\
&= (\overline{P} \vee Q) \wedge (P \vee \overline{Q})
\end{aligned}
$$

The connective 'exclusive or', that is, 'or but not both' also deserves mention. 'P or Q but not both' is different from $P \vee Q$. If P is true and Q is true, then $P \vee Q$, is true but 'P or Q but not both' is false. In symbols the latter can obviously be written as $(P \vee Q) \wedge (\overline{P \wedge Q})$. Table 5.7 is the truth table for this statement.

Table 5.7

P	Q	$P \vee Q$	$P \wedge Q$	$\overline{P \wedge Q}$	$(P \vee Q) \wedge (\overline{P \wedge Q})$
1	1	1	1	0	0
1	0	1	0	1	1
0	1	1	0	1	1
0	0	0	0	1	0

Boolean Algebra

We have described some rules of operations which hold for statements. Let us now give these rules an abstract interpretation. Let there be a set such that its elements P, Q, R, ... can have only either of the two values, 0 or 1. Let two binary operations '$\wedge$' and '$\vee$' be defined on the set such that the following axioms hold.

1a	$P \vee Q$ is in the set (the set is closed with respect to $\vee$)	1b	$P \wedge Q$ is in the set (the set is closed with respect to $\wedge$)
2a	$P \vee Q = Q \vee P$ ($\vee$ is commutative)	2b	$P \wedge Q = Q \wedge P$ ($\wedge$ is commutative)
3a	$P \vee (Q \vee R) = (P \vee Q) \vee R$ ($\vee$ is associative)	3b	$P \wedge (Q \wedge R) = (P \wedge Q) \wedge R$ ($\wedge$ is associative)
4a	$P \vee 0 = P$ (0 is the identity element with respect to $\vee$)	4b	$P \wedge 1 = P$ (1 is the identity element with respect to $\wedge$)
5a	$P \vee \overline{P} = 1$	5b	$P \wedge \overline{P} = 0$

(P is the complement of P governed by the above rules)

6a	$P \vee (Q \wedge R) = (P \vee Q) \wedge (P \vee R)$	6b	$P \wedge (Q \vee R) = (P \wedge Q) \vee (P \wedge R)$

(Distributive law with respect to both the operations holds)

These are the axioms of the abstract structure known as Boolean algebra. It will be noticed that we have not included in the list of axioms all the results obtained earlier. The reason is that all of them need not be treated as axioms. A minimum number is accepted as axioms, and the others, and many more, can be deduced from them. It is of course possible to include some others among the axioms and deduce the displaced ones from them.

It is interesting to compare the axioms of Boolean algebra with those of ordinary algebra, (page 61). In both algebras two binary operations are assumed. Instead of the symbols + and $\times$ of ordinary algebra, we have used $\vee$ and $\wedge$ in Boolean algebra, but symbols are after all symbols, and we could even use the same symbols in both the systems without doing any damage to either. In fact it is quite customary to use + and . in Boolean algebra. The first three axioms, namely, of closure, commutativity and associativity, are identical in the two lists. Also the fourth axiom which postulates the existence of identity elements with respect to both the operations is identical. The fifth axiom is slightly different, in that the identity elements 1 and 0 in Boolean algebra get interchanged between (5a) and (5b) as compared to their positions in ordinary algebra. Finally, the sixth axiom is the major difference. In ordinary algebra the distributive law over addition with respect to multiplication is valid, that is,

$$a \times (b + c) = (a \times b) + (a \times c),$$

but the distributive law over multiplication with respect to addition, that is,

$$a + (b \times c) = (a + b) \times (a + c)$$

is not valid. In Boolean algebra the distributive laws hold mutually over the two binary operations.

It will be observed that in the above list the axioms have been listed in pairs, each pair consisting of an axiom marked (a) and another marked (b). There is a definite correspondence between the two members of each pair. Every (b) axiom can be obtained from its corresponding (a) axiom by interchanging $\vee$ and $\wedge$ and 1 and 0. One is called the dual of the other. On account of this duality in the axioms, in Boolean algebra, for every theorem there exists another theorem, called its dual, obtained by the above rule of interchange of symbols.

Switching Circuits

There are other systems too whose behaviour can be described in terms of Boolean algebra. An important example is provided by electrical circuits consisting of networks of wires and switches. If a switch is on, a connection is made through it, and if it is off, the connection is broken. A switch is either off or on; it can have only one of the two possible states (or values). It is, therefore, in this respect similar to a statement.

Suppose two terminals are connected by a wire with a switch P on it. We denote the two states of the switch, on and off, by the two symbols 1 and 0, respectively. When the switch is on, we say that $P = 1$ and the current flows between the terminals. When it is off, we say that $P = 0$ and the current is cut off.

Suppose we introduce two switches, P and Q, in series on the line between the two terminals (Fig. 5.1). If both P and Q are on, the current flows; if either of the two or both are off, no current flows. In other words, if $P = 1, Q = 1$, the combined effect of the switches is 1, but if $P = 1, Q = 0$ or $P = 0, Q = 1$, or $P = 0, Q = 0$, the combined effect is 0. This information is presented in Table 5.8. It is identical with Table 5.2. A series combination of two switches P and Q is thus equivalent to 'and' operation between statements. A series circuit, therefore, may be called an 'and' circuit and two switches P and Q in series may be denoted as $P \wedge Q$.

Let us consider the switches P and Q in parallel (Fig. 5.2). In this case the current can flow between the terminals if any one or both of the switches are on, and is cut off if both together are off. Table 5.9 contains this information.

Table 5.8

		P	
	∧	1	0
Q	1	1	0
	0	0	0

Table 5.9

		P	
	∨	1	0
Q	1	1	1
	0	1	0

Fig. 5.1

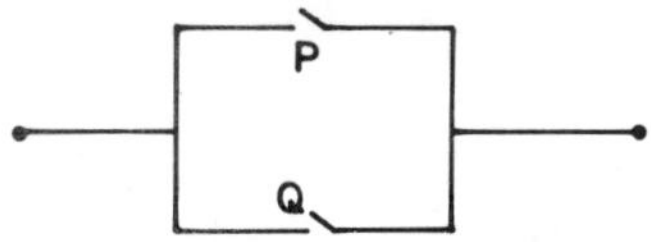

Fig. 5.2

It is identical with Table 5.1. A parallel circuit may, therefore, be called an 'or' circuit, and the two switches *P* and *Q* in parallel may be denoted as $P \vee Q$.

Also, for any switch *P* we may define a switch $\overline{P}$ such that if *P* is on, $\overline{P}$ is off, and vice versa. This is analogous to defining the complement or negation of a statement.

It is easy to construct switching circuits corresponding to Boolean expressions. Fig. 5.3 shows circuits which correspond to expressions $P \vee (Q \vee R)$ and $(P \vee Q) \vee R$.

That the two circuits are equivalent is obvious from physical considerations which verifies the validity of axiom 3a. The circuits corresponding to two

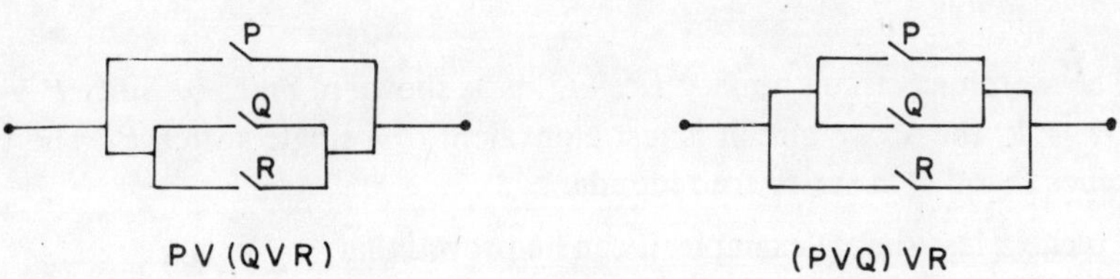

Fig. 5.3

expressions in the distributive law 6a are shown in Fig. 5.4. Fig. 5.5 shows the circuits for expressions in the other distributive law. It is easy to see that in each case the two circuits are equivalent which verifies the distributive laws.

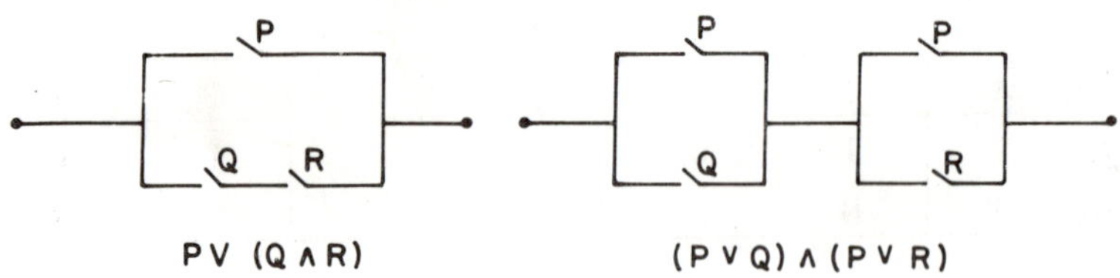

Fig. 5.4

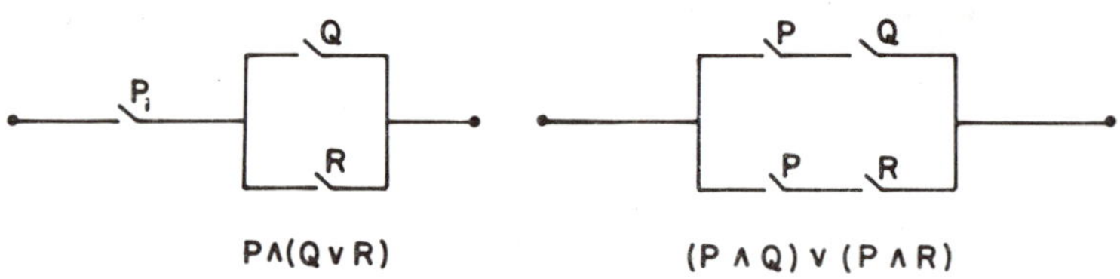

Fig. 5.5

As in ordinary algebra, so in Boolean algebra axioms provide rules for manipulating and simplifying Boolean expressions. If two Boolean expressions are proved equivalent to one another, then it follows that the corresponding switching circuits are also equivalent. This helps in designing circuits. To take a simple example, it can be proved by applying the rules of Boolean algebra that

$$P \vee (P \wedge Q) = P.$$

The proof goes as follows.

$$
\begin{aligned}
P \vee (P \wedge Q) &= (P \wedge 1) \vee (P \wedge Q), && \text{from axiom 4b,}\\
&= P \wedge (1 \vee Q), && \text{from axiom 6b,}\\
&= P \wedge 1\\
&= P
\end{aligned}
$$

The switching circuit for $P \vee (P \wedge Q)$ is as shown in Fig. 5.6. Since $P \vee (P \wedge Q) =$ P, the above circuit is just equivalent to a single switch P. The two switches P and Q in series are redundant.

To cite a less simple example, it can be proved that

$$[P \vee (Q \wedge R)] \vee [P \vee (R \wedge \overline{Q})] = P \vee R$$

from which it follows that the two circuits in Fig. 5.7 are equivalent.

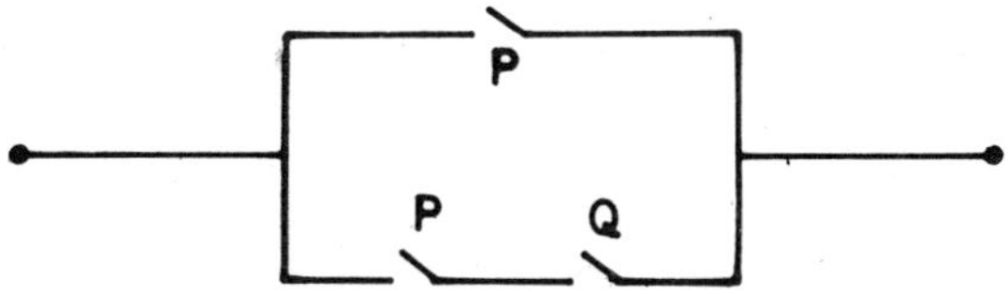

Fig. 5.6

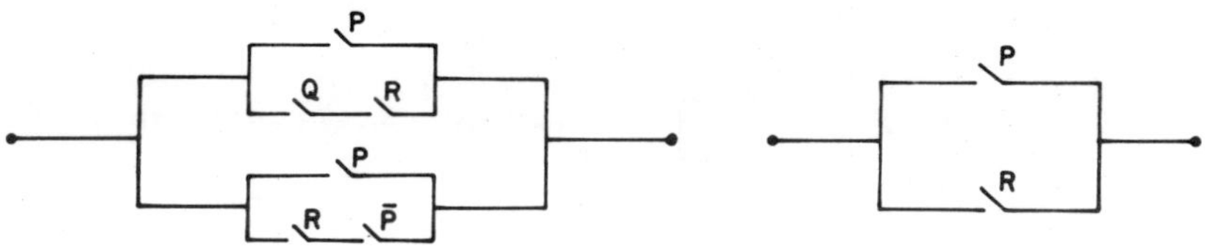

Fig. 5.7

Electronic Gates

Besides the switching circuits there are other types of electrical devices capable of implementing the three basic logical operations, 'and', 'or' and 'not'. There are electronic circuits, very small in size, with input and output points. They receive inputs as voltages at input points, and produce outputs as voltages at output points. The precise value of these voltages is not significant; it may differ from machine to machine. What is important is that there must be two levels of voltages, say V and zero, unambiguously distinguishable, so that an input or output point is either at voltage V or zero, representing the two binary digits 1 or 0 respectively.

The discussion of the physical nature of such a device is outside our scope. It lies in the area of electronic engineering and physics. We may take it as a black box. (A 'black box' is a term used for any package about whose contents we may know nothing. It should not be taken in its literal meaning.) It has terminals coming out on one side serving as input points, and terminals going out on the other side giving outputs.

These black boxes are called 'gates'. The black box of the 'and' gate contains an electronic circuit such that with P and Q as inputs, $P \wedge Q$ is the output (Fig. 5.8). In other words, if each of the input terminals is at voltage V, (that is $P = 1$, $Q = 1$) then the output terminal also acquires the voltage V ($P \wedge Q = 1$), but if either of the input terminals has a voltage zero then the output voltage is also

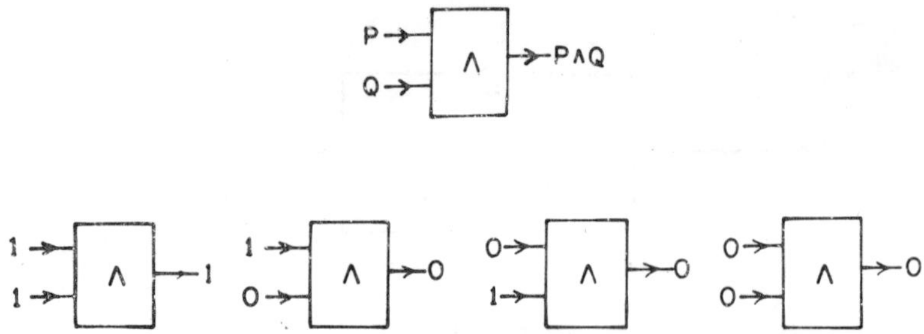

Fig. 5.8

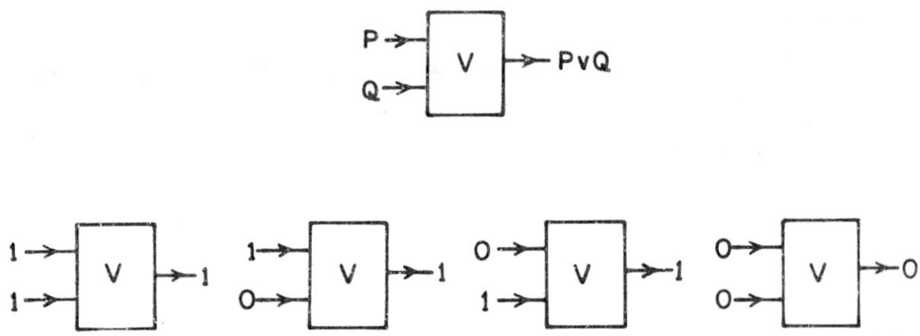

Fig. 5.9

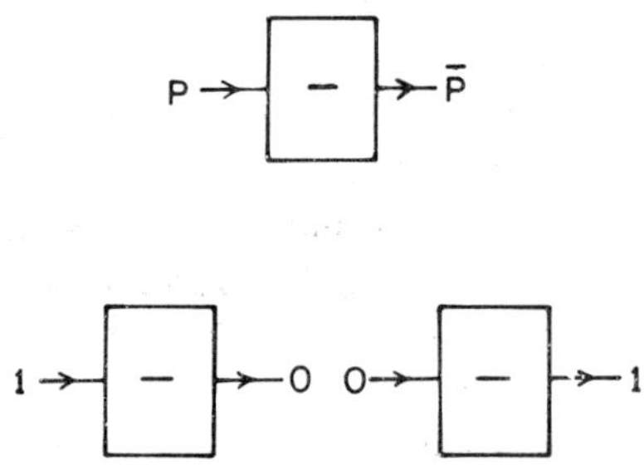

Fig. 5.10

zero ($P \wedge Q = 0$ for $P = 0, Q = 0$; $P = 1, Q = 0$; $P = 0, Q = 1$). All the four particular states of the 'and' gate are shown in Fig. 5.8.

Similarly, Fig. 5.9 shows an 'or' gate. In this circuit, with inputs P and Q, the output is always $P \vee Q$.

The third type of basic gate, the 'not' gate, is shown in Fig. 5.10. In this if the input is P, the output is $\bar{P}$, that is, if the input voltage is V, the output voltage is zero, and vice versa.

The Adder

Let us see how the basic gates can be joined together to produce the addition of two binary digits. Before proceeding further, the reader is advised to refer back to chapter 1 (page 8) to recollect the operations of addition, subtraction, multiplication and division of binary numbers. When two digits are added, the sum may be either in one digit or in two digits. The digit to the left in the two-digit answer may be called the carry over, because it is actually carried over when more than one-digit numbers are being added. When the answer is in one digit, we may say the carry over digit is zero. Thus, in every case when two digits, a, b, are added, we have in the answer a digit s which we shall call the sum digit, and a digit c called the carry over. Table 5.10 gives c and s for every combination of a, b. (Compare with the addition table in chapter 1.)

Table 5.10

$a + b = cs$

a	b	c	s
1	1	1	0
1	0	0	1
0	1	0	1
0	0	0	0

We notice that $c = a \wedge b$, and $s = (a \vee b) \wedge (\overline{a \wedge b})$ (a or b but not both, compare Table 5.7). We have to design a circuit with the 'and', 'or' and 'not' gates to produce two outputs, c and s, with two inputs, a and b, according to Table 5.10. The circuit shown in Fig. 5.11 does the trick.

There can be alternatives also. It can be proved by rules of Boolean algebra that

$$(a \vee b) \wedge (\overline{a \wedge b}) = (a \vee b) \wedge (\bar{a} \vee \bar{b}) = (a \wedge \bar{b}) \vee (\bar{a} \wedge b)$$

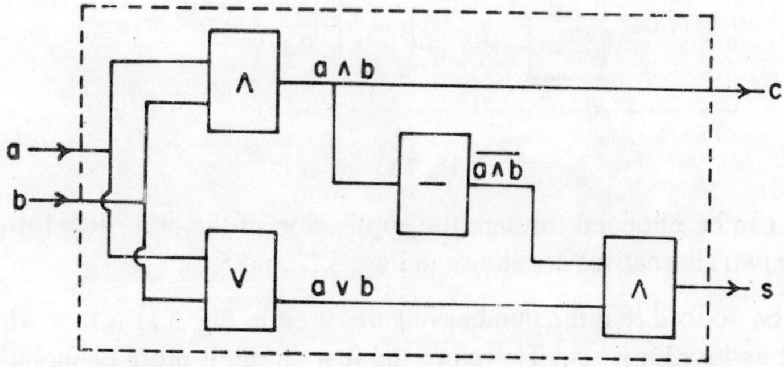

Fig. 5.11

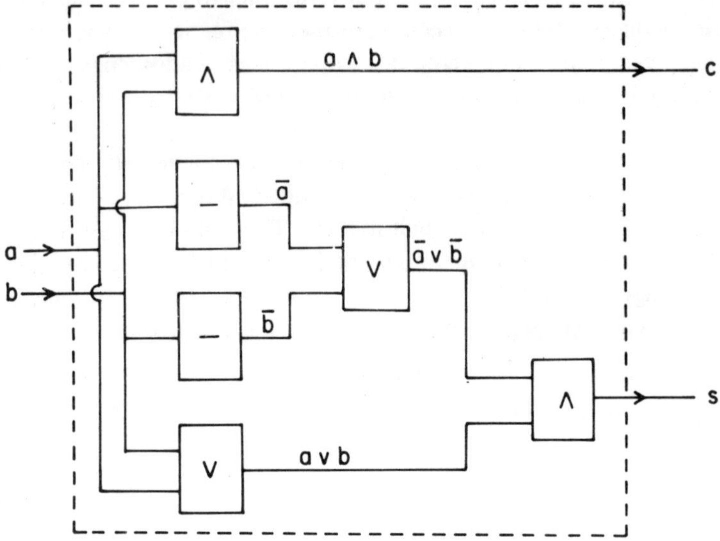

Fig. 5.12

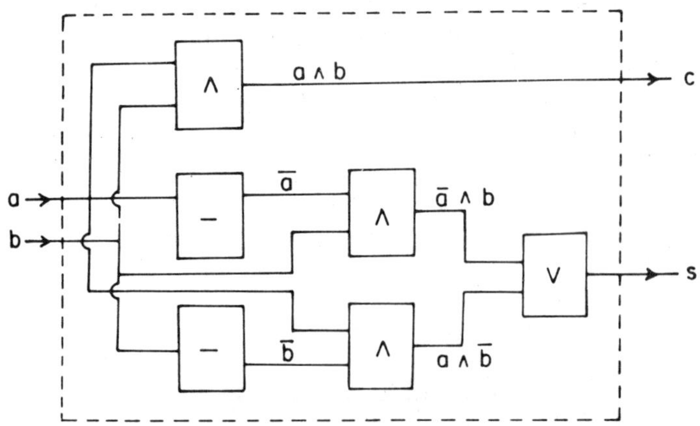

Fig. 5.13

Hence, s can be obtained through the application of the other two formulae also. The two alternatives are shown in Figs. 5.12 and 5.13.

It will be noticed that the number of gates used in Fig. 5.11 is four while in Figs. 5.12 and 5.13 it is six. Therefore the first circuit is more economical in terms of the number of gates. This example also illustrates how Boolean algebra can give us alternative solutions to a circuitry problem from which the most suitable solution from some point of view may be selected.

What we have described above is generally called a half adder. It can only add two digits. In general, in adding two numbers, we need to add three digits, two of the two numbers and one the carry over. A complete adder should therefore have a three-digit input and a two-digit output.

There can be many designs of the full adder. Fig. 5.14 shows one possibility. It consists of two half adders and one 'or' gate. a, b, c_0 are the digits to be

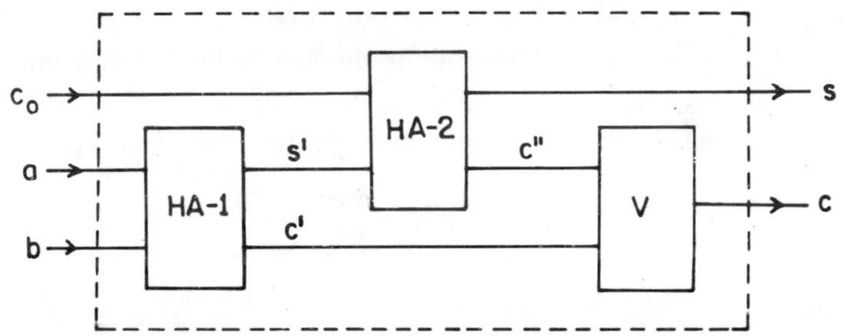

Fig. 5.14

added, c_0 being the carry over from the earlier sum; HA-1 and HA-2 are the boxes representing the half adders, each a circuit of the type shown in Fig. 5.11, 5.12 or 5.13. Table 5.11 shows how the final output c, s is the correct sum for each possible combination of inputs.

Table 5.11

Input			HA-1 output $(a + b)$		HA-2 output $(c_0 + s')$		gate output $c' \vee c''$	sum	
c_0	a	b	c'	s'	c''	s	c	c	s
0	1	1	1	0	0	0	1	1	0
0	1	0	0	1	0	1	0	0	1
0	0	1	0	1	0	1	0	0	1
0	0	0	0	0	0	0	0	0	0
1	1	1	1	0	0	1	1	1	1
1	1	0	0	1	1	0	1	1	0
1	0	1	0	1	1	0	1	1	0
1	0	0	0	0	0	1	0	0	1

Let us now see what arrangement can give the sum of any two binary numbers. Let the two numbers be

$$a_n\, a_{n-1} \ldots a_4\, a_3\, a_2\, a_1$$

and

$$b_n\, b_{n-1} \ldots b_4\, b_3\, b_2\, b_1,$$

whose sum is

$$c_n\, s_n\, s_{n-1} \ldots s_4\, s_3\, s_2\, s_1$$

where all the symbols stand for either 0 or 1. We have to begin adding the two digits a_1 and b_1, and then on to adding three digits, a_2, b_2, c_1, (c_1 being the carry over from the first addition), then a_3, b_3, c_2, and so on, till we add up the last three, a_n, b_n, c_{n-1}. The output should be the sum digits $s_1, s_2, s_3, \ldots s_n$ and the last carry over digit, c_n. A half adder would do the first addition, but from then on we need full adders, one for each addition. Fig. 5.15 shows the half adder (HA) and the adders (A) arranged in series which give the required output.

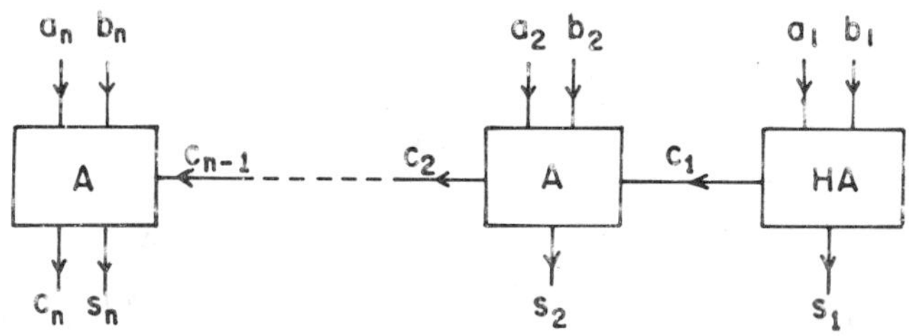

Fig. 5.15

It is possible to devise special circuits for the other arithmetical operations, but it is more convenient to perform these operations also through the adder. As we have seen in chapter 1 (page 10) subtraction of one binary number from another can be done by adding the complement of the first (the number obtained by changing 0 to 1 and 1 to 0) to the second. Multiplication and division can also be reduced to repeated additions. The adder, therefore, is a basic circuit through which other operations can also be done.

The theory of computer design is an intricate subject utilising many ideas of the new algebras quite beyond our present scope. What has been attempted here is to show how a different algebra, invented over a century ago, as a purely intellectual exercise to put logic in mathematical terms, has found application in a technological invention with mind-boggling potentialities for human civilization.

FROM THE GALLERY OF MATHEMATICIANS

George Boole

Self-taught son of a shoemaker, George Boole (British, 1815-1864) made the earliest attempt to mathematize logic. Neither mathematicians nor philosophers paid much attention to his remarkable achievement. Boole's notation was somewhat clumsy. In an improved and elegant form Boolean algebra today comprises of an abstract algebra in which symbols are not given any particular physical interpretation, but can be interpreted in different ways depending upon the physical situations which are sought to be analysed and studied through its applications. Boolean algebra provides the basic logic for the design of modern computers.

Boole was the pioneer in liberating mathematics from the narrow definition of the science of magnitude and number. In his work, the Mathematical Analysis of Logic, he proposed that 'mathematics is a method resting upon the employment of symbols whose laws of combination are known and general and whose results admit of constant interpretation'. He claimed for his calculus of logic a place among the acknowledged forms of mathematical analysis. In his second work, *Investigation of the Laws of Thought*, he laid the foundations of Boolean algebra.

Norbert Wiener

Son of a renowned scholar, Norbert Wiener (American, 1894-1964) was driven rather mercilessly forward by his father to becoming a scholar at a very young age earning reputation as something of a child prodigy. Getting his Ph.D. from Harvard University in 1913 at the age of nineteen, he went to Cambridge, England, and studied under Russell and Hardy. In 1919 he became Professor of Mathematics at the Massachusetts Institute of Technology. During World War II, Wiener was involved as a mathematician in work connected with anti-aircraft defence. As a result he grew interested in basic problems concerning communication and control and coined the word 'Cybernetics' for the new subject of Communication and Control in Men and Machines. Wiener was a thorough anti-vitalist denying any basic distinction between life and nonlife. In 1947 he announced that he would not contribute any further to any form of military research, and spent the rest of his life trying to alert humanity to the significance and problems of the coming age of automation.

John von Neumann

An outstanding mathematician of the present century, John von Neumann (Hungarian-American, 1903-1957) made fundamental contributions to knowledge basic to the design of computers. After studying in Germany and Switzerland he went to U.S.A. in 1930 and joined the Institute of Advanced

Study at Princeton. His great contibutions include the theory of competitive games and many advances in quantum theory.

EXERCISES

1. Construct the truth tables for

   (i) $P \wedge \overline{Q}$ (ii) $\overline{P} \vee Q$ (iii) $P \Leftrightarrow Q$

2. Construct the truth tables for

   (i) $P \vee (P \wedge Q)$ (ii) $P \wedge (P \vee Q)$

   and show that each of these expressions is equal to P. Assuming P, Q as switches, draw circuits to represent (i) and (ii).

3. Verify the validity of the following statements for all values of P, Q, R by constructing truth tables.

   (i) $(P \vee Q) \vee R = P \vee (Q \vee R)$

   (ii) $P \vee (Q \wedge R) = (P \vee Q) \wedge (P \vee R)$

   (iii) $\overline{P \wedge Q} = \overline{P} \vee \overline{Q}$

   (iv) $(P \vee Q) \wedge (\overline{P} \vee \overline{Q}) = (P \wedge \overline{Q}) \vee (\overline{P} \wedge Q)$

4. Prove that the two circuits of Fig. 5.7 are equivalent by constructing the truth tables for the corresponding Boolean expressions.

Chapter 6

Communicating with the Computer

"Aladin:	**Make something amusing, amazing, something the world has never seen.**
Genie:	**Tell me what.**
Aladin:	**Use your imagination.**
Genie:	**Imagination! I have no imagination. I can move mountains, turn deserts into oceans, but I have no imagination. You have to tell me what to do."**

— *The story of Aladin and the Wonderful Lamp.*

The computer is a machine. It is a material object created by man. Like any other machine, it has components designed and assembled to form a larger unit which can be made to perform certain operations. It does not do anything by itself. It needs a skilled person to operate it.

There is, however, one big difference between the computer and the usual types of machines. An ordinary machine needs a human operator at its controls, pulling levers, pressing buttons or turning wheels, to take it through the various stages of its operation to obtain the desired performance. Whether it is a hammer or a bulldozer, a wheelbarrow or a motor car, a spinning wheel or a sewing machine, it cannot be told in advance (except now through a computer) what sequence of physical states it should get into to accomplish a given job. It is the person at the controls who knows the job and decides when and how he has to manipulate the controls to get the desired work done.

A Programmable Machine

A computer, on the other hand, is a 'programmable' machine. In fact, it cannot function without a *programme*. What a computer does is determined by the set of instructions fed into it. Widely different things can be done by the same computer through different programmes. It is the flexibility in controlling its performance through instructions that makes the computer so versatile a machine. It can solve not only mathematical problems but can also run other machines to predetermined programmes. It has provided 'brains' to machines.

The programme or 'software', as it is called, is the 'soul' of the computer. The simile is indeed very appropriate. The 'hardware' – the physical body of the computer – is a dead object. The software puts 'life' into it. The software and the hardware are complementary to each other, and each is useless without the other. There are now people called software engineers, programmers or systems analysts whose job is accomplished with a pencil, a paper and a keyboard, and there are hardware technologists who design and assemble the physical components constituting the computer. Software is a subject falling entirely in the area of modern mathematics, and so deserves an elementary introduction in this book.

What is a Programme?

To appreciate the nature of a programme, let us take a simple illustration. Suppose you have a helper who is new to your town. You ask him to go and put a letter and a parcel in the mail box, and give him the following instructions.

This is a letter and this is a parcel.
Take these with you.
Go up the road.
Go straight through the first crossing.
Turn left on the second crossing.
Go straight about a hundred metres.
Look left for the building marked post office.
Enter the veranda of the building.
Look for a part of the wall painted red.
Look for the slit in the wall marked 'Letters'.
Drop the letter in it.
Look for the slit in the wall marked 'Parcels'.
Drop the parcel in it.
Come back.

These instructions constitute a programme of work for the man. You need not walk with him telling him at each step what to do. The instructions, in proper sequence, have been lodged in his mind; he will recall and use them as he proceeds.

Let us have another example. Suppose you need to find interest on different amounts of money at different rates for different times. You have an assistant who can multiply and divide but have no idea of what interest is and how to calculate it. You give him numbers arranged in the following table, and give him the following seven instructions.

	Amount in Rs.	Interest rate % per annum	Time in years	Interest in Rs.
Column	1	2	3	4
	4500	5	4	
	6800	9	8	
	7900	10	12	

Number	Instruction
1	Look at the first row
2	Pick up the numbers in columns 1, 2, 3.
3	Multiply them together.
4	Divide the result by 100.
5	Write the result in column 4.
6	Look at the next row.
7	If there are numbers in the row, repeat instructions 2, 3, 4, 5, 6, otherwise stop.

It is easy to see that, if the assistant were to follow the instructions exactly in the sequence they are written, he would be making the desired entries in column 4, and would stop after finishing with all the rows.

The computer acts somewhat similarly. It is not a living organism; it does not understand or think in the sense a person or an animal does. Yet, information and data can be supplied, stored, recalled and processed in it through operations performed according to a plan which is also fed into it. As with all machines, the user of the computer may not and need not know what is inside it, but he has to know how to use it. He has to have the skill to put his problem in a series of instructions which the computer can carry out. We shall see in this chapter what sort of instructions the computer can understand and carry out, and how to reduce our problem to such instructions. In short, we shall learn a little bit of programming.

However, before we start discussing programming, let us have a look at the hardware too – its appearance, its main components and a bare outline of how and what it does – in order to have an intelligent appreciation of its use.

The Hardware

What are the broad steps involved in a person receiving instructions to do a job, doing it and reporting back? First, these instructions should be communicated to him through writing which he reads or speech which he hears. His eyes and ears are the input mechanisms. His brain stores information received. The mind memorizes, recalls, thinks and acts. When the job is done, the result is reported back through his output mechanism – speech or writing.

The computer too has parts to do analogous duties. It has components which serve as input and output devices, and a part called the central processing unit which may be called its brain. It has a section which stores information and may be compared to the memory centres in the brain. Another section works as a processor. The physical body of the computer thus consists of three units shown diagrammetically in Fig 6.1.

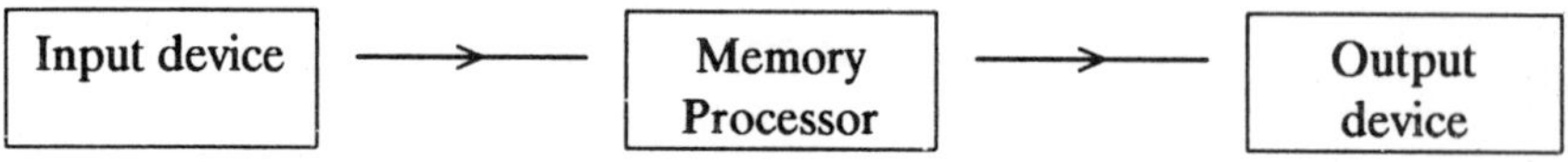

Fig. 6.1

Computers come in different sizes, ranging from big computers, with large capacity for memory and processing which may occupy a big room, to computers small enough to be held in hand. A computer system with sufficiently large memory, cheap enough to be owned by individuals and schools, is one with a processing unit of the size of a portable typewriter which, with the input-output accessories, can be arranged on an office table. Computers of this size are called microcomputers.

The smallest building block of a computer is a microscopically small electronic circuit. Millions of circuits systematically connected go into it. The technology of imprinting small electronic circuits on a small piece of silicon, which came to be called a 'chip', was developed in 1970's. It is now possible to arrange and integrate (that is connect systematically) tens of thousands of tiny circuits on a single chip as small as 3 mm square. Several chips fixed into a complex web of wires on a printed circuit board form the processor and the memory of computer. We have compared the hardware of the computer to the body and the software to the soul of a living organism. On the same analogy the chip could be compared to the living cell. Just as a living organism consists of a large number of cells, each cell basically the same and yet specially adapted to serve a particular purpose, similarly all chips are basically similar and yet they are joined to perform different functions in the body of the computer.

The input-output components of a computer system are, outwardly, a typewriter-like keyboard, a TV-like screen for video display, and a printer. Instructions and data can be 'typed' into the computer; they simultaneously appear on the screen. Whatever the computer does can also be made to appear on the screen. In fact, it is possible to carry on a sort of conversation with the computer. Through the keys of the keyboard all that we want the computer to do, and all that it does, can be sequentially displayed on the screen, and instructions can be inserted as work progresses. For a permanent record, the inputs and the outputs can be printed on a paper also through a typewriter-like printer.

The computer is run by electric power. Before it can do anything, it has to be activated by turning on the power switch. The moment it is turned off, everything in it – data, instructions, display on screen – is erased. If it is turned off in the middle of a problem, accidentally or otherwise, one has to begin again from the very beginning. You cannot pick up threads where you left.

It is, however, possible to store information in the computer on a more permanent basis also. Computers which are not general purpose but are meant to do the same job over and over again can be fitted with programmes which are not lost when switched off. But computers required for scientific, educational or other general purpose cannot have their memory locked permanently with special purpose programmes. Their memory should be as much free as possible to handle a variety of programmes. They may lose a programme completely when turned off.

The situation would have been vexing for different users, who cannot finish their work in one sitting, but for the magnetic tapes and discs. Devices to record sounds and pictures on magnetic tapes and play them back are now familiar things. Magnetic discs work on the same principle as magnetic tapes. The difference is that on a tape the recording track runs along its length while on a disc it runs in circles as in a gramophone record. It is possible to transfer information back and forth between a computer and a disc or a tape. Magnetic discs of size about 13 cm square (usually called diskettes) are generally used with microcomputers. Tapes and discs of other types are used generally on large computers. Any information that needs to be saved from being erased when the computer is turned off can be transferred to the disc or tape. It can stay there as long as we want. Magnetic discs and tapes have thus become essential accessories of a computer system to be used as storehouses of data and programmes which can be read into or written out of the computer as needed.

It is worthwhile having some idea of the speed and the capacity of the computer. Time for computer operations is measured in microseconds (a microsecond is a milionth part of a second). An arithmetical operation or an instruction may take only a fraction of a microsecond. What a person, working unaided by any machine, would do in years, with perhaps mistakes creeping in due to mental fatigue, a computer can do in minutes. Of course, people have to write programmes for it. To solve large problems or accomplish complicated tasks, it may take teams of highly trained persons months to produce an error free programme which computers execute in the twinkling of an eye.

The capacity of a computer to hold information is measured in 'bytes'. Every character – numeral, letter or any other symbol – is registered inside a computer as a code in terms of 'bits' (acronym for binary digits), a string of 0's and 1's, in a 'storage cell' of a chip. One character occupies one byte, usually equal to eight bits, of storage space. A microcomputer generally has at least a memory of 64 KB (kilobytes). One KB is equal to 1024 or 2^{10} bytes. A diskette may have a storage space of the order of 300 KB. With additional chips in the memory section of the computer and diskettes outside, the capacity of even a modest computer can be raised to thousands of kilobytes.

Programming Languages

Just as there are many human languages, there are many computer languages too. Deep down inside itself the computer understands only one language, the 'machine language', in which all the statements are made in binary digits, 0, 1. But for a person to write a programme in binary digits is very difficult, long and time consuming, and the absence of any alternative would have severely restricted the use of the computer. Other languages have been invented which are more akin to everyday language. When fed into the computer through its input device, these are translated into machine language. The translators, 'compilers' as they are called, are software programmes which act as interpreters. BASIC, FORTRAN, COBOL, ALGOL, PASCAL are the names of some of the languages in use. There are many more. BASIC (acronym for Beginners All-purpose Symbolic Instruction Code) is at present regarded as the easiest for beginners.

All computer languages have some common features based on the elementary operations the computer can perform. Once these are understood, it is easy to write a programme in any language with the help of manuals and guides. In fact a programmer can first write the steps in his own way, using any words he likes, clearly indicating the sequence of instructions which the computer will execute. Such a language is called a 'pseudo-language'. Transcribing a programme from a pseudo-language to any standard computer language is easy.

We shall use pseudo-language to introduce elementary ideas about programming, and also provide a glimpse into BASIC through some examples. We propose generally to write statements in two columns, in pseudo-language on the left and its equivalent in BASIC on the right. What follows should not be taken as sufficient to learn programming or BASIC. The objective in this chapter, as in the rest of the book, is to provide a general appreciation of the subject rather than working knowledge.

A computer programme consists of statements written in a standard form. The term 'statement' here is used to include every instruction, command or data. Each statement should begin on a new line. The programme is read into the computer through the keyboard. The computer executes the statements in a sequential order, and therefore they should be written in the correct order or the sequence indicated otherwise, as we shall see later. We first discuss the different types of statements that can go into a programme.

Arithmetical Operations

We have seen in Chapter 5 how an electronic circuit can be designed to add two numbers. We therefore start by accepting that circuitry can be designed to do all the elementary arithmetical operations, and that the processor can add, subtract, multiply, divide, and calculate the numerical value of an arithmetical expression involving these operations. The only requirement is that for the computer each expression should be written in one line. So we write division and exponentiation (or raising to power) also in one line. That is, we write division of *a* by *b* as *a*/*b*, and *a* raised to power *b* as *a* ↑ *b*. Generally the order of operations in an expression is the following.

(1) Within parentheses: ( )

(2) Exponentiation: ↑

(3) Multiplication and division: ×, /

(4) Addition and subtraction: +, −

It is always safe to ensure the correct order by introducing parentheses, whenever there is any doubt.

To take some examples, observe the expressions in the following table. In the left column they are written in the familiar form. In a computer programme they should be written as in the right column. Such expressions can be evaluated by the computer. The form of statement required for the purpose will be described later.

Ordinary form	Computer form
$9 \div 4$ or $\frac{9}{4}$	9/4
$(41.5+9.5) \times 7.8$	(41.5 + 9.5) × 7.8
$\frac{6.4(32.4-8.9)}{5.6-3.2}$	6.4 × (32.4 - 8.9) / (5.6 - 3.2)
$(3.6)^2$	3.6 ↑ 2
$\frac{4\times5^3-6}{7}$	(4 × 5 ↑ 3 − 6)/7

Location Address and Assignment

The memory circuits of a computer can be compared to a large number of drawers or pigeonholes in a cabinet. A number or any other small segment of information is stored in one pigeonhole. To make use of the information we should know in what pigeonhole it is stored, that is, it should be given a name or an address. It is done by setting up a 'variable'. A variable is a name we give to a location. The information stored in that location is the 'value' of the variable. What combinations of alphanumeric characters (letters of the alphabet and numerals) can be used as variables differ from language to language. In BASIC any letter of the alphabet followed by another letter or numeral is acceptable as a variable, except some standard words, such as LET, GOTO, IF, THEN, READ, PRINT and many more, which are given special meaning.

To store a number in the computer we first define a variable, and then assign the number to that variable. As an example, the following two statements will store the number 4 in the location named N. In BASIC a single statement does the trick.

Pseudo-language	BASIC
Set up variable N	LET N = 4
Assign to N value 4 or, briefly, N ← 4	

For convenience in our pseudo-language we use the symbol ← to indicate assignment. What is assigned to a variable may be an arithmetical number or expression or another variable or an expression in variables. Here are some examples.

Pseudo-language	BASIC
Variables M, N, MP, Q4	
M ← 17.3	LET M = 17.3
N ← 6.7	LET N = 6.7
MP ← M + N	LET MP = M + N
Q4 ← (MP + 20)/2	LET Q4 = (MP + 20)/2

This programme stores 17.3 in location M, 6.7 in location N, 24 in location MP and 22 in location Q4. In executing the statement, LET MP = M + N, the values of M and N are added first and then stored in location MP. Similarly it executes the last statement.

The value of a variable is changed by a subsequent statement assigning to the same variable a different value. It is the latest value that is used through the subsequent part of the programme, and the earlier value is lost. It is like changing the contents of a pigeonhole. The old contents are lost. Of course, if necessary, they can be stored in a different location before they are lost from the first. Consider the following sequence of statements.

Pseudo-language	BASIC
Variables A, B, C	
A ← 10	LET A = 10
B ← A	LET B = A
A ← A + 1	LET A = A + 1

First the number 10 is stored in location A. Then the value of A, namely 10, is stored in location B. Finally in the location A the existing value of A, namely 10, added to 1 is stored. Thus the net effect is that the number 10 is stored as the value of B and 11 as the value of A. Calling A subsequently will call the number 11 and not 10. The statement A = A + 1 in a programming language (it is so in BASIC and many other languages) looks enigmatic. In ordinary algebra such a statement is absurd. But let us remember that the sign = in programming does not indicate a mathematical equation, it indicates assigning the value on the right to the variable on the left. To clarify this point we have used the symbol ← rather than = in the pseudo-language.

Line Numbers and GOTO Statement

Normally the statements in a programme are executed in the order in which they are written. But it is possible to jump forward or backward to any statement. This is called 'transfer of control' from one statement to another. In the absence of any instruction the control goes from one statement to the next, but a GOTO statement can make it jump to any other.

To accomplish this it is obviously necessary that the statement one wants to jump to must be recognized by some name or number. In BASIC the rule is to label all statements by numbers. The numbers of successive statements should be in increasing order, for, in the absence of any 'transfer of control' order, the computer will execute the statements in the order they are numbered. The numbers may not necessarily be consecutive. In fact it is advisable to skip numbers betwen two successive statements so that if a new statement has to be inserted between two statements later on, it is possible to do so without changing the numbers of the statements already written.

The transfer of control is accomplished by a statement of the type

GOTO *n*

where *n* is the number of the statement where we want to go to. For example, consider the following statements in BASIC.

```
10  LET A = 10
20  LET B = A
30  LET A = A + 1
40  GOTO 20
```

The successive statements have been numbered as 10, 20, 30, 40. We could have used any other numbers, the only condition being that they have to be in ascending order. We could use the numbers 1, 2, 3, 4, or 10, 11, 13, 18, or 140, 149, 158, 200. Statement number 40, namely GOTO 20, sends the processor back to statement number 20. Then it proceeds on according to the general rule to the next statements, 30 and 40, and then again it goes back to 20, and so on. Such a 'going round and round' is called a 'loop'.

Let us see what this loop is doing. The successive steps result in the values of A and B as below.

(i) A = 10

(ii) B = 10

(iii) A = A + 1 = 10 + 1 = 11

(iv) B = 11 (last value of A)

(v) A = 11 + 1 = 12

(vi) B = 12

(vii) A = 13, and so on.

The computer starts with 10 as the value of A and goes on increasing it by 1 and storing it back in B. At any stage only the last values of A and B are in store. All the previous values are lost.

Comparison and Logical Decision

Another fundamental operation of great significance which the computer can perform is to decide whether a number is equal to, greater than or less than zero. It implies that given any two numbers x and y, it can decide whether $x = y$, $x < y$, or $x > y$. For, to decide this it has only to decide whether $x - y = 0$, < 0 or > 0.

This ability to compare is used to introduce conditional statements in a programme, like 'if it is so, then do this, otherwise do that'. Such statements are called 'IF' statements. The following is an example of an IF statement.

Pseudo-language	BASIC
If X > 5, then go to statement number 110, otherwise proceed normally	50 IF X > 5 THEN 110 60 ---------------- 70 ---------------- 110 ----------------

When the processor comes to statement 50, it examines whether X > 5. If yes, it jumps to statement 110 skipping the two intermediate statements, otherwise it proceeds sequentially through statements 60 and 70.

Input Output Statements

We now consider statements by which data can be put in or results printed out. A 'READ' statement does essentially the same thing as the LET statement described earlier, except that the former does it more economically. Suppose the variable X has to be successively assigned values 5, 8, 9, 21, 32, and with each of these values a programme has to be gone through. We may write a statement like 'READ X' and supply the list of values of X in an earlier line. In BASIC it is done as follows.

```
10   DATA 5, 8, 9, 21, 32
15   READ X
20   ---------------
25   ---------------
30   GOTO 15
```

First X is assigned the value 5 and all the instructions up to statement 25 are executed. Statement 30 sends the control back to statement 15, and now 8 (the next value in the data) is picked up for X, and again all the instructions carried out, and so on. If in the above example the READ statement is modified to

READ X, Y

then the first number in the data list is assigned to X and the second to Y, and the programme executed, then on return to the READ statement the next two numbers in the data list are assigned to X and Y respectively, again the programme executed, and so on until the data list is exhausted. This principle can be extended to assign data to any number of variables.

'PRINT' statement prints out whatever is required to be printed. A statement like

PRINT X, Y, Z

will print out the values of the variables X, Y, Z as they stand at that stage of the programme. It is also possible to print any text right as it is. In BASIC we have to put the text within quotes (" "). For example, the statement

PRINT "The problem is solved. The answer is"

will just print out the words in quotes.

The statement 'END' is essential to indicate the end of a programme. The statement 'STOP' will stop the execution of the programme at any stage we want.

Illustrative Problems, Flow Charts

There are many other types of commands and statements possible in different higher level languages which make programming of large and complicated problems convenient. But for our present purpose the statements described so far are sufficient, as with these it is possible to write programmes for a sufficiently wide variety of relatively simple problems. We take now a few simple problems and discuss how to set about writing programmes. We shall also at the same time introduce the idea of flowcharts which often are useful aids to programming.

Problem 1. A bank account has the following rules of calculating interest on a deposit. If the average amount of deposit in a month falls below Rs. 500, the bank charges Rs. 5 as rent and pays no interest; if the amount is Rs. 500 or more but less than Rs. 2000, the interest is 3% per annum; if the amount is Rs. 2000 or more, the interest is 6% per annum. Write a programme which prints out the rent or the interest on the amount of average deposit in any month.

Let us first analyse what we shall do if we are to solve the problem by hand, but confining our work only to those operations which the computer can do. Suppose Rs. P is the average deposit in a month, I the interest, and C the rent. We shall proceed as follows.

Read the numerical value of P
Compare P with 2000
If $P \geq 2000$, then $I = 6 \times P/(100 \times 12)$
If $P < 2000$, then compare P with 500
If $P \geq 500$, then $I = 3 \times P/(100 \times 12)$
If $P < 500$, then $C = 5$

We may indicate the above procedure through a diagram known as a flowchart. It is only an alternative way of showing the sequence of operations graphically.

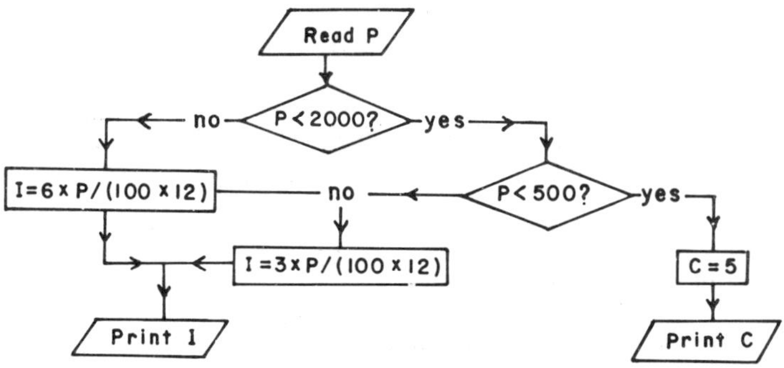

Flowchart

In a flowchart we write the statements in boxes and join them through directed lines to indicate the sequence. Conventionally, different shapes of boxes are used to distinguish between different types of operations. Statements indicating calculations and assignment of values to variables are enclosed in ▭. Inputs and outputs are shown in ▱. Stages at which decisions are made to do one thing or the other are shown as ◇. Straight lines with arrow-heads show the directions in which the work proceeds.

In the flowchart of the present problem, we start by reading the value of P. Then we compare it with 2000. To the question : Is P < 2000?, if the answer is no, we proceed to calculate I at the rate of 6%; if the answer is yes, we compare P with 500. If P < 500, we proceed to write the charge as 5; otherwise we go ahead to calculate I at the rate of 3%. Finally either the value of I or P is printed.

Writing a computer programme for this problem is now easy. As usual we shall write it in our own words, a pseudo-language, and also in BASIC.

Pseudo-language	BASIC
5 Value of P	5 DATA n
10 Read P	10 READ P
20 If P < 2000, go to 50, otherwise do the next statement	20 IF P < 2000 THEN 50
30 I = P × 6/(100 × 12)	30 LET I = P × 6/(100 × 12)
40 Print I and stop	40 GOTO 100
50 If P < 500, go to 80, otherwise do the next statement	50 IF P < 500 THEN 80
60 I = P × 3/(100 × 12)	60 LET I – P × 3/(100 × 12)
70 Print I and stop	70 GOTO 100
80 C = 5	80 LET C = 5
90 Print C and stop	90 PRINT "Charge"; C
	95 STOP
	100 PRINT "Interest"; I
	105 END

The letter 'n' against DATA should be replaced by the numerical value of P. The final print-out will be either 'Charge 5' or 'Interest x', x being the numerical value of I. Notice 'STOP' in the programme. It stops after the value of C is printed. Without the STOP statement execution of the next statement will be undertaken. As it will find no value of I to be printed, the print-out will indicate error.

Problem 2. Write a programme to find the sum of the squares of the first 20 natural numbers, that is, to find the value of

$$1^2 + 2^2 + 3^2 + 4^2 + \dots\dots + 20^2$$

Let us look at the problem like this. Suppose we denote the required sum by the variable S, or, in other words, store the sum in the location named S. We start with the first term, 1^2, and store it in S by the statement

$$S \leftarrow 1^2$$

The value of S after this operation is 1^2. Then calculate the second term, 2^2, and add this to the existing value of S. This can be done by the statement

$$S \leftarrow S + 2^2$$

which makes the present value of S as $1^2 + 2^2$, because the previous value of S was 1^2. Now calculate the third term, 3^2, and add it to the existing value of S by the statement

$$S \leftarrow S + 3^2$$

This makes the present value of S as $1^2 + 2^2 + 3^2$. We go on doing like this till we come to the last term, 20^2. Also we notice that if n^2 is the term added at one stage, $(n + 1)^2$ is the term added next. The number $n + 1$ is obtained by adding 1 to the previous number n. We might do this by defining a variable n, and increasing its value step by step by the statement $n \leftarrow n + 1$.

These observations suggest that in the programme we need set up only two variables, S and n. Initially let $S = 0$, and $n = 0$. Subsequently go on increasing n by 1 so that the new value of n is 1 added to its old valure, which we do by the statement

$$n \leftarrow n + 1.$$

Also set $$S \leftarrow S + n^2,$$

so that the new value of S is obtained by adding n^2 to its old value. We go on repeating these two operations till the required value of n, namely 20, is reached. The procedure is further clarified by the following flowchart.

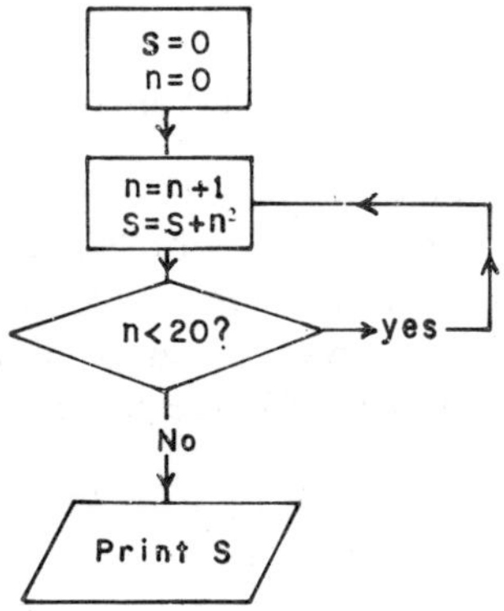

Flowchart

Let us follow step by step what the above flowchart indicates.

(i) $n = 0, S = 0$

(ii) $n = 0 + 1 = 1, S = 0 + 1^2.$

(iii) Is $n < 20$? Yes. Go back and set

(iv) $n = 1 + 1 = 2$, $S = 1^2 + 2^2$

(v) Is $n < 20$? Yes. Go back and set

(vi) $n = 2 + 1 = 3$, $S = 1^2 + 2^2 + 3^2$

... ...

... ...

$n = 19 + 1 = 20$, $S = 1^2 + 2^2 + \dots 20^2$
Is $20 < 20$? No.
Print S.

It becomes easy now to write this programme in BASIC

```
10   LET S = 0
11   LET N = 0
12   LET N = N + 1
13   LET S = S + N²
14   IF N < 20 THEN 12
15   PRINT S
16   END
```

Dialogue with the Computer

Programming for the computer is now a highly skilled art and a continuously developing science. It is possible to write programmes which enable one to carry on a dialogue with the computer. One can play games with it – backgammon, chess, checkers, etc. It can be used as a teaching and learning aid in schools. Here is an example of a conversation that a child can have with the computer by running a particular programme. It is meant to be a multiplication test. As it is run the following lines appear on the video screen. After every question there is a pause for the answer which the child provides by typing it himself.

What is your name?
Sanjay (typed by the child)
Hello, Sanjay, let's try this question.
What is 8 × 6?
40 (typed by the child)
Wrong. Try again.
42 (typed by the child)
Wrong. Try again.
48 (typed by the child)
Right. Well done, Sanjay.

The programme behind the print-out is quite simple. The answers are taken as inputs. The name is accepted as input in the blank of the sentence "Hello, ..., let's try this question". The numbers 40, 42, 48 are compared with the value of 8 × 6. If the two are equal, the printer prints the last sentence, otherwise it prints "Wrong. Try again".

Conclusion

As was emphasized in the beginning, the computer is a machine. If you do not have a machine to examine and work, no amount of verbal des ription can help you to appreciate it fully. This chapter, therefore, may have its limitations for those who have no access to a computer. The computer has already become a familiar appliance in millions of homes, offices and schools in the developed world. In India too it is becoming fairly common. It is the base for future technology. Ability to communicate with the computer – computer literacy, as it is being called – will become as essential a part of one's education as the three R's. Elements of programming would be a necessary constituent of school mathematics. In the past mathematics has been an ornament and pursuit of scholars, in the present times it is an important factor contributing to the growth of civilization, but in future mathematics is going to be the very basis of civilization.

OF HISTORICAL INTEREST

Humanity's quest for calculating machines goes into antiquity. The abacus was the earliest and the simplest calculating device. In its advanced form it is still widely used in China and Japan. The Japanese experts of abacus can compete with the computer in speed of calculation. But till about forty years back a book of logarithmic tables or a slide rule was the only generally available aid to arithmetical calculations. With the advent of the electronic pocket calculator, they have been rendered not only obsolete but look crude and antiquated.

The first successful attempt to produce a machine which could be programmed to perform calculations is attributed to Sir Charles Babbage (1791–1871). It was a large and elaborate combination of gears, wheels and axles, which in logical terms, though not in mechanical, is regarded as the forerunner of the modern electronic computer. For this reason Babbage is sometimes thought of as the father of the modern computer. But apart from the commercial adding machines which used the mechanistic principles of gears and axles, not much progress could be made till the middle of the present century.

The first electronic digital machines were invented during World War II (1939–45). In 1943 a machine called Collosus was set up at Bletchley Park, England, which aided war effort by decoding the German and Japanese secret military codes. About the same time a machine called ENIAC (Electronic Numerical Integrator and Calculator) was built at the University of Pennsylvania in U.S.A. These machines filled whole rooms with vacuum tubes to give calculating power less than a modern programmable pocket calculator, but the principles underlying the modern electronic computer had been discovered and successfully applied.

The revolution came in about 1950 with the invention of the transistor which replaced the cumbersome and easily fusable vacuum tube. It brought down the size and the cost and proportionately increased the capacity and reliability of the machine.

The second major breakthrough came in the seventies with the development of the technology of imprinting integrated circuitry on microscopically small silicon chips. This has brought the computer into offices, schools and homes, and has laid the foundation of a computer-oriented civilization. In 1950 the electronic computer filled large rooms and cost crores of rupees. Every ten years its cost came down by a factor of ten. A microcomputer system today can be placed on a small table and is available for less than fifty thousand rupees. The trend continues.

EXERCISES

1. What does the following programme do and what does it print?

```
DATA 4, 5
READ X, Y
LET S = X ↑ 2 + Y ↑ 2
LET U = X × Y
LET V = S/U
PRINT V
END
```

2. Draw a flowchart of the following programme. What does it accomplish and what number is printed out?

```
10   DATA 2, 8, 14, 20, 26, 32
20   LET S = 0
30   LET N = 0
40   READ X
50   LET S = S + X
60   LET N = N + 1
70   IF X = 32 THEN 90
80   GOTO 40
90   PRINT S/N
100  END
```

3. The population of a town increases by 25% every ten years. Its population in 1970 was 50,000. Write a programme in BASIC to print the population in years 1980, 1990 and 2000.

4. Write a programme in your own pseudo-language to print the ten natural numbers 1, 2, ... 10, their squares and cubes.
5. What programme does the following flowchart show?

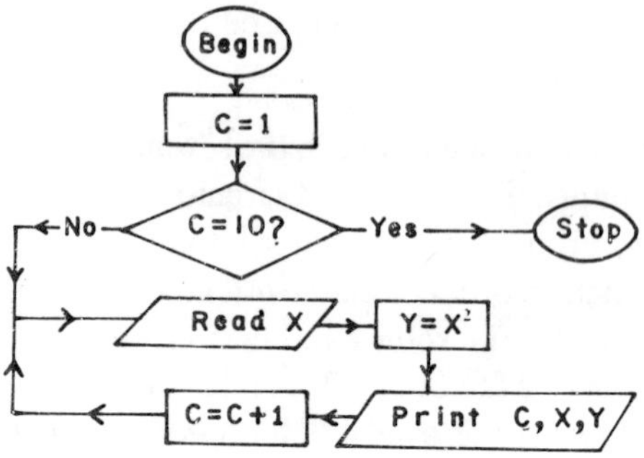

Flowchart

ANSWERS

1. Calculates S, U, V for X = 4, Y = 5, and prints the value of V which is 2.05.
2. The numbers are added one by one and stored in S. The sum is finally divided by 6, and the result which is the average of the six numbers is printed.

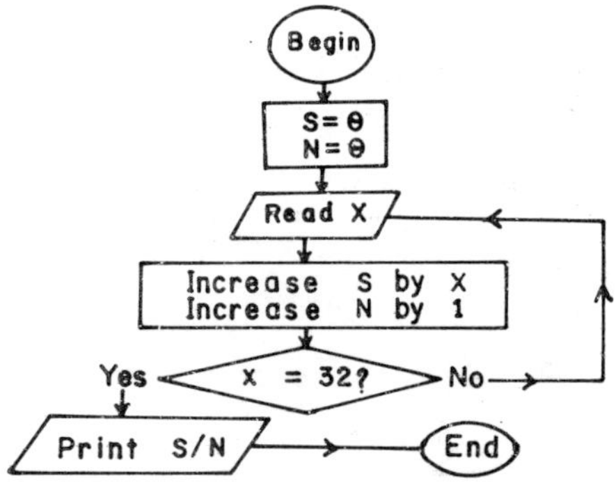

Flowchart

3.
```
10  Y = 1970
20  P = 50000
30  I = P × 25/100
40  P = P + I
50  Y = Y + 10
60  PRINT Y, P
70  IF Y = 2000 THEN 90
80  GOTO 30
90  END
```

4.
```
    Set N = 1
15  Print the values of N, N², N³
    Increase N by 1
    If N = 11 then stop
    otherwise go to statement number 15.
```

5. It will read the value for the variable X nine times. At the tenth time it will stop. So we should have a data of nine numbers. The serial number, the given number and its square will be printed in one line, nine lines in all.

Chapter 7

Vectors and Matrices

"Mathematics, however abstract and however precise, is a science of experience"

— *C. Truesdell, American (1919–)*

Number is a useful concept to describe a variety of attributes of things. Generally, whenever a measure of the size of a thing is required, the real number system provides a suitable scale. Whether it is the weight of a baby or the quantity of milk he needs, the population of a country or the amount of its food production, the degree of fever of a sick man or the cost of building a hospital, the height of a mountain or the distance of the moon, it is always a real number that describes the idea satisfactorily. But quite often one real number alone is not sufficient for an adequate description of an idea or a thing.

Vectors

Suppose we want to describe the position of a place A with respect to another place O on a plane map (Fig. 7.1). The real number r measuring the length of the straight line OA in some suitable units gives some information about the position of A, but it is not sufficient to unambiguously fix it. The direction of OA has also to be indicated. We may further specify that with a standard direction, say east, denoted by OE in the figure, OA makes an angle whose

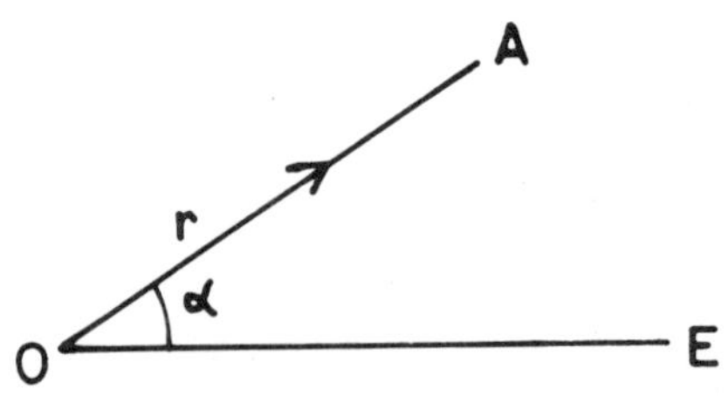

Fig. 7.1

measure in some units is given by the real number α. The two numbers r and α, understood in the sense described above, give a complete specification of the place A with respect to O. In other words, a line of a certain length drawn out from O in a certain direction fixes the position of A exactly.

The position of one point with respect to another is not the only idea that can be satisfactorily described by a line of definite length and direction. There are many other notions for which a *directed line segment* (as a line with a definite length and direction is called) is a suitable model of representation. Displacement of a very small body or particle from a point A to another point B is measured by the line AB which is also a directed line segment. Force is another similar concept. It is common experience that the effect of a force upon a body depends not only on its magnitude but also on its direction. The effect of pushing a body away from you is different from pulling it towards you, even if the effort you make (that is, the magnitude of the force) in each case is the same. A force, for its complete specification, needs a magnitude and a direction. It can also therefore be represented by a directed line segment, the length of the line being a measure of the magnitude of the force and the direction of the line indicating the direction of the force. Motion is also a similar idea. It involves change in position with time, change in distance as well as direction. Velocity is the precise term describing this concept which associates direction with speed.

A concept which can be represented by a directed line segment is called a *vector*. Position of a point with respect to another point, displacement, force, velocity are examples of vectors. To distinguish one vector from another, we can give a vector a name or, which is the same thing, a symbol. '**P** is a vector' means there is a certain vector which we agree to call **P**. **P** is not a number; it is a symbol which stands for a pair of properties, a magnitude and a direction. We diagrammatically represent **P** by a line of a fixed length and direction.

Algebra of Vectors

It has been possible to define meaningful rules of operations between symbols denoting vectors. Such rules constitute the algebra of vectors.

First, the sum of two vectors is defined as follows.

If a vector **P** is represented by OA and a vector **Q** by OB, Fig. 7.2(a), (we can always draw two such lines to represent **P** and **Q**), then the diagonal OC of the parallelogram $OACB$ defines the sum of the two vectors, written as $\mathbf{P} + \mathbf{Q}$. If the sum vector is denoted by **R**, then

$$\mathbf{P} + \mathbf{Q} = \mathbf{R}$$

Since OB and AC are equal and parallel, AC also represents **Q**, and so we might obtain **R** by drawing OA and AC to represent **P** and **Q** and then joining OC, Fig.

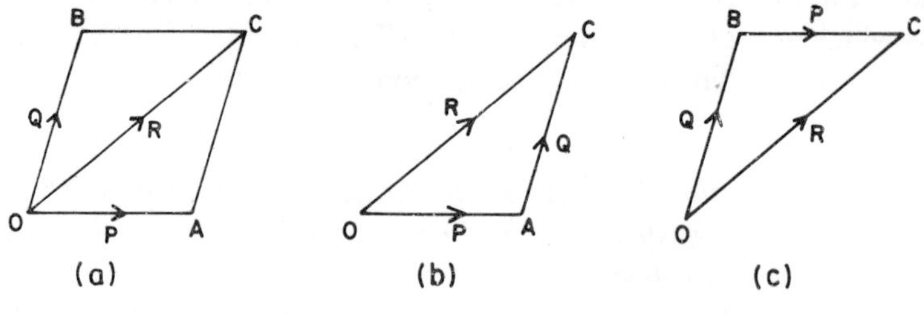

Fig. 7.2

7.2(b). We could also draw first *OB* to represent **Q** and then *BC* to represent **P** and then get *OC* to represent **Q** + **P**, Fig. 7.2(c). We thus find that

$$\mathbf{Q} + \mathbf{P} = \mathbf{P} + \mathbf{Q}$$

that is, the addition of two vectors is commutative.

That this definition of the sum of two vectors is meaningful can be seen by referring to any physical concept which is a vector. Suppose **P** and **Q** represent displacements. If a particle is first displaced through **P** represented by *OA* and then through **Q** represented by *AC*, its final displacement from the original position *O* is clearly *OC* which, by definition, is the vector **P** + **Q**. Thus the rule of addition is meaningful in the case of displacements. Again, if **P** represents the position of *A* with respect to *O* and **Q** the position of *C* with respect to *A*, **P** + **Q**, by definiton, indicates the position of *C* with respect to *O*, which also makes sense. If **P** and **Q** are forces acting at a point *O*, it is experimentally verifiable that the vector $\mathbf{R} = \mathbf{P} + \mathbf{Q}$ represents the force which is the combined physical effect of **P** and **Q**. Similarly, if a body has two velocities imposed on it, one **P** represented by *OA* and the other **Q** represented by *OB*, its net velocity will be **P** + **Q** represented by *OC*. As an example of this, one can imagine a boat in a river. If the boatman tries to row with a velocity **P** and the river flows with a velocity **Q**, then the boat will actually move with a velocity $\mathbf{R} = \mathbf{P} + \mathbf{Q}$.

Corresponding to every vector one can imagine a vector equal in magnitude but opposite in direction. If *OA* and *OB* are two line segments equal in length but opposite in direction (Fig. 7.3), and if *OA* represents a vector **P**,

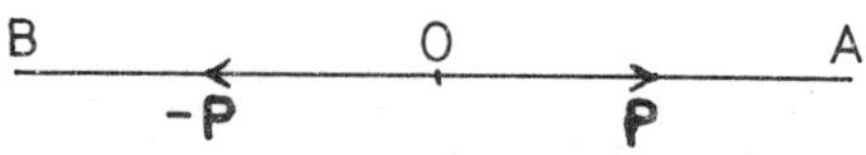

Fig. 7.3

then the vector represented by *OB* is customarily denoted by **–P**. The sum of two vectors **P** and **–P** is a *null* or a *zero* vector, written as

$$\mathbf{P} + (-\mathbf{P}) = \mathbf{P} - \mathbf{P} = \mathbf{0}$$

Intrepreted physically, it makes sense. If a body is given two displacements equal in magnitude but opposite in direction, the net result is no displacement. If two equal and opposite forces act at a point, they merely cancel the effect of each other. If a boat is rowed against the current but with the same speed as the current, it would remain where it is.

Further, we agree to denote by $m\mathbf{P}$, where m is a positive real number, a vector whose direction is the same as of $\mathbf{P}$ but magnitude m times that of $\mathbf{P}$. Thus $2\mathbf{P}$ is a vector with the same direction as $\mathbf{P}$ but with double the magnitude. We may also verify that

$$\mathbf{P} + \mathbf{P} = 2\mathbf{P}$$

by applying the rule of addition of two vectors given earlier. Also multiplication of a vector $\mathbf{P}$ by a negative real number $-m$ is written as $-m\mathbf{P}$ and is interpreted to mean a vector of the same magnitude as $m\mathbf{P}$ but opposite in direction.

We define a *unit vector* in a certain direction as a vector of unit magnitude in that direction, that is, a vector represented by a directed line of unit length. Suppose $\mathbf{p}$ is a unit vector in the same direction as $\mathbf{P}$. If p denotes the magnitude of $\mathbf{P}$, by what we have said above,

$$\mathbf{P} = p\mathbf{p}$$

Let Ox, Oy be two perpendicular directions which we agree to regard as standard reference directions (like, for instance north and east on the ground), (Fig. 7.4).

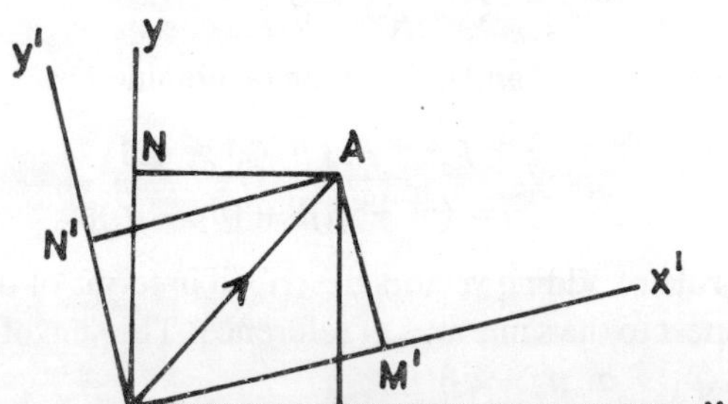

Fig. 7.4

Let $\mathbf{P}$ represented by OA be any vector in the plane determined by them. Let AM and AN be perpendiculars to Ox and Oy from A. Let the vectors represented by OM and ON be denoted by $\mathbf{P}_1$ and $\mathbf{P}_2$. Since OA is the diagonal of the parallelogram with sides OM and ON, $\mathbf{P}$ is the vector sum of $\mathbf{P}_1$ and $\mathbf{P}_2$:

$$\mathbf{P} = \mathbf{P}_1 + \mathbf{P}_2$$

$\mathbf{P}_1$, $\mathbf{P}_2$ are called the *components* of $\mathbf{P}$ in the two directions Ox, Oy.

Let p, p_1, p_2 be the magnitudes of the vectors **P**, $\mathbf{P}_1$, $\mathbf{P}_2$, respectively. Since these magnitudes are represented by the lengths OA, OM, ON respectively,

$$p = OA, \quad p_1 = OM, \quad p_2 = ON.$$

If the directions Ox, Oy and the numbers p_1, p_2 are given, the rectangle $OMAN$ is fixed, and so the length and direction of its diagonal OA are fixed, specifying thereby the vector **P**. A vector can thus be completely defined in terms of two ordered real numbers (p_1, p_2) with the understanding that they are numbers measuring distances in two specified perpendicular directions. An ordered pair of real numbers is thus an alternative way of describing a vector. But the ordered pair is not unique. If the reference axes are changed, the ordered pair changes, even though the vector remains the same. For instance, in Fig. 7.4, if Ox', Oy' are the axes of reference, the components of **P** are OM', ON', and then **P** is described by the ordered pair of numbers (p_1', p_2') where $p_1' = OM', p_2' = ON'$. The same vector is specified by different pairs of numbers if the reference directions change. The direction of a vector is after all described with respect to some standard direction, and if the latter is changed, the terms in which the former is described should naturally change.

If we denote by **i** and **j** the unit vectors in the directions Ox and Oy respectively, the vectors $\mathbf{P}_1$ and $\mathbf{P}_2$ may be denoted as $p_1\mathbf{i}$ and $p_2\mathbf{j}$, and then

$$\mathbf{P} = p_1\mathbf{i} + p_2\mathbf{j}$$

If **Q** is another vector described with respect to the same axes by the pair of numbers (q_1, q_2), then

$$\mathbf{Q} = q_1\mathbf{i} + q_2\mathbf{j}$$

The sum of the two vectors **P** and **Q** can then be obtained as

$$\begin{aligned} \mathbf{P} + \mathbf{Q} &= p_1\mathbf{i} + p_2\mathbf{j} + q_1\mathbf{i} + q_2\mathbf{j} \\ &= (p_1 + q_1)\mathbf{i} + (p_2 + q_2)\mathbf{j} \end{aligned}$$

This gives us the rule of adding vectors described in terms of ordered pairs of numbers with respect to the same axes of reference. The sum of the two vectors (p_1, p_2), (q_1, q_2) is $(p_1 + q_1, p_2 + q_2)$.

We have so far considered vectors in a plane. In general they can be in three-dimensional space of which we are most naturally conscious. The position of a point in it can be conveniently described with respect to three lines mutually perpendicular and meeting in a point. The simplest example of such lines is provided by the lines in which two adjacent walls and the floor of a rectangular room meet each other.

Let Ox, Oy, Oz be three such lines forming the axes of reference, and let OP represent a vector **P** (Fig. 7.5). Draw the perpendicular PM from P on the plane xOy, complete the rectangle $ONMK$ in that plane and then complete the rectangular solid of height MP and base $ONMK$. The lines ON, OK, OL can

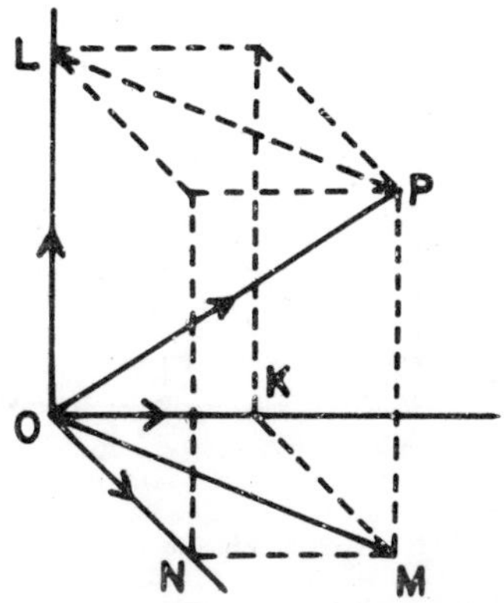

Fig. 7.5

represent three vectors. Denoting their lengths by p_1, p_2, p_3 and the unit vectors in the *Ox, Oy, Oz* directions by **i, j, k**, we may denote the vectors *ON, OK, OL* as $p_1\mathbf{i}, p_2\mathbf{j}, p_3\mathbf{k}$ respectively.

We may now apply the rule of addition to these three vectors to find their sum. In the rectangle *ONMK*, *OM* is the diagonal and *ON* and *OK* are the two adjacent sides. Therefore,

$$\text{vector } OM = \text{vector } ON + \text{vector } OK$$

or

$$\text{vector } OM = p_1\mathbf{i} + p_2\mathbf{j}$$

Also, *OMPL* is a rectangle in which *OM* and *OL* are two adjacent sides and *OP* is the diagonal. Hence

$$\text{vector } OP = \text{vector } OM + \text{vector } OL$$

or

$$\mathbf{P} = p_1\mathbf{i} + p_2\mathbf{j} + p_3\mathbf{k}.$$

The line *OP* (that is, the vector **P**) is fixed in direction and magnitude if the three lengths *ON* ($= p_1$), *OK* ($= p_2$) and *OL* ($= p_3$) in the three standard directions *Ox, Oy, Oz*, respectively are given. We may, therefore, say that the vector **P** can be described in a three-dimensional space by an ordered triplet of numbers (p_1, p_2, p_3) with respect to three standard directions.

Scalar Product

Two other binary operations on vectors deserve mention. Suppose a body is placed on a level ground at *A* and a man has to move it by pulling it by force **P** applied through a rope (Fig. 7.6). The greater the distance through which the body is to be moved, the more tired the man would feel after moving it. This feeling of tiredness is described mathematically by the concept of *work*. It

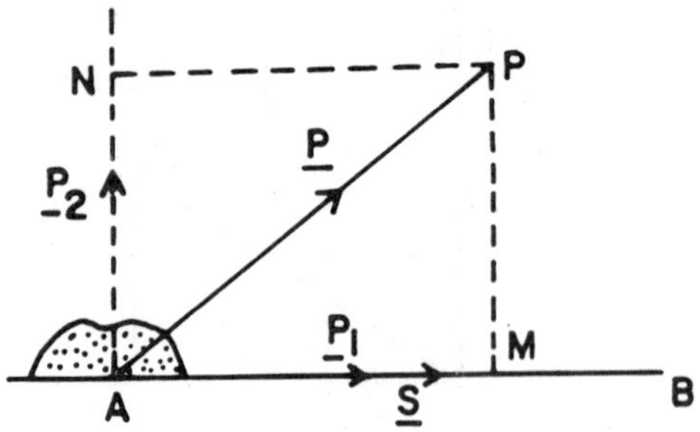

Fig. 7.6

depends both upon the force **P** which is a vector, and the distance $AB = \mathbf{s}$ through which the body moves, which is also a vector. We can regard **P** as the sum of two vectors, one $\mathbf{P}_1$ in the direction AB, of magnitude $p_1 = AM$, and another $\mathbf{P}_2$ in a direction perpendicular to the floor, of magnitude $p_2 = AN$. It is common experience that the body cannot be moved from A to B by any force acting perpendicular to the line AB. For example, you cannot move a body along the floor by pulling it up only perpendicular to the floor. You have to apply at least a part of the force along the floor in the direction in which the body is to be moved. We are therefore justified in concluding that work depends upon the component of the force in the direction of displacement. Work done by the force **P** in moving the body through the distance **s** is, accordingly, defined as

$$W = p_1 s$$

where s is the magnitude of **s**, the displacement vector, and p_1 is the magnitude of the vector $\mathbf{P}_1$, the component of the force **P** in the direction of **s**.

Work is not a vector. The feeling of tiredness has a magnitude but no direction. It is a notion expressed in terms of a single real number. The product $p_1 s$ certainly depends upon the two vectors **P** and **s** (not only on their magnitudes but their directions also), but it is itself a real number without any direction associated with it.

It can be proved that in terms of the alternative notation for vectors as ordered triplets with respect to three mutually perpendicular axes of reference, if

$$\mathbf{P} = p_1\mathbf{i} + p_2\mathbf{j} + p_3\mathbf{k}$$

and $$\mathbf{s} = s_1\mathbf{i} + s_2\mathbf{j} + s_3\mathbf{k},$$

then $$W = p_1 s_1 + p_2 s_2 + p_3 s_3$$

$p_1, p_2, p_3, s_1, s_2, s_3$ being real numbers, the above expression for W is a real number or a *scalar*. To distinguish it from a vector, a physical quantity representable by a single real number is often called a scalar.

Taking clue from the notion of work, which is a meaningful concept, we may now generalize and define a binary operation between two vectors **P** and **Q** as

$$\mathbf{P}.\mathbf{Q} = p_1q_1 + p_2q_2 + p_3q_3$$

where, in terms of ordered triplets, $\mathbf{P} = (p_1, p_2, p_3)$ and $\mathbf{Q} = (q_1, q_2, q_3)$. It is also equal to the product of the magnitude of any one of the vectors and the magnitude of the component of the other in the direction of the first. This binary operation is given the name *scalar product* of two vectors. It is also called the *dot product* because it is always indicated by a dot between the symbols for the two vectors. Work is only one example of scalar product. In physics and other branches of knowledge where vectors find application, one comes across many other examples where scalar product of vectors is a useful idea.

Vector Product

There is another binary operation between two vectors, called the vector product, which is also a useful idea. We shall again first illustrate the concept by a physical example.

Suppose a bolt AB is to be tightened by applying a force **Q** at the end C of a spanner AC (Fig. 7.7a) Let the bolt AB be vertical and the spanner AC and the force **Q** be in a horizontal plane. It is common experience that the ease with which the bolt can be turned depends upon the length of the spanner. The longer the spanner, the less the force required to produce a certain turning effect. Also, to get the best effect the force must be applied in a direction perpendicular to the spanner. Any effort, pull or push, applied along the length of the spanner is a waste so far as the turning effect is concerned. If **P** is the vector representing the length of the spanner in a position when it is held straight and about to be turned, and **Q** is the force vector, the magnitude of the

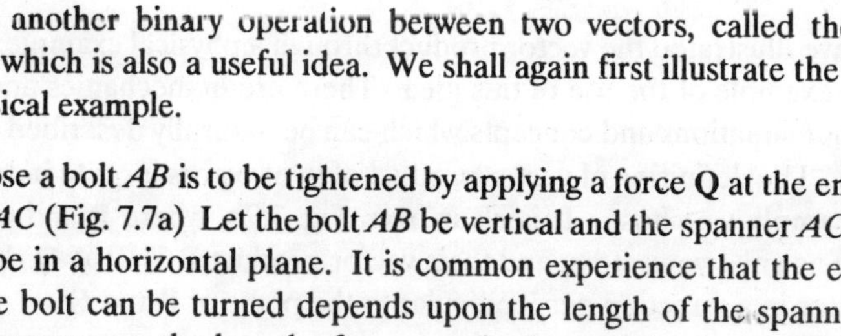

Fig. 7.7

effect produced on the bolt depends upon both **P** and **Q**. Also the effect is to move the bolt perpendicular to the plane of **P** and **Q**. Thus the effect on the bolt has a magnitude and also a direction associated with it, and therefore it can be described as a vector. It is a vector whose direction is perpendicular to the plane of **P** and **Q**. Its magnitude depends upon the magnitude of **P** (length of the spanner) and the magnitude of the component of **Q** perpendicular to **P** (magnitude of the effective force). In Fig. 7.7b, the vectors **P** and **Q** are shown as line segments meeting at the point *O*, and $\mathbf{Q}_2$, the component of **Q** perpendicular to **P** is also marked. It is the product of the magnitudes of **P** and $\mathbf{Q}_2$ which can be taken as a measure of the turning effect.

To sum up, we can say that the turning effect produced by the force **Q** acting on the spanner represented by the vector **P** is a vector **R** depending upon **P** and **Q** such that its direction is perpendicular to the plane of **P** and **Q** and its magnitude is pq_2, where p is the magnitude of **P** and q_2 that of $\mathbf{Q}_2$, the component of **Q** perpendicular to **P**. It is customary to write the vector **R** as

$$\mathbf{R} = \mathbf{P} \times \mathbf{Q}$$

It is called the *vector product* or the *cross product* (because a cross is always used between the two vectors to denote this operation) of the vectors **P** and **Q**.

We have illustrated the vector product through a physical example. But it is only one example of the use of this idea. There are in mechanics and physics many other situations and concepts which can be naturally described as vector products. The definition of vector product of two vectors is quite independent of the example we chose. It is clear from Fig. 7.7b, where **P** and **Q** may be regarded as any two vectors, and their vector product $\mathbf{R} = \mathbf{P} \times \mathbf{Q}$ shown as a third vector in a direction perpendicular to the plane of **P** and **Q**.

But a plane has two directions perpendicular to it. As in Fig. 7.8, the plane *AOB* has two perpendicular directions, one *OC* and the other *OD*. Let us take the directions *OA* and *OB* to make a right angle between them, so that the three

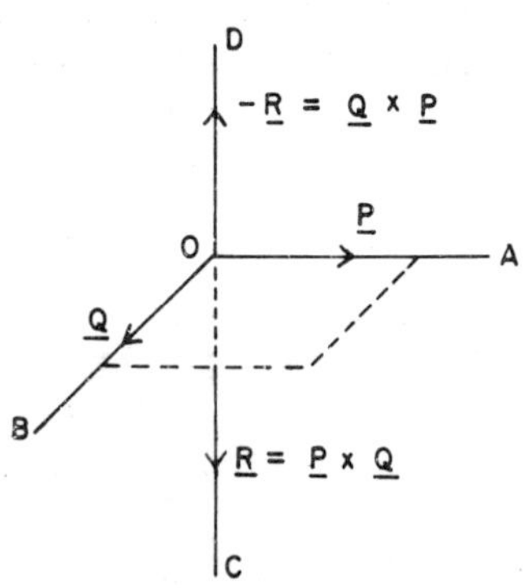

Fig. 7.8

directions OA, OB, OC (or OD) are mutually perpendicular. Let **P** and **Q** be two vectors along OA and OB respectively. Then the question is – what is the direction of **R** (= **P** × **Q**), OC or OD ?

The convention is that **P**, **Q**, **R** form a right-handed system of axes. In other words it means that if you look at the plane of **P** and **Q** (plane AOB) as if it were the face of a clock with **P** pointing towards 12 and **Q** towards 3, then **P** × **Q** is in the direction into the clock. This gives the direction OC in figure 7.8. If the same rule is applied to determine the direction of **Q** × **P**, then **Q** is imagined to point towards 12 and **P** towards 3, and then the direction of **Q** × **P** would be OD. Thus we conclude that it would be reasonable to postulate that if

$$\mathbf{P} \times \mathbf{Q} = \mathbf{R},$$

then

$$\mathbf{Q} \times \mathbf{P} = -\mathbf{R},$$

or

$$\mathbf{P} \times \mathbf{Q} = -(\mathbf{Q} \times \mathbf{P})$$

The vector product is thus found to be an example of a noncommutative binary operation, because **P** × **Q** is not the same thing as **Q** × **P**.

If **i**, **j**, **k** are the unit vectors in the three mutually perpendicular directions OA, OB, OC, (Fig. 7.8), then from what has been said above,

$$\mathbf{i} \times \mathbf{j} = \mathbf{k}, \quad \mathbf{j} \times \mathbf{i} = -\mathbf{k}.$$

Since each of the three vectors is relatively similarly placed with respect to the other two, we conclude that

$$\mathbf{i} \times \mathbf{j} = \mathbf{k}, \quad \mathbf{j} \times \mathbf{k} = \mathbf{i}, \quad \mathbf{k} \times \mathbf{i} = \mathbf{j},$$

$$\mathbf{j} \times \mathbf{i} = -\mathbf{k}, \quad \mathbf{k} \times \mathbf{j} = -\mathbf{i}, \quad \mathbf{i} \times \mathbf{k} = -\mathbf{j}.$$

These constitute the basic rules of vector multiplication between unit vectors in three standard directions. These were the first binary operations to be discovered, rather postulated, which violated the commutative law. It heralded the beginning of new ideas in the field of algebra.

Matrices

We have seen how an ordered pair of real numbers can represent a vector in a plane (or two-dimensional space) and an ordered triplet of real numbers a vector in the natural space around us which is three-dimensional. The mathematician's urge to generalize raises the question – can we talk of an ordered set of four real numbers as a vector in a four-dimensional space, or, in general, an ordered set of n real numbers in an n-dimensional space. It does not worry the mathematician that even four-dimensional space, much less a higher dimensional, is beyond the comprehension of our senses and hence impossible of geometrical visualization. He is quite accustomed to deal with figments of his own imagination. There is no problem in defining a four-dimensional vector as a collection of four ordered real numbers written in a row or a column as

$$[x_1\ x_2\ x_3\ x_4] \quad \text{or} \quad \begin{bmatrix} x_1 \\ x_2 \\ x_3 \\ x_4 \end{bmatrix}$$

obeying certain axioms or laws of manipulation which are in conformity with those applicable to two- or three-dimensional vectors. And again, as it happens repeatedly in the development of mathematics, the extended framework of ideas proves to be useful.

Why stop at a column or a row of numbers ? What about an array of numbers ? Can we deal with an arrangement of numbers like, for example,

$$\begin{bmatrix} 1 & 3 & -5 & -1 \\ 4 & 0 & 2 & 2 \\ 6 & -7 & 9 & 4 \end{bmatrix}$$

as a single entity? It has three rows and four columns. In general there can be an array of objects with m rows and n columns, m and n being any positive integers. We call it a *matrix* of order $m \times n$, or, in short, an $m \times n$ matrix. The objects forming the array are called the *elements* of the matrix. In the above example the elements are numbers, but in further generalizations they may be symbols conveying other ideas. We shall keep matters simple by confining our discussion to matrices (plural of matrix) of numbers only. We may devise rules of operations on such arrangements of numbers, and we shall have invented an algebra of matrices. It is customary to put the array within square brackets to indicate that it is a matrix. There are alternative notations also in vogue. Before we present the definitions and axioms of matrix algebra in an abstract sense, let us see how arrays forming matrices can arise naturally, and what sort of operations would be useful in describing realistic situations.

Meaningful Arrays

Consider the following situation. A Public Services Commission holds a common examination for recruitment to various high level services in the government. Each candidate has to choose two written papers (each of 50 marks) from each of the following three sections: (i) Literatures and Languages (L), (ii) Sciences (S), (iii) Humanities (H). In addition, the personality of the candidate is also judged in two separate interviews (I) (also each of 50 marks). To keep the magnitude of the problem small without sacrificing its essential features, suppose the scores of three candidates, A, B, C, in the first paper in each of the three written sections and in the first interview are as follows:

	L	S	H	I
A	22	43	34	20
B	28	35	25	25
C	32	20	18	38

We may standardize the format for tabulation, drop the names of candidates against rows and the subject headings on columns, and write the scores as a 3×4 matrix with the understanding that the rows and columns are to be interpreted as before. We denote this matrix by P_1:

$$P_1 = \begin{bmatrix} 22 & 43 & 34 & 20 \\ 28 & 35 & 25 & 25 \\ 32 & 20 & 18 & 38 \end{bmatrix}$$

Suppose the scores of the same students in the second paper of each section and in the second interview are arranged in another similar format denoted by P_2:

$$P_2 = \begin{bmatrix} 18 & 41 & 20 & 25 \\ 20 & 40 & 11 & 40 \\ 35 & 30 & 20 & 40 \end{bmatrix}$$

To get the total marks obtained by each candidate in each subject (out of a total of 100), we have only to add every entry of P_1 to the corresponding entry of P_2 and get a new matrix P. Calling this operation *addition* between two matrices, we write

$$P = P_1 + P_2 = \begin{bmatrix} 40 & 84 & 54 & 45 \\ 48 & 75 & 36 & 65 \\ 67 & 50 & 38 & 78 \end{bmatrix}$$

If we subtract each entry in P_2 from the corresponding entry in P, we shall get the matrix P_1. We may indicate this as

$$P_1 = P - P_2$$

Thus the operations of addition and subtraction between two matrices are defined. Obviously these operations can be performed only if the two matrices are of the same order, that is, they have the same number of rows and the same number of columns (3 and 4 in the present example).

Now suppose the Public Services Commission, through this common examination, wants to select candidates for two different services, one administrative and the other technical. For the administrative service the relative weightage of the four sections L, S, H, I is 2 : 1 : 2 : 2, or, in other words, Languages, Humanities and the Interview carry 200 marks each while Sciences carry 100 marks. For the technical services this proportion is 1 : 3 : 2 : 1, that is, L and I carry 100 marks each, S carries 300 marks and H 200.

Let us form the matrix

$$R = \begin{bmatrix} 2 & 1 \\ 1 & 3 \\ 2 & 2 \\ 2 & 1 \end{bmatrix}$$

whose columns give the weightages in the two cases. It is a 4 × 2 matrix. We do a certain operation between P and R which we agree to call *multiplication*. Through this operation a new matrix denoted by PR is obtained as follows:

$$PR = \begin{bmatrix} 40 & 84 & 54 & 45 \\ 48 & 75 & 36 & 65 \\ 67 & 50 & 38 & 78 \end{bmatrix} \begin{bmatrix} 2 & 1 \\ 1 & 3 \\ 2 & 2 \\ 2 & 1 \end{bmatrix}$$

$$= \begin{bmatrix} (40 \times 2) + (84 \times 1) + (54 \times 2) + (45 \times 2) & (40 \times 1) + (84 \times 3) + (54 \times 2) + (45 \times 1) \\ (48 \times 2) + (75 \times 1) + (36 \times 2) + (65 \times 2) & (48 \times 1) + (75 \times 3) + (36 \times 2) + (65 \times 1) \\ (67 \times 2) + (50 \times 1) + (38 \times 2) + (78 \times 2) & (67 \times 1) + (50 \times 3) + (38 \times 2) + (78 \times 1) \end{bmatrix}$$

$$= \begin{bmatrix} 362 & 445 \\ 373 & 410 \\ 416 & 371 \end{bmatrix}$$

The four elements of the first row of P are multiplied respectively with the four elements of the first column of R and the products are added. Thus we get 362, the entry in the first row and the first column of the resulting matrix. This number represents the aggregate marks of A for the Administrative Service. Similarly multiplying the elements of the first row of P with those in the second column of R, each to each, and adding we get 445 which are A's marks for the Technical Service. Multiplying the second row of P with the first and second columns of R in the same way we get 373 and 410 as B's marks for the two services. Similarly we obtain C's marks as 416 and 371. Thus the matrix obtained by a certain operation between P and R which we have named multiplication (quite arbitrarily; in fact we could have given it any other name) gives the information required by the Public Services Commission.

This is an example providing some justification for defining a matrix. A stronger motivation comes from the problem of simultaneous equations which we proceed to discuss.

Simultaneous Equations

Simple simultaneous equations appeared early in the history of algebra. Ancient works on mathematics in India dating back to over fifteen hundred years contain problems which lead to the formulation and solution of simultaneous equations. To take one such simple problem: a father is 24 years older than his son; five years hence the father's age will be five times that of the son; find their ages. Denoting the ages of the father and the son by x_1 and x_2 years respectively, we get the following equations connecting x_1 and x_2.

$$x_1 - x_2 = 24$$

$$x_1 + 5 = 5(x_2 + 5)$$

These are equivalent to

$$\begin{aligned} 1x_1 - 1x_2 &= 24 \\ 1x_1 - 5x_2 &= 20 \end{aligned} \qquad (1a)$$

To get the values of x_1, x_2 satisfying these equations, we eliminate one of the unknowns, say x_1, from one of the equations with the help of the other, to get

$$\begin{aligned} 1x_1 - 1x_2 &= 24 \\ 4x_2 &= 4 \end{aligned} \qquad (2a)$$

which lead to

$$\begin{aligned} 1x_1 - 1x_2 &= 24 \\ 1x_2 &= 1 \end{aligned} \qquad (3a)$$

finally giving us

$$\begin{aligned} 1x_1 &= 25 \\ 1x_2 &= 1 \end{aligned} \qquad (4a)$$

or $x_1 = 25,\ x_2 = 1.$

Instead of symbols x_1, x_2 any other pair of symbols could be used. The solution is independent of these symbols; it depends upon the numerical coefficients of these symbols and the numbers 20 and 24 in equations (1a). This numerical data of the problem can be arranged as

$$\begin{bmatrix} 1 & -1 & 24 \\ 1 & -5 & 20 \end{bmatrix} \qquad (1b)$$

which may be called the matrix of equations (1a). Subtracting the second row from the first, we can obtain the matrix representation of equations (2a):

$$\begin{bmatrix} 1 & -1 & 24 \\ 0 & 4 & 4 \end{bmatrix} \qquad (2b)$$

Dividing the second row by 4, we obtain the matrix corresponding to equations (3a):

$$\begin{bmatrix} 1 & -1 & 24 \\ 0 & 1 & 1 \end{bmatrix} \qquad (3b)$$

Finally, in (3b) adding the second row to the first we obtain the matrix

$$\begin{bmatrix} 1 & 0 & 25 \\ 0 & 1 & 1 \end{bmatrix} \tag{4b}$$

which may be interpreted to represent equations (4a) giving the answer.

The problem thus could be looked upon as one of matrix manipulation. The method of solution remains essentially the same; only it has been written in a more compact form doing away with repetitive and redundant use of the symbols $x_1, x_2, =$.

Equations (1a) could be written in another matrix form also. We could write (1a) as

$$\begin{bmatrix} 1x_1 - 1x_2 \\ 1x_1 - 5x_2 \end{bmatrix} = \begin{bmatrix} 24 \\ 20 \end{bmatrix} \tag{1c}$$

an equation between two 2×1 matrices with the understanding that the equality is row-wise, that is, each row on the left is equal to the corresponding row on the right. Equation (1c) may be looked upon as a matrix equation.

Further by the rule of multiplication of two matrices, the left side of (1c) may be obtained as a product of two matrices:

$$\begin{bmatrix} 1 & -1 \\ 1 & -5 \end{bmatrix} \begin{bmatrix} x_1 \\ x_2 \end{bmatrix} = \begin{bmatrix} 1x_1 - 1x_2 \\ 1x_1 - 5x_2 \end{bmatrix}$$

The first matrix on the left is the 2×2 matrix of coefficients of x_1 and x_2 in the equations, and the second is a 2×1 matrix of the same x_1, x_2. The multiplication has been done according to the rule explained earlier.

The equations (1c) can now be written as

$$\begin{bmatrix} 1 & -1 \\ 1 & -5 \end{bmatrix} \begin{bmatrix} x_1 \\ x_2 \end{bmatrix} = \begin{bmatrix} 24 \\ 20 \end{bmatrix}$$

or

$$AX = C$$

where A, X, C denote the respective matrices. This is the matrix form of equations (1a).

The importance or the power of the matrix notation is not apparent from the above examples. It should, however, be clear that the solution of the equations depends upon the matrix of coefficients (such as A in the above example) and the matrix of constants on the right (such as C above). Simultaneous equations with many unknowns occur frequently in the applications of mathematics. The numerical work involved in the solution of these equations by the method of successive elimination (as exemplified above) increases rapidly with the number of equations. In two equations with two unknowns, the number of additions, subtractions, multiplications and divisions is at most nine, in three equations this number is 28, while in ten equations it is over 800. In modern engineering and economics it is not unusual to come across thousands of equations in thousands of unknowns. Matrix notation makes the handling of such large number of equations possible, and matrix theory helps to investigate the nature of such equations and the type of solutions they are expected to have.

Simultaneous equations are not the only motivation for the study of matrices. Matrix notation and theory are found useful wherever problems with many variables and parameters occur.

Matrix Operations

We may now define a matrix and operations connected with it in general terms. These constitute the algebra of matrices. It is convenient to denote a general matrix of order $m \times n$ as

$$A_{mn} = \begin{bmatrix} a_{11} & a_{12} & \cdot & \cdot & a_{1j} & \cdot & \cdot & a_{1n} \\ a_{21} & a_{22} & \cdot & \cdot & a_{2j} & \cdot & \cdot & a_{2n} \\ \cdot & \cdot & \cdot & \cdot & \cdot & \cdot & \cdot & \cdot \\ a_{i1} & a_{i2} & \cdot & \cdot & a_{ij} & \cdot & \cdot & a_{in} \\ \cdot & \cdot & \cdot & \cdot & \cdot & \cdot & \cdot & \cdot \\ a_{m1} & a_{m2} & \cdot & \cdot & a_{mj} & \cdot & \cdot & a_{mn} \end{bmatrix}$$

It is a matrix of m rows and n columns, a_{ij} denoting the element in the ith row and the jth column. This notation has the obvious advantage that the subscripts indicate the position of the element in the matrix. Thus a_{13} is the element in the first row and the third column, and a_{62} is the element in the sixth row and the second column. When the elements are not required to be explicitly written, it is customary to denote a matrix by a symbol like A_{mn}, the subscripts denoting the number of rows and columns in the matrix. When not explicitly required, even the subscripts like mn are dropped, and a single letter (usually capital) is used to denote a matrix.

The binary operation of *addition* is defined only between two matrices of the same order. If A_{mn} and B_{mn} are matrices, both of order $m \times n$, then

$$A_{mn} + B_{mn} = C_{mn}$$

where C_{mn} is also an $m \times n$ matrix whose element c_{ij} is given by the sum of the corresponding elements a_{ij} and b_{ij} of the matrices A_{mn} and B_{mn}. For example,

$$\begin{bmatrix} a_{11} & a_{12} \\ a_{21} & a_{22} \\ a_{31} & a_{32} \end{bmatrix} + \begin{bmatrix} b_{11} & b_{12} \\ b_{21} & b_{22} \\ b_{31} & b_{32} \end{bmatrix} = \begin{bmatrix} a_{11}+b_{11} & a_{12}+b_{12} \\ a_{21}+b_{21} & a_{22}+b_{22} \\ a_{31}+b_{31} & a_{32}+b_{32} \end{bmatrix}$$

To take a numerical example,

$$\begin{bmatrix} 3 & 2 & 4 \\ 1 & -2 & 3 \\ 0 & 4 & 6 \end{bmatrix} + \begin{bmatrix} 1 & -1 & 0 \\ 2 & 4 & -1 \\ 5 & 6 & 2 \end{bmatrix}.$$

$$= \begin{bmatrix} 3+1 & 2-1 & 4+0 \\ 1+2 & -2+4 & 3-1 \\ 0+5 & 4+6 & 6+2 \end{bmatrix} = \begin{bmatrix} 4 & 1 & 4 \\ 3 & 2 & 2 \\ 5 & 10 & 8 \end{bmatrix}$$

The binary operation called *multiplication* is defined between two matrices provided the number of columns in the first matrix is equal to the number of rows in the second. If A_{mn} and B_{np} are two matrices, then a product matrix $C_{mp} = A_{mn} B_{np}$ is obtained by a certain rule. The rule is that c_{ij}, the element in the ith row and the jth column of C_{mp}, is the sum of the products of the elements of the ith row of A_{mn} with the elements of the jth column of B_{np}, elements being multiplied each to each. As an example, let

$$A_{23} = \begin{bmatrix} a_{11} & a_{12} & a_{13} \\ a_{21} & a_{22} & a_{23} \end{bmatrix}, \quad B_{32} = \begin{bmatrix} b_{11} & b_{12} \\ b_{21} & b_{22} \\ b_{31} & b_{32} \end{bmatrix}$$

Since the number of columns in A_{23} is equal to the number of rows in B_{32}, the product $A_{23}\, B_{32}$ is defined and is obtained as follows.

$$A_{23}\, B_{32} = \begin{bmatrix} a_{11} & a_{12} & a_{13} \\ a_{21} & a_{22} & a_{23} \end{bmatrix} \begin{bmatrix} b_{11} & b_{12} \\ b_{21} & b_{22} \\ b_{31} & b_{32} \end{bmatrix}$$

$$\begin{bmatrix} a_{11}b_{11} + a_{12}b_{21} + a_{13}b_{31} & a_{11}b_{12} + a_{12}b_{22} + a_{13}b_{32} \\ a_{21}b_{11} + a_{22}b_{21} + a_{23}b_{31} & a_{21}b_{12} + a_{22}b_{22} + a_{23}b_{32} \end{bmatrix}$$

The binary operation of multiplication is noncommutative. It may happen that two matrices may be multiplicable in one order, but not in the reverse order. For instance, the product $A_{mn}\, B_{np}$ is defined, but not $B_{np}\, A_{mn}$, if $m \neq p$.

Example:

Let

$$A_{23} = \begin{bmatrix} 1 & -1 & 0 \\ 2 & 0 & 2 \end{bmatrix} \quad B_{31} = \begin{bmatrix} 2 \\ 1 \\ -2 \end{bmatrix}$$

Then

$$A_{23}\, B_{31} = \begin{bmatrix} 1 \\ 0 \end{bmatrix}$$

but $B_{31}\, A_{23}$ is not defined.

For two matrices of the type A_{mn}, B_{nm}, both the products $A_{mn}\, B_{nm}$ and $B_{nm}\, A_{mn}$ can be worked out, but the product in the first case is an $m \times m$ matrix and in the second $n \times n$ matrix. Thus the two products are different and so the operation is noncommutative.

Example:

Let

$$A_{23} = \begin{bmatrix} 1 & 3 & 2 \\ -1 & 2 & -3 \end{bmatrix}, \quad B_{32} = \begin{bmatrix} 4 & 1 \\ 2 & -1 \\ 1 & 0 \end{bmatrix}$$

Then

$$A_{23}\,B_{32} = \begin{bmatrix} 1 & 3 & 2 \\ -1 & 2 & -3 \end{bmatrix} \begin{bmatrix} 4 & 1 \\ 2 & -1 \\ 1 & 0 \end{bmatrix} = \begin{bmatrix} 12 & -2 \\ -3 & -3 \end{bmatrix}$$

and

$$B_{32} A_{23} = \begin{bmatrix} 4 & 1 \\ 2 & -1 \\ 1 & 0 \end{bmatrix} \begin{bmatrix} 1 & 3 & 2 \\ -1 & 2 & -3 \end{bmatrix} = \begin{bmatrix} 3 & 14 & 5 \\ 3 & 4 & 7 \\ 1 & 3 & 2 \end{bmatrix}$$

A matrix in which the number of rows is equal to the number of columns is called a *square* matrix. Two square matrices of the same order can be multiplied both ways, but the resulting matrices are, in general, still different, though they are of the same order.

Example:

Let

$$A_{22} = \begin{bmatrix} 3 & 2 \\ -1 & 4 \end{bmatrix}, \qquad B_{22} = \begin{bmatrix} 4 & 1 \\ 1 & -2 \end{bmatrix}$$

Then

$$A_{22}\,B_{22} = \begin{bmatrix} 3 & 2 \\ -1 & 4 \end{bmatrix} \begin{bmatrix} 4 & 1 \\ 1 & -2 \end{bmatrix} = \begin{bmatrix} 14 & -1 \\ 0 & -9 \end{bmatrix}$$

and

$$B_{22} A_{22} = \begin{bmatrix} 4 & 1 \\ 1 & -2 \end{bmatrix} \begin{bmatrix} 3 & 2 \\ -1 & 4 \end{bmatrix} = \begin{bmatrix} 11 & 12 \\ 5 & -6 \end{bmatrix}$$

Null and Unit Matrices

A matrix with all the elements zero is called a zero or *null* matrix. It plays the same role among matrices as zero among numbers. The addition of any matrix to a null matrix (the two being of the same order, else the sum is not defined) leaves the former unchanged:

$$\begin{bmatrix} a_{11} & a_{12} & a_{13} \\ a_{21} & a_{22} & a_{23} \end{bmatrix} + \begin{bmatrix} 0 & 0 & 0 \\ 0 & 0 & 0 \end{bmatrix} = \begin{bmatrix} a_{11} & a_{12} & a_{13} \\ a_{21} & a_{22} & a_{23} \end{bmatrix}$$

From an example like

$$\begin{bmatrix} 4 & 6 \\ -2 & -3 \end{bmatrix} + \begin{bmatrix} -4 & -6 \\ 2 & 3 \end{bmatrix} = \begin{bmatrix} 0 & 0 \\ 0 & 0 \end{bmatrix}$$

it can be surmised that if

$$A_{mn} + B_{mn} = O_{mn}$$

where O_{mn} is the null matrix of order $m \times n$, then the elements of B_{mn} and A_{mn} differ only in sign. We then say that

$$B_{mn} = -A_{mn}\,,\; A_{mn} = -B_{mn}$$

Further, if any matrix is multiplied by a null matrix, (provided the two are multiplicable), the result is a null matrix. For example,

$$\begin{bmatrix} a_{11} & a_{12} \\ a_{21} & a_{22} \\ a_{31} & a_{32} \end{bmatrix} \begin{bmatrix} 0 & 0 \\ 0 & 0 \end{bmatrix} = \begin{bmatrix} 0 & 0 \\ 0 & 0 \\ 0 & 0 \end{bmatrix}$$

In a square matrix the elements lying along the diagonal from the left top corner to the right bottom corner are called the *diagonal elements*. A square matrix is called a unit matrix if all its diagonal elements are 1 and all its other elements zero. The name is suggested from the fact that this matrix behaves with respect to matrices as 1 behaves with respect to numbers. Just as a number on multiplication by 1 remains unchanged, so does a matrix on multiplication with a unit matrix. As examples,

$$\begin{bmatrix} a_{11} & a_{12} & a_{13} \\ a_{21} & a_{22} & a_{23} \end{bmatrix} \begin{bmatrix} 1 & 0 & 0 \\ 0 & 1 & 0 \\ 0 & 0 & 1 \end{bmatrix} = \begin{bmatrix} a_{11} & a_{12} & a_{13} \\ a_{21} & a_{22} & a_{23} \end{bmatrix}$$

$$\begin{bmatrix} 1 & 0 \\ 0 & 1 \end{bmatrix} \begin{bmatrix} a_{11} & a_{12} & a_{13} \\ a_{21} & a_{22} & a_{23} \end{bmatrix} = \begin{bmatrix} a_{11} & a_{12} & a_{13} \\ a_{21} & a_{22} & a_{23} \end{bmatrix}$$

It is customary to denote the unit matrix of order $n \times n$ by I_n.

If the product of two square matrices of the same order (otherwise they are not multiplicable) is a unit matrix, one is called the inverse of the other. Thus two square matrices, A, B, both of the same order, are inverse of each other, if

$$A\,B = I,$$

where I is the unit matrix of the same order. (We may drop the subscript n from I if it is not explicitly required). We then write

$$B = A^{-1},\; A = B^{-1}$$

For example,

$$A = \begin{bmatrix} 2 & -1 & 3 \\ 4 & 0 & 1 \\ 1 & -2 & 5 \end{bmatrix},\quad B = \begin{bmatrix} -2 & 1 & 1 \\ 19 & -7 & -10 \\ 8 & -3 & -4 \end{bmatrix}$$

are the inverse of each other, that is $A = B^{-1}$ and $B = A^{-1}$, because

$$\begin{bmatrix} 2 & -1 & 3 \\ 4 & 0 & 1 \\ 1 & -2 & 5 \end{bmatrix} \begin{bmatrix} -2 & 1 & 1 \\ 19 & -7 & -10 \\ 8 & -3 & -4 \end{bmatrix} = \begin{bmatrix} 1 & 0 & 0 \\ 0 & 1 & 0 \\ 0 & 0 & 1 \end{bmatrix}$$

Suppose we have three simultaneous equations in three unknowns x_1, x_2, x_3 as follows.

$$2x_1 - 1x_2 + 3x_3 = 4$$
$$4x_1 + 0x_2 + x_3 = 5$$
$$1x_1 - 2x_2 + 5x_3 = 4$$

In matrix notation we may write them as

$$\begin{bmatrix} 2 & -1 & 3 \\ 4 & 0 & 1 \\ 1 & -2 & 5 \end{bmatrix} \begin{bmatrix} x_1 \\ x_2 \\ x_3 \end{bmatrix} = \begin{bmatrix} 4 \\ 5 \\ 4 \end{bmatrix}$$

or

$$AX = C$$

where

$$A = \begin{bmatrix} 2 & -1 & 3 \\ 4 & 0 & 1 \\ 1 & -2 & 5 \end{bmatrix}, \quad X = \begin{bmatrix} x_1 \\ x_2 \\ x_3 \end{bmatrix}, \quad C = \begin{bmatrix} 4 \\ 5 \\ 4 \end{bmatrix}$$

If we multiply both sides of this matrix equation by A^{-1}, we get

$$A^{-1} A X = A^{-1} C$$

But $A^{-1}A = I$, a unit matrix. So

$$IX = A^{-1}C.$$

But, since I is a unit matrix, $IX = X$, and therefore

$$X = A^{-1}C.$$

From the last numerical example we know that

$$A^{-1} = B = \begin{bmatrix} -2 & 1 & 1 \\ 19 & -7 & -10 \\ 8 & -3 & -4 \end{bmatrix}$$

Hence writing the equation $X = A^{-1}C$ explicitly in terms of matrices,

$$\begin{bmatrix} x_1 \\ x_2 \\ x_3 \end{bmatrix} = \begin{bmatrix} -2 & 1 & 1 \\ 19 & -7 & -10 \\ 8 & -3 & -4 \end{bmatrix} \begin{bmatrix} 4 \\ 5 \\ 4 \end{bmatrix}$$

or, on multiplying the two matrices on the right,

$$\begin{bmatrix} x_1 \\ x_2 \\ x_3 \end{bmatrix} = \begin{bmatrix} 1 \\ 1 \\ 1 \end{bmatrix}$$

which means that $x_1 = 1, x_2 = 1, x_3 = 1$. It can be verified that this is the solution of the simultaneous equations.

Thus, the inverse of the matrix of the coefficients of the unknowns in a set of simultaneous equations can easily give the solution of the equations. It is, however, not always easy to find the inverse of a matrix, particularly if the order of the matrix is large. There are other more convenient methods of solving simultaneous equations. But the concept of the inverse of a matrix plays an important role in the study of matrices in general.

Not all matrices have inverse. A square null matrix, for instance, has no inverse, because it is not possible to find a matrix which when multiplied by a null matrix would give a unit matrix. (It is analogous to the property of zero among numbers which has no inverse in the sense that there is no number which on multiplication with zero would give 1). Null matrices are not the only matrices which have no inverse. There is a whole class of square matrices with nonzero elements which have no inverse. There are also simultaneous equations which have no unique solution, and as is natural to expect, such equations give rise to matrices which have no inverse.

Conclusion

Matrices were invented in the middle of the nineteenth century but they remained buried in the archives of mathematics as their usefulness was not realised as long as problems involving one, two or three variables, at the most, were faced. In this century, and particularly in the last fifty years, mathematicians have been coming to grips with large problems, problems with many dimensions and many variables, and it is in connection with these that matrices have assumed importance. Matrices not only provide a concise notation, they often separate the essentials from the not-so-essentials in a problem. It is often the pattern of a matrix—the distribution of zeros in it and the relative positions of positive and negative numbers—that determines the nature of a problem. Matrix theory has now become an important subject and there is scarcely an area of application of mathematics where matrices are not used with advantage.

FROM THE GALLERY OF MATHEMATICIANS

William Rowan Hamilton

Acclaimed as the greatest mathematician of the British Isles after Isaac Newton, Hamilton (Irish, 1805-1865) showed remarkable intellectual ability since early childhood. By the age of fourteen, in addition to his own language English, he could speak and write French, Italian, Latin, Greek, Hebrew, Arabic and Sanskrit. His interest turned to mathematics at the age of fifteen, and soon he became famous as a mathematical prodigy. At twenty-one, while still an undergraduate, his ability was recognised in an unusual and unprecedented manner by his being appointed professor of astronomy at Dublin.

Though a celebrity in his lifetime, Hamilton's work has been fully appreciated only in the present century. His researches in mechanics proved to be of fundamental importance in the development of physics (quantum mechanics) in the early part of this century. In his efforts to go beyond the complex numbers, he tried to work with ordered triplets and quadruplets of numbers and stumbled into noncommutative binary operations. It was in his study of quaternions (ordered quadruplets) that he postulated the rules which are now presented as $\mathbf{i} \times \mathbf{j} = \mathbf{k}$, $\mathbf{j} \times \mathbf{i} = -\mathbf{k}$, etc. of vector algebra.

The credit for developing vector algebra based on Hamilton's work goes largely to J.W. Gibbs (American, 1839-1903).

Arthur Cayley, James Joseph Sylvester

Arthur Cayley (1821-1895) and James Joseph Sylvester (1814-1897), these two British mathematicians were close friends and inspired each other in their work on matrices and related topics. On the basis of publications, the invention of matrices is attributed to Cayley in 1858, but both Cayley and Sylvester, in their writings and lectures, recognised the debt each owed to the other for their contributions in mathematics.

To the German physicist Heisenberg goes the credit of bringing matrix algebra out from the archives of mathematics, where it had laid for sixty-seven years after Cayley had invented it, for his work in quantum mechanics in 1925.

EXERCISES

1. A stream is flowing with a speed of 5 km per hour, and a boatman rows with the same speed perpendicularly across the current. In what direction and with what speed the boat is moving as observed from the land? [*Hint*: The two vectors of speed are equal in length but perpendicular to each other in direction. The diagonal of the square formed by the vectors gives the resultant speed.]

2. The following three figures show two wires in a horizontal plane stretched from the top of a vertical pole. In each case the tension in the wires is equal to the weight of 100 kg, but the angle between the two wires is 60° in case (i), 90° in case (ii), and 120° in case (iii). Show that the effective pull on the pole is the least in case (iii) and the greatest in

case (i). How should the wires be stretched so that there is no pull on the pole?

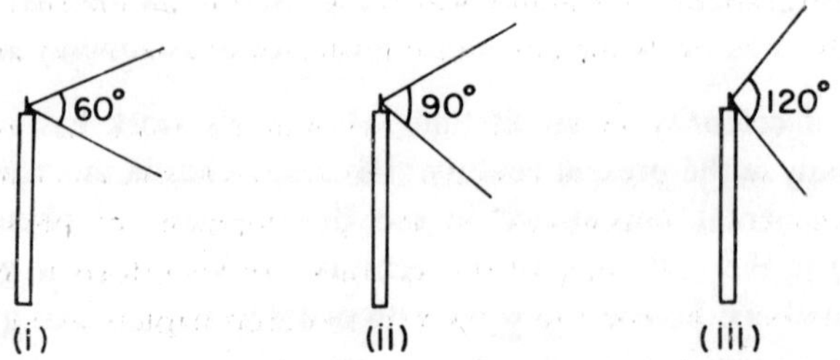

[*Hint*: Draw parallelograms in each case. It is easy to see that the diagonal is the smallest in case (iii) and the largest in case (i). For no pull, the two wires should be in the same line but in opposite directions.]

3. The vector *OP* giving the position of the point *P* with respect to *O* has components (3,1) with respect to the *x* and *y* axes. Similarly the vector *OQ* giving the position of the point *Q* has components (4,4). What are the components of the vector *PQ*? What are the magnitudes of the vectors *OP*, *OQ* and *PQ*?

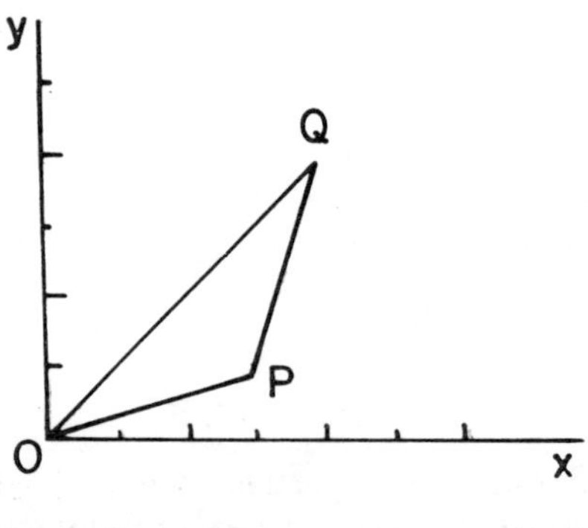

4. You have the choice of two spanners, one twice as long as the other. Which one would need lesser effort to turn and why? What will be the ratio of the efforts required in the two cases?

5. $$A = \begin{bmatrix} -3 & 4 \\ 2 & 0 \\ -4 & 6 \end{bmatrix}, \quad B = \begin{bmatrix} 7 & 2 \\ -6 & -2 \\ -3 & 4 \end{bmatrix},$$

$$C = \begin{bmatrix} 3 & 2 & 4 \\ 6 & -1 & 4 \end{bmatrix}, \; D = \begin{bmatrix} 2 & 3 & -4 \\ 1 & 0 & 2 \end{bmatrix},$$

find (i) $A + B$, $C–D$;
(ii) AC, BC, CA, DB;

Are the following defined?
(iii) $A + C$, $D + B$, CB, CA, CD.

6. Find x, y, z, w in the following equations.

(i) $$\begin{bmatrix} 4 & 1 \\ 3 & -9 \end{bmatrix} + \begin{bmatrix} x & y+1 \\ z & w-1 \end{bmatrix} = \begin{bmatrix} 0 & 0 \\ 0 & 0 \end{bmatrix}$$

(ii) $$\begin{bmatrix} x & 2 \\ 3 & y \end{bmatrix} - \begin{bmatrix} 3 & z \\ w & 5 \end{bmatrix} = \begin{bmatrix} 1 & 0 \\ 0 & 1 \end{bmatrix}$$

7. Solve the equations:

$$7x + 2y = 4$$
$$x - y = 7$$

by working on the matrix

$$\begin{bmatrix} 7 & 2 & 4 \\ 1 & -1 & 7 \end{bmatrix}$$

8. Show that the matrices

$$\begin{bmatrix} 2 & -3 \\ -3 & 5 \end{bmatrix} \quad \text{and} \quad \begin{bmatrix} 5 & 3 \\ 3 & 2 \end{bmatrix}$$

are inverse of each other. Using this fact, solve the equations

$$2x - 3y = 3$$
$$-3x + 5y = -4$$

9. Multiply:

$$\begin{bmatrix} a_{11} & a_{12} & a_{13} \\ a_{21} & a_{22} & a_{23} \\ a_{31} & a_{32} & a_{33} \end{bmatrix} \begin{bmatrix} 0 & 1 & 0 \\ 1 & 0 & 0 \\ 0 & 0 & 1 \end{bmatrix}$$

[Notice that the matrix on the right is obtained from the unit matrix by interchanging its first two columns, and the effect of multiplication is to bring about the same change in the matrix on the left. It can be conjectured that in the multiplication AI' of a matrix A by any matrix I', obtained by interchanging the columns of a unit matrix in any manner, will bring about the same type of interchange of columns in the matrix A.]

Write the product matrix in the following by observation, and then verify by actual multiplication.

$$\begin{bmatrix} 3 & 5 & 4 \\ 6 & 0 & 5 \\ -1 & 2 & 3 \end{bmatrix} \begin{bmatrix} 0 & 0 & 1 \\ 1 & 0 & 0 \\ 0 & 1 & 0 \end{bmatrix}$$

10. Multiply

$$\begin{bmatrix} 0 & 1 & 0 \\ 1 & 0 & 0 \\ 0 & 0 & 1 \end{bmatrix} \begin{bmatrix} a_{11} & a_{12} & a_{13} \\ a_{21} & a_{22} & a_{23} \\ a_{31} & a_{32} & a_{33} \end{bmatrix}$$

and make the same type of conjecture as in the above problem.

ANSWERS

1. Direction makes an angle of 45° with that of the current; speed: $5\sqrt{2}$ km/hr.

3. (1,3); $\sqrt{10}$, $\sqrt{32}$, $\sqrt{10}$.

4. The longer spanner would need half the effort.

5. (i) $\begin{bmatrix} 4 & 6 \\ -4 & -2 \\ -7 & 10 \end{bmatrix}$, $\begin{bmatrix} 1 & -1 & 8 \\ 5 & -1 & 2 \end{bmatrix}$

(ii) $\begin{bmatrix} 15 & -10 & 4 \\ 6 & 4 & 8 \\ 24 & -14 & 8 \end{bmatrix}$, $\begin{bmatrix} 33 & 12 & 36 \\ -30 & -10 & -32 \\ 15 & -10 & 4 \end{bmatrix}$,

$\begin{bmatrix} -21 & 36 \\ 36 & 48 \end{bmatrix}$, $\begin{bmatrix} 8 & -18 \\ 1 & 10 \end{bmatrix}$

(iii) No, no, yes, yes, no.

6. (i) $x = -4$, $y = -2$, $z = -3$, $w = 10$.

(ii) $x = 4$, $y = 6$, $z = 2$, $w = 3$.

7. $$\begin{bmatrix} 7 & 2 & 4 \\ 1 & -1 & 7 \end{bmatrix} \approx \begin{bmatrix} 7 & 2 & 4 \\ 7 & -7 & 49 \end{bmatrix} \approx \begin{bmatrix} 0 & 9 & -45 \\ 1 & -1 & 7 \end{bmatrix}$$

$$\approx \begin{bmatrix} 0 & 1 & -5 \\ 1 & -1 & 7 \end{bmatrix} \approx \begin{bmatrix} 0 & 1 & -5 \\ 1 & 0 & 2 \end{bmatrix},$$

hence $x = 2, y = -5$.

8. The product of the two matrices is

$$\begin{bmatrix} 1 & 0 \\ 0 & 1 \end{bmatrix};$$

hence they are inverse of each other.

The given equations are

$$\begin{bmatrix} 2 & -3 \\ -3 & 5 \end{bmatrix} \begin{bmatrix} x \\ y \end{bmatrix} = \begin{bmatrix} 3 \\ -4 \end{bmatrix}$$

Multiplying both sides by

$$\begin{bmatrix} 5 & 3 \\ 3 & 2 \end{bmatrix}$$

$$\begin{bmatrix} 1 & 0 \\ 0 & 1 \end{bmatrix} \begin{bmatrix} x \\ y \end{bmatrix} = \begin{bmatrix} 5 & 3 \\ 3 & 2 \end{bmatrix} \begin{bmatrix} 3 \\ -4 \end{bmatrix}$$

or

$$\begin{bmatrix} x \\ y \end{bmatrix} = \begin{bmatrix} 3 \\ 1 \end{bmatrix};$$

hence $x = 3, y = 1$.

9. $\begin{bmatrix} 5 & 4 & 3 \\ 0 & 5 & 6 \\ 2 & 3 & -1 \end{bmatrix}$

10. The product $I'A$, where I' is unit matrix with its rows interchanged in any manner, is obtained by interchanging the rows of A in the same manner.

Chapter 8

Fusion of Algebra and Geometry

"Mathematical ideas originate in empirics. Once they are so conceived the subject begins to live a peculiar life of its own governed by almost aesthetical motives."

—John Von Neumann, Hungarian-American mathematician (1903-57).

Mathematics is often defined as the science of number and space. Number is the basis of arithmetic and its generalised form algebra. Space is the basic theme of geometry. Algebra and geometry were the two main divisions of mathematics till about two and a half centuries ago when calculus was added as a third. These are still the three main streams of mathematics, but only in the broadest sense, for they do not flow in separate channels. There are no boundaries dividing them. Each mingles freely with the other. Basically all mathematics is one.

Geometry

Geometry, as its name implies, arose from man's need to measure and divide land and build houses. Measurement involved numbers, and so geometry needed arithmetic and algebra. Geometrical problems were often problems of arithmetic and algebra, and consequently some algebraical problems could be interpreted in terms of geometry. The solution to a problem arising in one area often came from the other. There was a geometric approach different from algebraic because geometry had a practical side to it – that of actually drawing and measuring instead of calculating. For this reason, instead of always growing hand in hand, algebra and geometry have sometimes grown, specially during their earlier history, at the expense of each other. Greeks developed geometry and brought it to a level of logical perfection unattained by any other branch of science or mathematics for more than two thousand years. Only in the present century efforts have been made to put all mathematics on a logical footing similar to that of Euclid's geometry. On the other hand, algebra received greater attention at the hands of Indians and Arabs and grew more as working rules and procedures rather than a self-contained system of deductive logic.

Space

Geometry deals with the study of figures in space like triangles, circles, ellipses, spheres, pyramids, etc. Matter occupies space and different material objects all around us occupy portions of space of different sizes and shapes. It is the portions of space, and not their material contents, that geometry studies. It is therefore essentially concerned with the properties of space independent of the matter distributed in it.

It is difficult to define space in physical terms. Whatever our senses detect through touch, sight, smell, taste or hearing is either matter or energy, which are only alternative forms of each other. Light, sound, electricity etc are forms of energy. Matter and energy are coexistent and inextricably bound with each other; in fact they are interconvertible. Imagine the withdrawal of all matter; what still remains is space. Imagine, for example, a vessel from which all air has been sucked out by powerful pumps. The vessel, emptied of all matter, still contains space. This intuitive comprehension of space, though, is not without difficulties. Can we really create vacuum? Even with the most powerful vacuum pumps matter cannot be completely removed from within a vessel. The walls of the vessel itself would give out material in highly rarefied form. Does it then make sense to talk of space without matter, or matter without space? This is a difficult question. Einstein, through his celebrated theory of relativity, established not only that matter and energy are two forms of the same entity (1905), but also that space and matter are manifestation of the same reality (1915). Let us, however, not get lost in the deep waters of science and philosophy – the culmination of mathematical and scientific investigations extending over centuries. Let us begin at the very beginning and agree that we intuitively understand space and can imagine objects like points, lines and surfaces in it through illustrations of the following type.

Points, Lines and Surfaces

Take a glass containing water. The water makes a distinction between the space where it is and where it is not. To get from one to the other one must cross the *surface* of the water. This surface is the boundary which separates the space where the water is from the space where it is not. Part of this surface is against the air and part against the glass. In getting from one part to the other, we have to cross the *line* which divides these two parts; it is the circular edge where water, air and glass meet. Suppose further that the glass had a colour design on its surface such that the circular line is divided into two parts, one against the colour and the other against the colourless glass. If we imagine to move along the line from one part to the other, we have to cross the *point* which separates them. We thus come to the notions of surface, line and point. We may say that

> the boundary of a solid (or part of space) is a surface;
> the boundary of a surface, or a part of it, is a line;
> the boundary of a line, or a part of it, is a point.

The process ends here. The point has no extension in space. It has no parts, no boundaries.

We may reverse the process and generate lines from points, surfaces from lines, and solids from surfaces. Imagine a line as an aggregate of points, a surface as an aggregate of lines, and a solid as an aggregate of surfaces, (Fig. 8.1). Surface as an aggregate of lines is also an aggregate of points, rather a double aggregate or an aggregate of an aggregate of points. We call the line a one-dimensional aggregate and the surface a two-dimensional aggregate of points. Extending the idea, we call the solid a three-dimensional aggregate of points. Our space of which we are intuitively conscious is, in this sense, three-dimensional. It is the limit, so far as our sense perceptions go. But, as usual, limitations of the senses are no bar to the imagination of the mathematician. He easily constructs higher-dimensional spaces, and not without use or advantage. To these we shall come later. Just now let us look closely at the basic concepts behind the familiar space of elementary geometry.

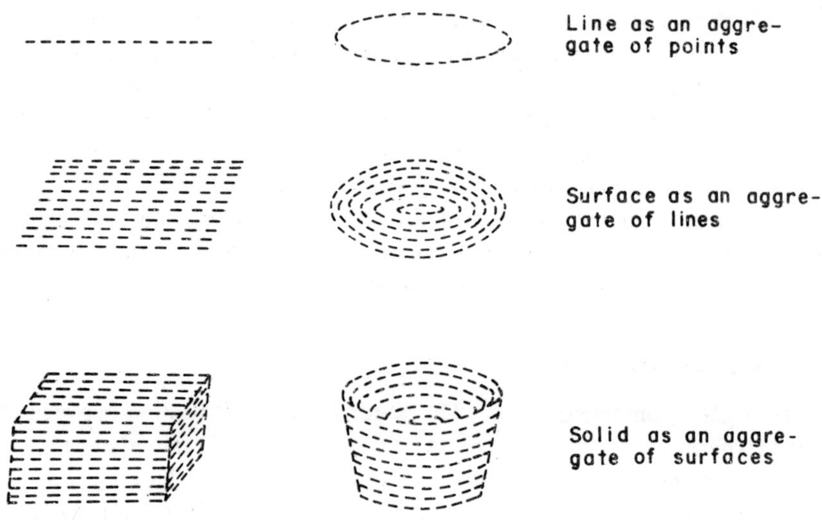

Fig. 8.1

Properties of Space

Space is an aggregate of points. But any aggregate of points is not space. The aggregate has to have further properties before it can be called space. We shall identify these properties by intuitive understanding and practical demonstration. They cannot be proved. In a strictly logical system they are assumed as axioms or postulates.

The first property is of *continuity*. Space is a continuous aggregate of points. It is the same thing as to say that along a line between any two points, however close, there are innumerable other points. This is similar to the property of real numbers and provides a basis for comparison of relative positions of points in terms of numbers. However, before this can be done, another property, that of *distance* between two points, has to be defined.

The manner in which we have defined a line makes a thin flexible inextensible string (such as a silk thread) a good representation of a line. We can compare the lengths of different pieces of flexible string by laying them side by side, and decide which one is the shortest. Between any two points in space any number of lines can be drawn with their ends at the two points. Fig. 8.2 shows a few lines joining points A, B. Imagine each line replaced by a thin string. The line corresponding to the shortest of all possible strings that can be laid between the two points is called a *straight line*. It is always possible to draw a straight line joining two points. The measure of this straight line (terminating at the two points) is a measure of the distance between them.

It is customary to call a straight line just a *line*. We shall follow this practice henceforth. Any line other than straight shall be called curved line or simply a *curve*.

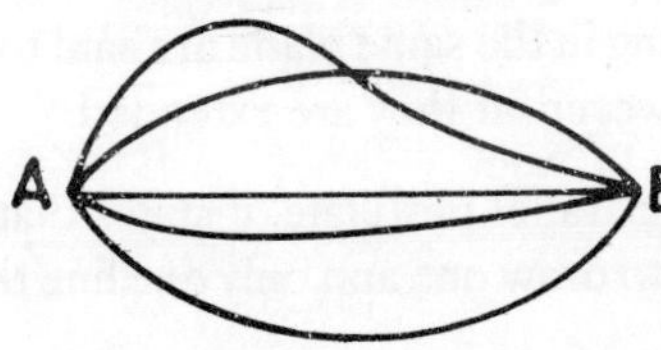

Fig. 8.2

In addition to the above two postulates about continuity and distance, there are three more postulates which form the basis of elementary geometry. One is that given any two points A and B, it is always possible to find a third point C such that the distance AC is equal to the sum of the distances AB and BC, (Fig. 8.3). It is equivalent to saying that a line can be extended in either direction along its length indefinitely.

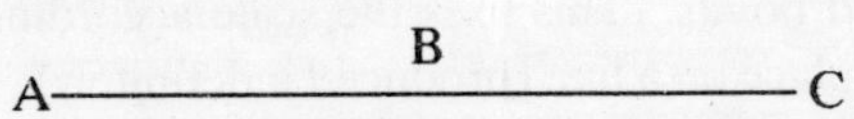

Fig. 8.3

The notion of inclination between two lines passing through a point leads to the postulate about the right angle. Two intersecting lines form four angles between them (marked 1,2,3,4, in Fig. 8.4a). It is possible for two lines to intersect such that all these four angles are equal to one another (Fig. 8.4b). Each one of them is called a *right angle*. It is assumed that one right angle is always equal to another right angle, however far removed in space one may be from the other.

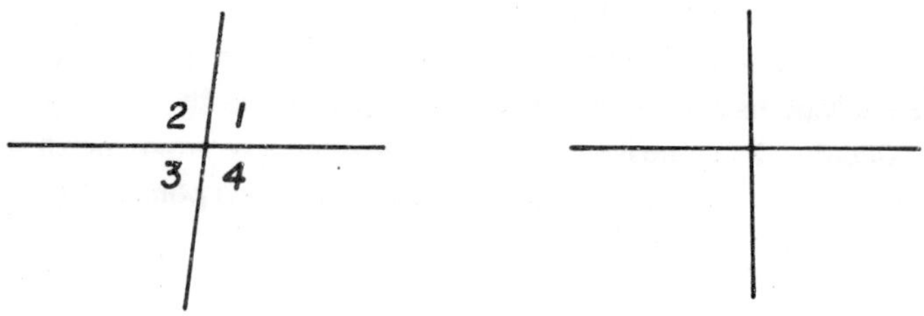

(a) (b)

Fig. 8.4

The fifth and last postulate, known as the parallel postulate, has become famous in the history of mathematics for reasons we shall see in chapter 10. To enunciate it, we shall first define a plane. A *plane* is a special type of surface which has the property that the line joining any two points on the surface has all its points lying on the surface. A plane is completely determined by two intersecting lines, or three points not in the same line, or a line and a point outside it. Two lines lying in the same plane are said to be *parallel* to each other if they do not meet, however far they are extended.

Now to come to the parallel postulate, it states that given a line and a point outside it, it is possible to draw one and only one line through the point parallel to the line

These five postulates or axioms are the basis of Euclid's geometry. In other words, these postulates define space in which theorems of Euclid's geometry hold.

Measuring Lines and Surfaces

The use of real numbers to measure the length of a line or, which is the same thing, the distance between two points, establishes the basic relationship between algebra and geometry. The distance is not measured in any absolute sense. Any distance may be taken as a standard unit by associating the number 0 and 1 with its end points. This fixes the scale according to which the real numbers find their place on a line (produced indefinitely). Any other distance can be measured by comparison with this line. This is the principle of the straight edge scale, the simplest instrument to measure length.

Since each line has a number associated with it which measures its length (relative to some standard unit length), we may reverse the argument and say that each real number can be represented by a line. We can go further and represent arithmetical operations on numbers by geometrical constructions. It is easy to give geometrical interpretation to the operation of addition. $b + c = d$ means that a line of length b extended through a distance c becomes a line of length d. The geometrical interpretation of multiplication is more interesting. It leads to the measurement of surfaces.

If two lines AB and AC, (Fig. 8.5a), each of unit length, intersect to make a right angle at A, we can make a four-sided figure $ABDC$, called a square, by drawing CD parallel to AB and BD parallel to AC. This square, which we call a *unit square*, is a portion of a plane surface and may be taken as a unit measure of area, area being the term used for the magnitude or the extent of the surface. Now, if the two lines AB and AC, intersecting at right angles, are of lengths, say 3 and 2 respectively, (Fig. 8.5b), by the same construction as before, they form a rectangle whose area is the sum of six (3×2) unit squares, as is clear from the figure. We therefore represent the multiplication of two numbers b and c by the area of a rectangle whose sides are of length b and c. This provides a geometrical interpretation of the operation of multiplication.

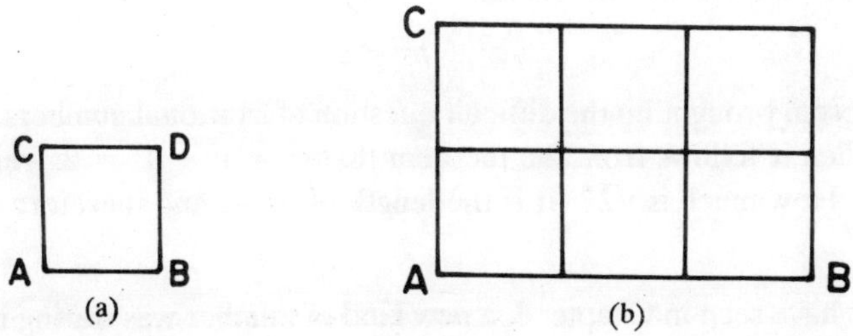

Fig. 8.5

As an example of proving an algebraic result geometrically, consider the algebraic statement

$$(a + b)^2 = a^2 + 2ab + b^2$$

The truth of this statement for all values of a and b is easily established by multiplying $a + b$ by itself according to the rules of algebra. Its geometrical proof is provided by Fig. 8.6. A large square of side $a + b$ is divided into two smaller squares of sides a and b respectively and two rectangles, each of sides a and b. The large square is equal to the sum of the two smaller squares and the two rectangles, which establishes the truth of the algebraic statement.

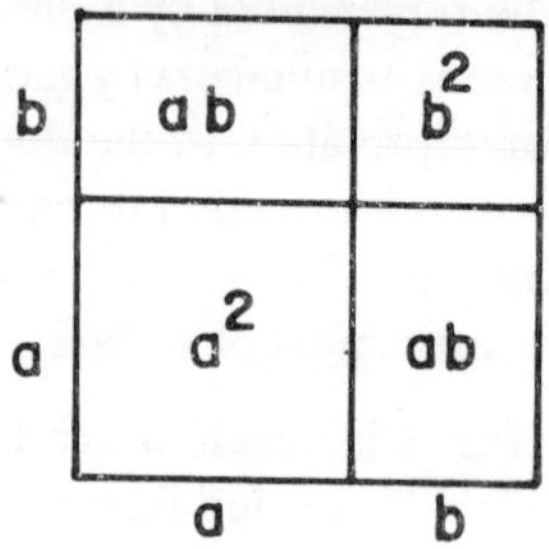

Fig. 8.6

Theorem of Pythagoras

Of all the theorems of elementary geometry, a theorem about the right-angled triangle, known as the theorem of Pythagoras, has contributed most in bringing algebra and geometry together. A right-angled triangle is one in which one angle is a right angle. The side opposite to the right angle is called the hypotenuse. The theorem states that the square on the hypotenuse is equal to the sum of the squares on the other two sides, (Fig. 8.7). If a and b are the lengths of the two sides adjacent to the right angle, and c is the length of the hypotenuse, then in algebraic terms

$$a^2 + b^2 = c^2$$

This theorem brought up the difficult question of irrational numbers. If $a = 1$, $b = 1$, then it follows from the theorem that $c^2 = 1^2 + 1^2 = 2$, which means $c = \sqrt{2}$. How much is $\sqrt{2}$? It is the length of a line and therefore must be a number.

As we have seen in Chapter 3, a new kind of number was staring in the face of mathematicians, and it took them many centuries before they could feel at

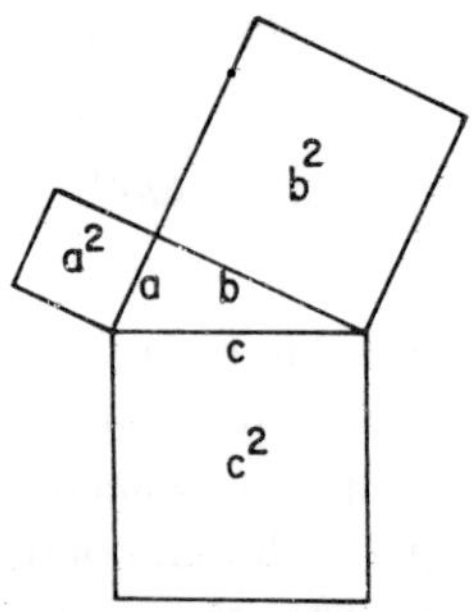

Fig. 8.7

home with it. The Greeks side-tracked the issue by concentrating on geometry rather than algebra. The Indians tamed such numbers by devising correct rules of operating on them. It was only in the sixteenth century that a big step was taken by the famous French mathematician and philosopher Descartes which brought geometry within the range of algebraic methods, and thus paved the way of unification of the two.

Coordinate axes

The position of a point on a line can be described by a real number which measures its distance from any arbitrarily chosen standard point on the line. Thus all points on the line will come to have unique numbers associated with them. Each point on the line can be identified by one real number.

Points on a plane present a different picture . They do not all lie on a line, but the plane on which they lie is uniquely determined by any two intersecting lines lying in the plane, and with respect to any such pair of lines the position of a point in the plane can be uniquely described. It is simplest to take a perpendicular pair of lines as the standard reference lines, because in that case by using the theorem of Pythagoras the distance between any two points can be most easily calculated. The reference lines are called the coordinate axes, usually designated as the x-axis ($x'ox$) and the y-axis ($y'oy$) intersecting at the origin O, (Fig. 8.8).

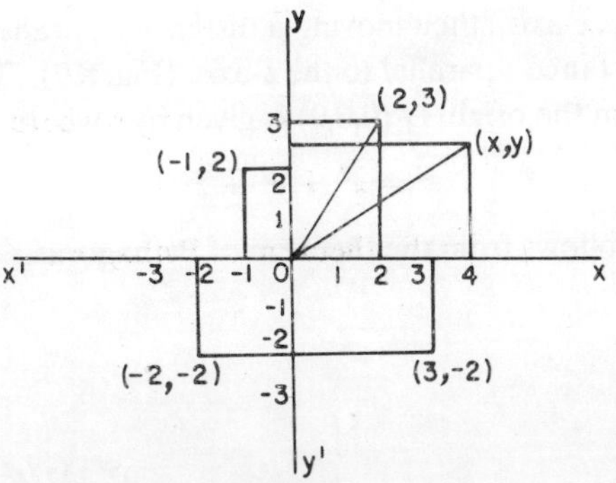

Fig. 8.8

Any point in the plane can be reached from O by moving first along the x-axis through a certain distance and then parallel to the y-axis through another distance. The two numbers, usually denoted by (x, y), giving measures of these distances, (positive in one direction, negative in the other), fix a definite point in the plane. Every pair of real numbers corresponds to a definite point in the plane, and every point in the plane has a unique ordered pair of real numbers, called its *coordinates*, describing its position with respect to the axes. As examples, note the points described by the pairs (2, 3), (3, –2), (–2, –2), (–1, 2) in Fig. 8.8.

By the theorem of Pythagoras, the distance of the point (2, 3) from the origin O, which is the point (0,0), is $\sqrt{2^2 + 3^2} = \sqrt{13}$. In general the distance s of any point (x, y) from (0, 0) is given by the relation

$$s^2 = x^2 + y^2$$

Since any point can be chosen as the origin, the formula is perfectly general and can be used to find the distance between any two points. This seemingly simple formula is of fundamental significance, for it incorporates the properties of space which we have assumed as postulates. The ordered pairs (x, y) of real numbers constitute a two-dimensional continuous aggregate of points, and when we further postulate that the shortest distance between two points is given by the above formula, we have assumed the theorem of Pythagoras. The theorem, for its proof, depends upon the axioms about the shortest distance, right angles and parallel lines. We have thus by implication assumed all the properties of space.

Points in three-dimensional space can be likewise described with respect to three coordinate axes. Three mutually perpendicular lines Ox, Oy, Oz intersecting at the origin O could be taken as reference lines. The position of any point P in space could be described with respect to these axes by an ordered triplet of real numbers (x, y, z) such that P is reached from O by moving a distance x along the x-axis,, then moving a distance y parallel to the y-axis, and finally moving a distance z parallel to the z-axis, (Fig. 8.9). The distance of the point P (x, y, z) from the origin O (0,0,0) is given by s where

$$s^2 = x^2 + y^2 + z^2$$

This formula also follows from the theorem of Pythagoras.

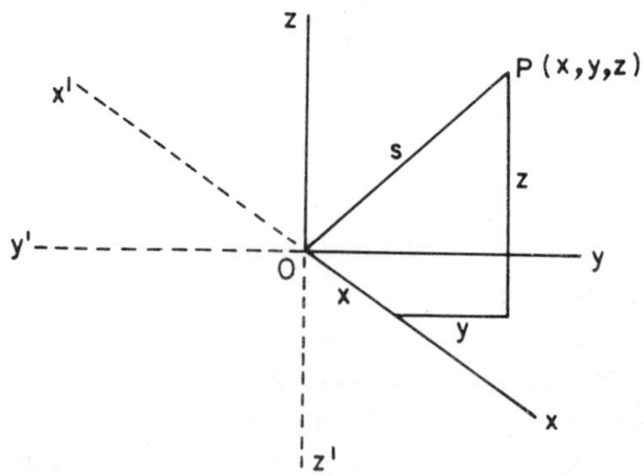

Fig. 8.9

Algebraic Geometry

An equation, logically speaking, is a statement which may be true or false. Consider, for example, the equation

$$3x - 2y = 6$$

This is a statement which is true for some values of x and y and false for others. If $x = 2$ and $y = 0$, the statement is true. It is also true for $x = 0, y = -3$. But it is false for $x = 1, y = 1$. A pair of values of (x, y) for which the statement is true is called a solution of the equation. There is an infinity of pairs of real numbers which are solutions to this equation. Corresponding to each such pair a point can be uniquely fixed in a plane with respect to some chosen coordinate axes. The set of points corresponding to all pairs which are solutions of the equation is called the graph of the equation. It can be theoretically proved as well as practically seen by actual construction that the graph of $3x - 2y = 6$ is a line, (Fig. 8.10). Every point on this line has coordinates which satisfy the equation, and every pair of values of (x, y) satisfying the equation corresponds to a point on the line (produced indefinitely). It can be proved as a general rule that the graph of any first degree equation in x, y like $ax + by + c = 0$, where a, b, c are real numbers, is a line.

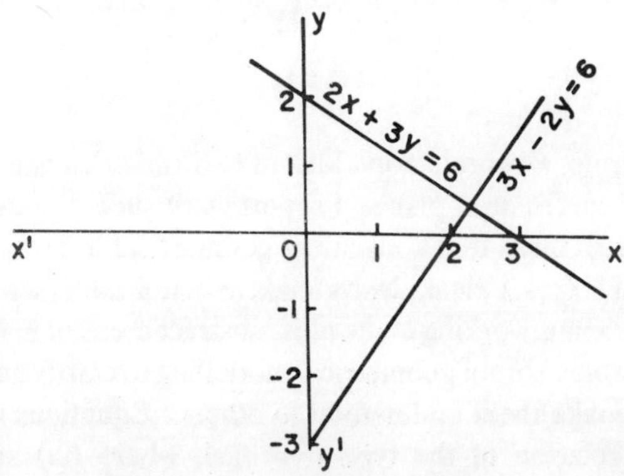

Fig. 8.10

Consider the pair of equations

$$3x - 2y = 6, \quad 2x + 3y = 6.$$

By algebraic methods these can be solved as simultaneous equations. Their solution is $x = 30/13$, $y = 6/13$. It means that this pair of values of (x, y) is the common solution of the two equations. The point corresponding to it should lie on the graphs of both the equations. It is therefore the point of intersection of the two lines representing the two equations, (Fig. 8.10). Thus we have a geometrical method of solving two algebraic simultaneous equations.

To take another type of example, consider the equation

$$x^2 + y^2 = 4.$$

Any number of pairs of real values of (x, y) can be found which are solutions of this equation. To cite a few, (0,2), (0,–2), (2,0), (–2,0), $(\sqrt{2},\sqrt{2})$, $(\sqrt{2}, -\sqrt{2})$, $(1,\sqrt{3})$ are all solutions of this equation. We have seen that $x^2 + y^2$ is the square of the distance of the point (x, y) from the origin. Any point whose distance from the origin is 2, therefore, gives a solution of the equation. In fact the set of points distant 2 from the origin corresponds to the set of solutions of this equation. Such a set of points is the circle with centre at the origin and radius 2, (Fig. 8.11). Thus this circle is the graph of the equation $x^2 + y^2 = 4$.

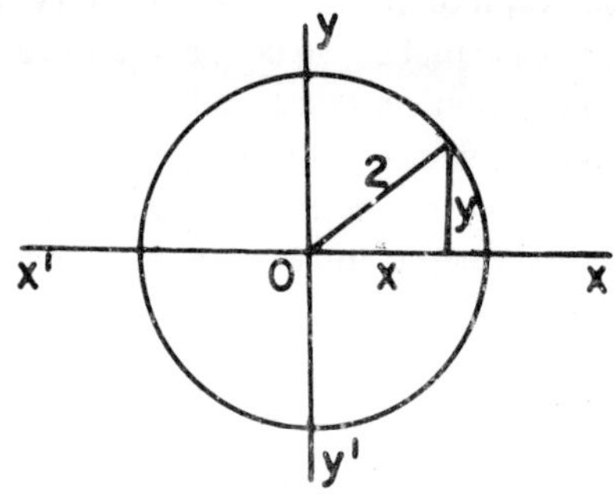

Fig. 8.11

As a general rule, algebraic equations in two variables can be represented geometrically as curves on a plane. Properties of such equations and results deduced from them often find convenient geometrical interpretations. Visual representation of abstract ideas always leads to better understanding. Even the best of mathematicians working in the most abstract areas of mathematics often take recourse to some sort of geometrical modelling to clarify and develop their own ideas or to make them understood to others. Equations in two variables always imply a relation of the type $y = f(x)$, where $f(x)$ stands for some mathematical expression in x. (A more correct name for $f(x)$ is 'function of x' which we shall explain more fully in the next chapter.) For example,

$$x^2 + y^2 = 4$$

is equivalent to

$$y = +\sqrt{4 - x^2} \quad \text{or} \quad -\sqrt{4 - x^2},$$

and

$$3x - 2y = 6$$

means the same thing as

$$y = \tfrac{1}{2}(3x - 6).$$

The graph of an equation like $y = f(x)$ is characteristic of the mathematical expression $f(x)$, and is often called the graph of the function $f(x)$. The properties of a function are often conveniently studied and appreciated through its graph.

Equations in three variables x, y, z can be similarly interpreted as graphs in three-dimensional space. An equation like

$$ax + by + cz + d = 0,$$

where a, b, c, d are real numbers, represents a plane in the sense that every point lying in the plane has coordinates which satisfy the equation, and every triplet of values of (x, y, z) which satisfy the equation represents a point on the plane.

As another example, the equation

$$x^2 + y^2 + z^2 = r^2$$

represents a sphere with its centre at the origin and radius r, because the points whose coordinates satisfy the above equation are distant r from the origin and so are on the surface of the sphere. In general, an equation in x, y, z represents a surface in space. If the equation is put in the form

$$z = f(x, y),$$

where $f(x, y)$ is some expression involving x, y, then the surface may be regarded as the graph of the function $f(x, y)$.

Giving geometrical interpretations to algebraic problems gives concrete shape to abstract ideas. It makes algebra easier to visualize. The benefit, however, is mutual. If geometry gives some shape to algebra, algebra liberates geometry from the limitations of shapes. Geometrical curves and surfaces can be described in algebraic terms, and all the numerous theorems and innumerable results following from them by Euclidean methods can be obtained by algebraic reasoning too. The algebraic method has greater flexibility, for algebraic logic has greater variability than verbal logic which is the sheet anchor of Euclid's method. Freed from the necessity of drawing figures on a plane or making models in space, geometry could leave the narrow confines of the three-dimensional space, and fly on the wings of algebra to explore the world of higher dimensions.

Extension to Higher Dimensions

Postulating a space of four, five or higher dimensions and describing geometrical objects in it was an easy matter of formal generalization of algebraic forms; its visualization in terms of figures and shapes was an impossibility. A single real number represented the position of a point along a line (one-dimensional space), an ordered pair (x_1, x_2)* represented a point in a plane (two-dimensional space), an ordered triplet (x_1, x_2, x_3)* described the position of a point in

* It is convenient to replace the notations (x, y) with (x_1, x_2) and (x, y, z) with (x_1, x_2, x_3), as the suffixed symbols are more suitable for higher dimensions.

a three-dimensional space, therefore, almost effortlessly, one can say that an ordered collection of four real numbers (x_1, x_2, x_3, x_4) represents a point in a four-dimensional space, and so on. A four-dimensional space is the set of all points described by the ordered collections of four real numbers. Conceptually a point in a four-dimensional space is nothing else but four ordered real numbers, and the space is nothing else but the set of all such sets of four real numbers. The thing is not different from its mathematical description. Upto three dimensions, perhaps for all except some mathematical philosophers, space is something which exists independently of numbers, and numbers are used only to describe some properties of it. But beyond three, (we keep the four-dimensional world of relativity theory out of consideration for the present), space is purely a mathematical idea. In fact it is merely a term without any meaning outside its mathematical definition. The development is quite in keeping with all other mathematical developments resulting from generalizations. In its initial stages all mathematics starts as an aid or a tool to deal with something outside itself; in its generalizations the tool becomes the thing, mathematics deals with mathematics only, it investigates itself.

Higher-dimensional geometries do not arise from sense experience. They are purely mathematical structures created through generalizations of mathematical forms. For example, since, by the theorem of Pythagoras, $x_1^2 + x_2^2$ is the square of the distance of the point (x_1, x_2) from the origin in a plane, and $x_1^2 + x_2^2 + x_3^2$ is the square of the distance of the point (x_1, x_2, x_3) from the origin in a three-dimensional space, we postulate that $x_1^2 + x_2^2 + x_3^2 + x_4^2$ is the square of the distance of the point (x_1, x_2, x_3, x_4) from the origin in a four-dimensional space, and $x_1^2 + x_2^2 + x_3^2 + ... + x_n^2$ is the similar quantity in an n-dimensional space. Thus the theorem of Pythagoras is formally extended to higher-dimensional spaces purely as an algebraic idea providing a definition of distance between two points. The definitions of geometrical figures follow easily. For instance, as

$$x_1^2 + x_2^2 = r^2$$

is the set of all points distant r from the origin and represents a circle of radius r on a plane, and likewise

$$x_1^2 + x_2^2 + x_3^2 = r^2$$

is a sphere of radius r in a three-dimensional space, we imagine a *hypershere* of radius r as a *surface* in an n-dimensional space every point of which is at the same distance r from a fixed point. It can be described by an equation of the type

$$x_1^2 + x_2^2 + x_3^2 + \ldots + x_n^2 = r^2.$$

As another example, as

$$a_1x_1 + a_2x_2 + a_3 = 0$$

represents a line in a plane, and

$$a_1x_1 + a_2x_2 + a_3x_3 + a_4 = 0$$

a plane in three-dimensional space, we imagine that an equation of the type

$$a_1x_1 + a_2x_2 + a_3x_3 + \ldots\ldots + a_nx_n + a_{n+1} = 0$$

describes a *hyperplane* in an n-dimensional space. Just as lines can be drawn to enclose a polygon, and planes can be drawn to enclose a polyhedron, we can imagine hyperplanes to form polyhedra in higher dimensions. So on with many other geometrical notions.

The geometrical terms like lines, hyperplanes, hyperspheres, polyhedra and many others used freely in spaces of higher dimensions do not denote constructible shapes but only algebraic forms. But geometrical names do serve a purpose. They are reminders of possible geometrical visualization and graphical representation of corresponding ideas in two or three dimensions, and help to indicate fruitful directions of mathematical reasoning. Moreover, they lead to complete synthesis of algebra and geometry, and enable mathematicians to freely make use of notions and terminology of either algebra or geometry and switch from one to the other, whenever convenient or desirable.

More Generalized Spaces

Spaces defined in the aforesaid manner are called Euclidean. They are formal extensions of the space of Euclid's geometry, in which points are defined as collections of ordered real numbers and distances are given by the generalized Pythagoras theorem. However, roads to further generalizations are still open.

Pythagoras theorem is not sacrosanct. One may define the distance between points in other ways. As an example of a different measure of distance, consider the following.

We imagine a plane with a very peculiar property, namely, that it is possible to move in that plane only in two mutually perpendicular directions shown as *OX, OY* in Fig. 8.12. If one has to go from the origin *O* to the point *P*, then one can take steps alternately parallel to x-axis and y-axis, but there is no way to move obliquely cutting across lines parallel to the axes. One can go along *OM* and *MP* or *ON* and *NP*, or along more zigzag paths (such as shown broken in Fig. 8.12). There can be several such paths. The smallest of these paths we take as the measure of the distance between *O* and *P*. It is apparent that the paths *OMP*, *ONP* and the one shown by ...... are all of the same length and the shortest. The path shown by · — · — · — · is longer. We thus notice that the 'line' denoting the shortest distance between two points is not unique. Except in the special case when the two points are along the same horizontal or vertical line (that is, parallel to either of the axes), the 'lines' representing the shortest distance between two points are infinitely many. This is a property very different from that of the Euclidean plane in which the line of shortest distance is unique.

The distance of any point (x,y) from the origin, with our present definition, is given by $|x| + |y|$. $|x|$ denotes the absolute or the positive value of x irrespective of its algebraic sign, similarly $|y|$. It is convenient to use such a notation, for the distance of the point (–2, 2) from the origin is $|-2| + |2| = 2 + 2 = 4$, and the distance of (3,–1) from the origin is $|3| + |-1| = 3 + 1 = 4$. The distance between (–2, 2) and (3, –1) is easily seen to be $|-2| + |2| + |3| + |-1| = 2 + 2 + 3 + 1 = 8$. (Fig. 8.12)

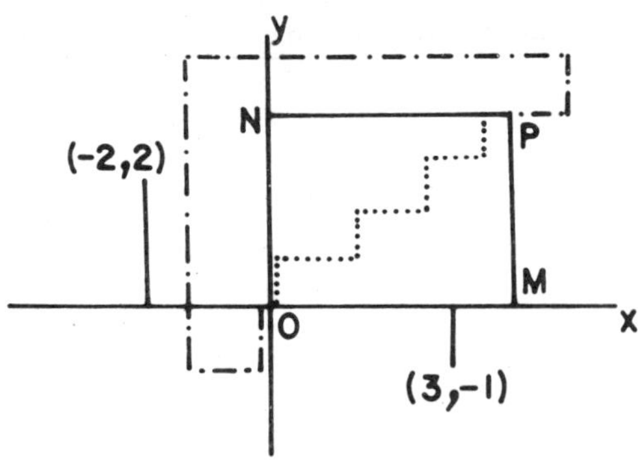

Fig. 8.12

Defining a circle as the set of points equidistant from a fixed point, it is interesting to see what shape the 'circle' takes in this plane. Taking O as the centre of the 'circle', (Fig. 8.13), it can be seen that the boundary of the figure

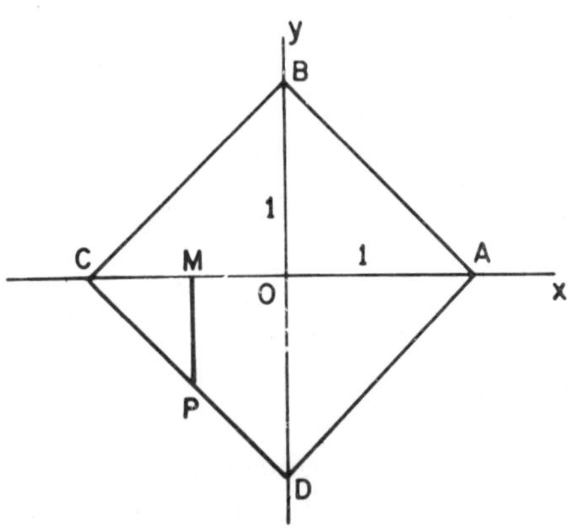

Fig. 8.13

ABCD is such that every point on it is distant 1 from *O*. For example, the distance $OP = OM + MP$ which is equal to 1. Thus *ABCD* is a 'circle' of unit radius. This is only one example of how, by logically pursuing the consequences of our definition of distance, we would arrive at results totally different from that of Euclidean geometry. We have really discovered, rather constructed, a new geometry.

It is not only with the definition of distance that one can play about. Even points can be defined differently. Real numbers or ordered collections of them are not the only way to define points. One may have complex numbers, or collections of them, to represent 'points'. Things are still more complicated when functions are taken as 'points', and distance between two 'points' as some significant measure of difference between the two functions. Such abstract spaces are the subject of study in functional analysis, a branch of modern mathematics which has assumed fundamental importance in mathematics itself as well as its applications.

Topology

Another subject which started as a branch of geometry but was soon generalized through algebraic methods is topology. Two geometrical shapes are said to be topologically equivalent when one can be obtained from the other by deformations consisting of bending, stretching, contracting or twisting, but not tearing or coalescing. It is possible to describe topologically equivalent figures by imagining them to be made of rubber or plasticine which can be bent, stretched, contracted or twisted in any manner and to any extent without tearing or joining.

For example, considering one-dimensional figures or curves first, the curves of Fig. 8.14 are all topologically equivalent to each other, but topologically different from the curves of Fig. 8.15, because a curve with two ends cannot be deformed into a closed curve without joining the two ends. All the curves of Fig. 8.15 are of the same topological class. In Fig. 8.16, curves (a) and (b) are topologically similar to each other but different from (c) as well as from those of Figs. 8.15 and 8.14. One can pinch a circle to form the figure of 8 but it would mean joining two points which originally were apart, which would make the two figures topologically different.

Fig. 8.14

Fig. 8.15

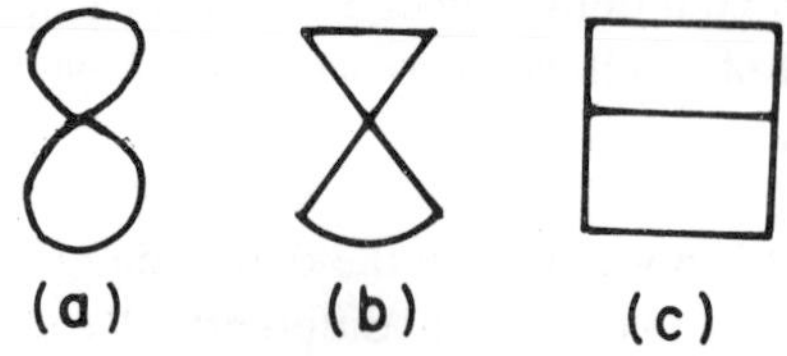

Fig. 8.16

To take the examples of surfaces, the part of a plane enclosed in a triangle, a circle or any polygon are topologically equivalent figures. Even if a plane is replaced by a curved surface like a sphere, a cylinder or, in fact, any irregular but continuous surface with 'hills' and 'valleys', a part of such a surface enclosed by any closed curve, (Fig. 8.17), is topologically equivalent to any other part enclosed by any other closed curve, since one can be deformed into another by stretching, bending and twisting alone. But the shapes in Fig. 8.18 are of a different nature. They are topologically similar to each other but none of them can be obtained by deforming any of the shapes of Fig. 8.17.

In three-dimensional space, a sphere can be deformed into a cube, an egg-shaped solid or a bowl, (Fig. 8.19), but not into a torus or a tea cup,

Fig. 8.17

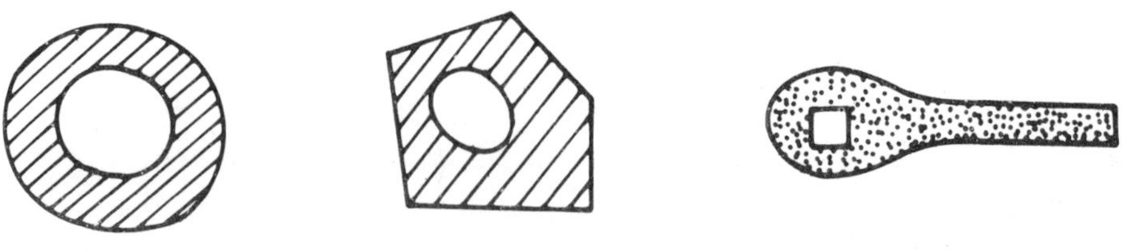

Fig. 8.18

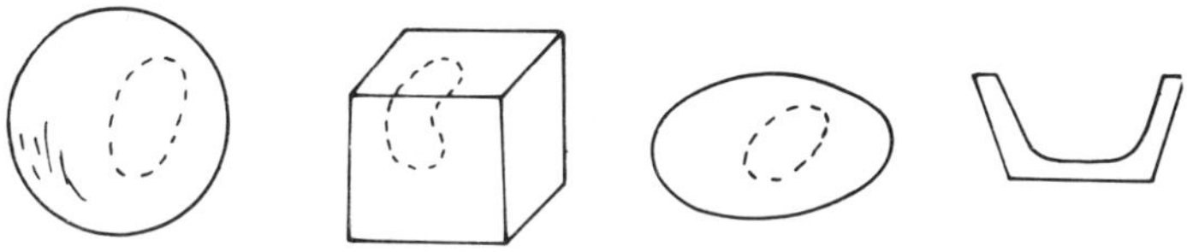

Fig. 8.19

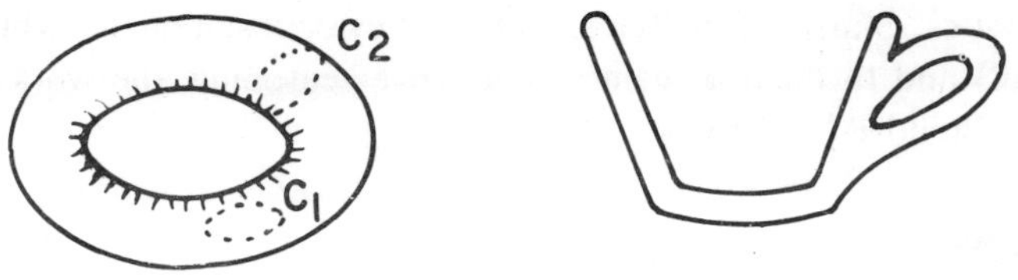

Fig. 8.20

(Fig. 8.20). A little consideration will show that a tea cup with one handle and a torus shown in Fig. 8.20 are topologically of the same class.

In general terms, a topological space is a set of points in which the concepts of continuity and neighbourhood are defined. Each point has its neighbourhood of points, and during deformation these neighbourhoods should remain unchanged.

The topological equivalence of figures, particularly in higher dimensions, is not always easy to see. Topology aims to discover definitive properties so that if two figures possess these properties, they must be topologically equivalent. As an example of such a property, if one draws any closed curve (shown dotted) on the surface of any of the solids of Fig. 8.19, the curve bounds a region of the surface. It is not possible to draw a closed curve on the surface of any of these solids which does not become a boundary of a portion of the surface of that solid. But this is not so on the torus of Fig. 8.20. One can, of course, draw such curves on this solid also, (for example, the closed curve C_1 encloses a part of the surface of the torus), but there are other types of curves also which do not do so. For example, closed curve C_2 does not enclose any part of the surface of the torus. So the characteristic property of solids of the same topological class as of Fig. 8.19 is that any and every closed curve on them encloses a part of their surface.

Beginning with geometrical notions, topology too has been extended through algebra to abstract spaces. It has assumed a position of central importance in mathematics with applications in various fields.

There have been generalizations of geometry from another point of view also which have had profound influence on the scientific view of the universe. This will be discussed in Chapter 10.

FROM THE GALLERY OF MATHEMATICIANS

Euclid

Euclid (Greek, about 300 B. C.) unified the work of many individuals and schools spread from Sicily and Italy to Asia Minor, and produced his masterly work called the Elements. It was the model of a logical structure given to geometry, a model which after two millennia was to become the structure of all mathematics. Starting from ten axioms (self evident statements which needed no proof) and through a chain of deductive reasoning, the work contained some five hundred theorems.

Rene Descartes

Philosopher, mathematician and scientist, Rene Descartes (French, 1596-1650) was among the foremost thinkers who pulled European thought out of the morass of medieval outlook, turned it from the blind alley of Aristotelian ideas, and laid the foundations of modern scientific method. Mathematics and philosophy, physics and physiology, matter and mind, all came under the sweep of his intellect. Many of his theories, particularly in physics and physiology, were soon found to be erroneous, but the emphasis he laid on the importance of mathematics as a basis of deductive reasoning in science, and his faith that the cause- and- effect chain in nature can be explained through mathematical analysis of motion of material particles proved to be the sheet anchor of scientific development for the next three centuries.

Descartes' lasting contribution to mathematics is his bringing together geometry and algebra by expressing geometrical ideas in algebraic terms and vice versa. The word 'cartesian' so commonly used as an adjective in mathematics is a fitting homage to the genius of this great revolutionary thinker.

EXERCISES

1. The geometrical proof of the algebraic identity

$$(a + b)^2 = a^2 + 2ab + b^2$$

is given on page 145. In a similar way prove geometrically the following identities.

$$(a - b)^2 = a^2 - 2ab + b^2$$

$$(a + b).(a - b) = a^2 - b^2.$$

2. Plot the points (0,5), (8,3), (–4,6), (–8,7) on a plane with respect to two perpendicular lines chosen as axes of x and y, and show that they all lie on the line whose equation is $x + 4y = 20$. Find two other points on this line.

3. Find the distance of the points $(\sqrt{2},\sqrt{2})$, $(\sqrt{3},1)$, $(-1,\sqrt{3})$ from the origin, and show that all these points lie on the circle whose centre is the origin and radius is 2. Write the equation of the circle.

4. Show that in a three- dimensional space the points

$$\left(\frac{1}{\sqrt{3}}, \frac{1}{\sqrt{3}}, \frac{1}{\sqrt{3}}\right), \left(\frac{1}{\sqrt{2}}, \frac{1}{\sqrt{2}}, 0\right), (1, 0, 0)$$

with respect to three mutually perpendicular axes x, y, z are at the same distance from the origin, and lie on the sphere whose equation is $x^2 + y^2 + z^2 = 1$. Find one other point on the sphere.

5. Suppose we define the distance of any point (x, y) from the origin in a two-dimensional space as the larger of the two positive numbers $|x|$ and $|y|$. With this definition the distance of the point (3,–4) from the origin is the larger of the two numbers $|3|$ and $|-4|$, that is, of 3 and 4, which is 4. Similarly, find the distance of the following points from the origin.

$$(3,-1), (-3,-8), (4,2), (-3,0).$$

Show that the two points (8,1), (–2,–8) are at the same distance from the origin.

Show that the square of side 2, placed on the x-y plane such that the origin is the centre of the square and its sides are parallel to the x and y axes, has all its points distant 1 from the origin.

ANSWERS

3. $x^2 + y^2 = 4$
5. 3, 8, 4, 3.

Chapter 9

From Discrete to Continuous

"In mathematical science connections between things are exhibited which, apart from the agency of human reasoning, are extremely unobvious."

—*A.N. Whitehead, British mathematician and philosopher, (1861–1947).*

The universe is continuously changing. Nothing is static, nothing is permanent in our world of experience; everything is in a state of flux. The mystics call it an illusion. But science deals with this 'illusion', and the primary motivation behind mathematics has been to have a logical framework to describe it.

Our perception of the flow of time, irreversible and beyond our control, is perhaps caused by the succession of events our consciousness records. Events recorded deliberately are called observations. They are always discrete or separately identifiable, and, however many, are finite in number. Through a stretch of imagination we pack observations closely to produce a continuous chain of events.

The mathematicians have invented a logically perfect continuous system in the set of real numbers. Whatever appears to us as a continuously varying phenomenon can usually be described through real numbers. Whether a phenomenon or a sequence of events is fundamentally discrete or continuous is what the philosophers from times immemorial and scientists in modern times have endlessly debated, and a final answer may never come. But this is beside the point in our present discussion. The relevant point is that whatever chain of events we want to regard as continuous can be described by the ideally perfect continuum of real numbers. In fact, the mathematician reverses the argument, and calls a system continuous if it can be described in terms of variables which can assume all values lying along the entire real line or any part of it.

Mathematical Model

Let us consider an example. Table 9.1 gives the measurements of the height of a small plant at equal intervals of time as it sprouts and grows into maturity.

Regarding both time and height as variables, measurable in terms of real numbers, we represent time by points along one line and height by points along a perpendicular line. The pairs of numbers in the table, one denoting the time and the other the height, can then be represented by points in the plane of the two lines (Fig. 9.1). We call it the graph of the data. These are isolated points and the data they represent is discrete. We could have measured height each day and we would have got more points on the graph. We *believe* that we could have reduced the interval of observations to an hour or to a minute or to a second, and we could still get numbers giving height corresponding to each instant of time. The smaller the interval of observations, the closer the points. We finally *imagine* that a continuous or unbroken curve passing through such points represents the height of the plant at different times. Each instant of time between 0 and 30 days is a real number between 0 and 30, and for each such number there is a real number which measures the height. There are no gaps in between successive points. Thus, from discrete data we have arrived at the notion of a continuous phenomenon describable in terms of real numbers.

Table 9.1

Time in days	0	5	10	15	20	25	30
Height in cm	0	15	26	34	38	40	40

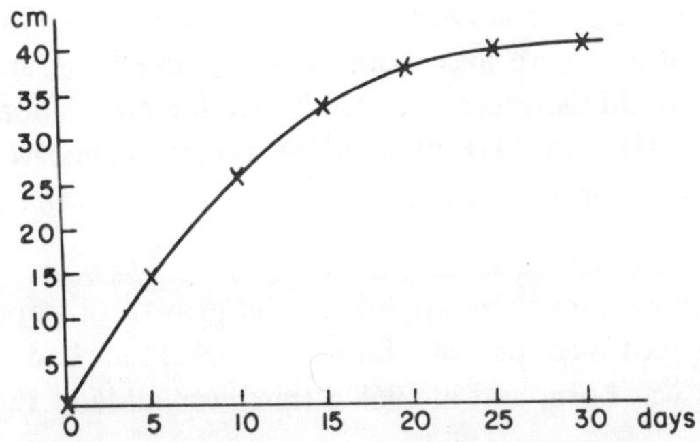

Fig. 9.1

It cannot be asserted that this mathematical model is the exact representation of the physical phenomenon. The height of a plant grows through accretion of matter. The creation of matter in its most elementary form may not be continuous but spontaneous. By spontaneous we mean that there is no interval of time between the non-being and the being of a particle. If we could measure height to the accuracy of a single particle, we would get two heights at the same instant, and our model of continuous growth would break down. Since such a degree of accuracy is beyond our perception, it does not upset the usefulness of the continuous model in the present case. But it is easy to cite examples where the continuous model is not tenable.

Take, for example, the process of growth of population. Points in Fig. 9.2 give roughly the population of India in the years from 1931 to 1971 at intervals of ten years. Though the population does not grow continuously but in jumps

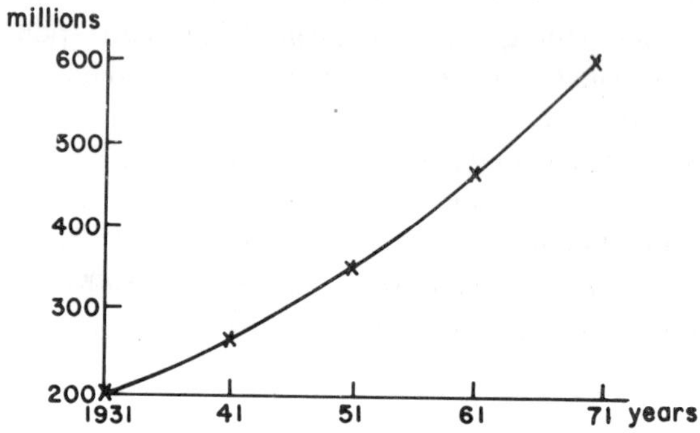

Fig. 9.2

of least magnitude one, these jumps are too small as compared to the numbers indicating total population, (1 is small as compared to 100 million). Therefore, one can imagine that if the census were taken every month, every day or every hour, the points will get more and more closely packed. A smooth curve through the points would therefore reasonably give the population of India at any time between 1931 and 1971, though the points themselves represent discrete data. In other words, it may be assumed that the growth of population is continuous.

The same reasoning cannot be applied to the growth of population in a family. Suppose in 1961 a couple was childless, in 1963 they had one child, in 1966 another child was born, and in 1968 a third was added. Fig. 9.3 is the

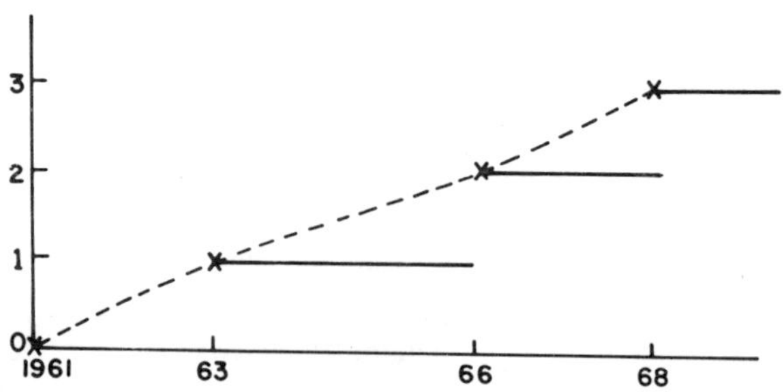

Fig. 9.3

graph of the number of children during the period. From 1961 to 1963 the couple was childless, from 63 to 66 they had one child, and so on. Therefore the graph consists of straight line segments parallel to the time axis. There is a jump from 0 to 1 in 1963, from 1 to 2 in 1966, and so on. The graph is not one continuous curve. A smooth curve (shown dotted) through the four points would not represent the growth of the family correctly. It would be meaningless to draw such a curve.

The examples illustrate the principle that mathematical models describe ideal situations. Whether a mathematical description is applicable to a situation depends on how closely the physical nature of the problem approximates to the ideal.

The notion of continuous change represented by a continuous curve led to the invention of differential calculus, the powerful tool of analysis of phenomena and processes which could be regarded as continuous. For over two hundred years since the beginning of the eighteenth century, the history of mathematics has been dominated by sharpening and refining of this tool and applying it in various branches of science. So widespread was its use in mechanics, physics and astronomy, and so spectacular the advancements achieved through it, that in their theoretical aspects these subjects became indistinguishable from mathematics. What generally came to be regarded as applied mathematics was mathematics applied to mechanics of the material world ranging from atoms and molecules to stars and galaxies.

Function

Each of the examples in the foregoing section involves a correspondence between two sets of numbers. To each number indicating day, there is a number indicating height of plant. To each number indicating year, there is a number denoting population of a country or children in a family. In each case there is a set A and a set B, and corresponding to every element of the set A there is a definite and unique element of the set B. Such a relation between two sets is given the name *function*. If x denotes any element of set A and y denotes an element of set B, and corresponding to every x there is one definite y, then y is said to be a function of x, generally written as $y = f(x)$. Here f is not a number multiplying x but merely a symbol to denote a relationship between x and y of the type defined above. The symbols x and y are also called *variables* as they vary over (or denote) different elements of some sets.

The variables x and y may be discrete or continuous. As we have seen, we can, if necessary, intuitively imagine a variable as continuous in the sense that it can take all possible values lying between two real numbers (usually called the interval between two numbers). In the foregoing examples some discrete values of x and the corresponding discrete values of y are given, and the pairs of values of (x, y) are plotted as points on a graph. It is assumed that x can vary continuously in some interval and the value of y corresponding to any value of x can be read from the curve, continuous or broken, passing through the points.

Instead of some discrete values of (x, y) defining the relationship between the pair, suppose we know of a rule or a procedure by which for every value of x we can find the corresponding value of y. Then the rule defines the function. The rule may be written in mathematical form. As an example, let the rule be

$$y = \tfrac{1}{2}x^2, \quad 0 \le x \le 2,$$

which means that x takes all possible real values in the interval between and including 0 and 2, and for each such value, y is equal to half the square of the value of x. We may represent the function graphically by drawing a smooth curve through the points representing pairs of values of (x, y) on some chosen coordinate axes, (Fig. 9.4).

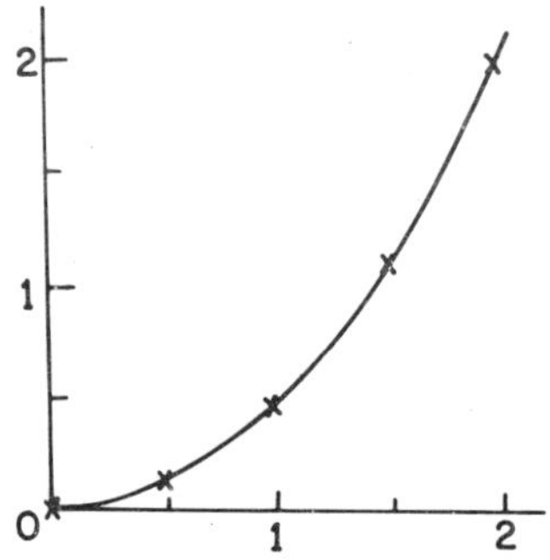

Fig. 9.4

Consider another example. Let the rule connecting y with x be

$$y = \tfrac{1}{2}x^2, \quad 0 \le x \le 1,$$

$$y = \tfrac{1}{2}, \quad 1 < x \le 2.$$

x can still take all values between and including 0 and 2, but for x from 0 to 1, y is equal to half the square of x, and for x greater than 1 but less than or equal to 2, y is always $\frac{1}{2}$. The graph of this function is as shown in Fig. 9.5.

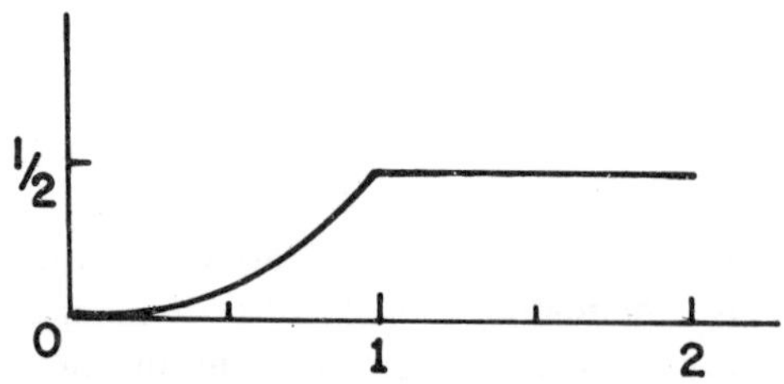

Fig. 9.5

Consider yet another example. Let the function be

$$y = \tfrac{1}{2}x^2, \quad 0 \le x \le 1,$$

$$y = 1, \quad 1 < x \le 2.$$

Fig. 9.6 shows the graph of this function.

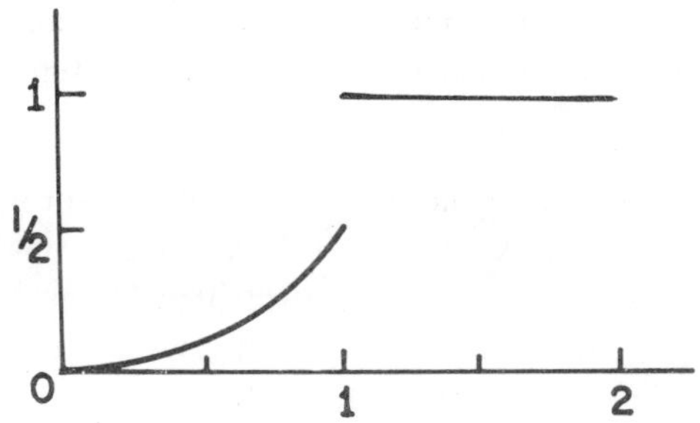

Fig. 9.6

The above three examples illustrate two basic concepts in connection with functions: continuity and smoothness. The curves in Figs. 9.4 and 9.5 are unbroken; there is no gap, no jump. These curves, and the corresponding functions, are said to be continuous at every point in the interval for which they are defined. The technical term for this property is *continuity*. The curve in Fig. 9.6 shows a break and a jump at the point $x = 1$. At $x = 1, y = \frac{1}{2}$, but as soon as x exceeds 1, y jumps to the value 1. The curve, and the corresponding function, is discontinuous at $x = 1$. It is, however, continuous at every other point in the interval of definition.

The other concept relates to what in popular language may be called smoothness. The curve in Fig. 9.4 has no sharp turns or corners, whereas that in Fig. 9.5 has a corner at the point $x = 1$. As one moves along the curve of Fig. 9.4 from one end to the other, the direction of movement changes gradually, but in Fig. 9.5 it changes abruptly with a sudden turn at $x = 1$. One may say that as in the break of continuity there is a sudden jump in the value of the function, in the break of smoothness there is a sudden change in the direction of the curve representing the function. In Fig. 9.6 there is a break in continuity as well as smoothness at the point $x = 1$.

Rate of Change; Differentiation

Assuming that a function $y = f(x)$ is continuous and smooth, the next question of interest is how y changes with respect to x. As an example of practical interest, consider the motion of a railway train between two stations. If x denotes the time and y the distance of the train from the first station, the change in y during a unit change in x is a measure of the speed of the train. Suppose at time x_1 the distance is y_1, and at a subsequent time x_2 it is y_2. Then the train goes a distance $y_2 - y_1$ in time $x_2 - x_1$, and its speed in this interval may be taken as $(y_2 - y_1)/(x_2 - x_1)$, (distance covered in unit time). But the speed might not have been uniform in this interval. All that we can say is that the average speed in the interval is this, or, in other words, if the speed of the train is uniformly this, it would cover a distance $y_2 - y_1$ in time $x_2 - x_1$. We can thus get an average speed for any interval of time. But, however small the interval, the speed during it may be changing. It may indeed be changing continuously. Will then such an idea as speed at a particular instant of time make any sense? Can we determine it?

The closer x_2 is to x_1, the smaller is the time interval for which the average speed can be calculated. Also as time interval is made smaller, the distance covered in that interval, $y_2 - y_1$, also gets smaller. To get a measure of the speed at time x_1, we are tempted to make the interval $x_2 - x_1$ equal to zero. But since the distance covered in zero time is always zero, whatever the speed, $y_2 - y_1$ also becomes zero. The ratio $(y_2 - y_1)/(x_2 - x_1)$ then becomes 0/0 which has no definite value as such. We know that for every number p, $p \times 0 = 0$, and so $0/0 = p$, which means that 0/0 can be equal to any number. 0/0 is an expression which does not indicate any definite number. It is like 'all things to all men', and therefore means nothing definitely. In algebra it is considered meaningless. Does it mean then that the idea of speed at a particular instant of time is meaningless?

Let us look at the problem from another angle. Suppose the function $y = f(x)$ is represented by a smooth curve, (Fig. 9.7). Let P and Q be the points (x_1, y_1) and (x_2, y_2), respectively. Then $PM = x_2 - x_1$, $QM = y_2 - y_1$, and

$$\frac{y_2 - y_1}{x_2 - x_1} = \frac{QM}{PM}$$

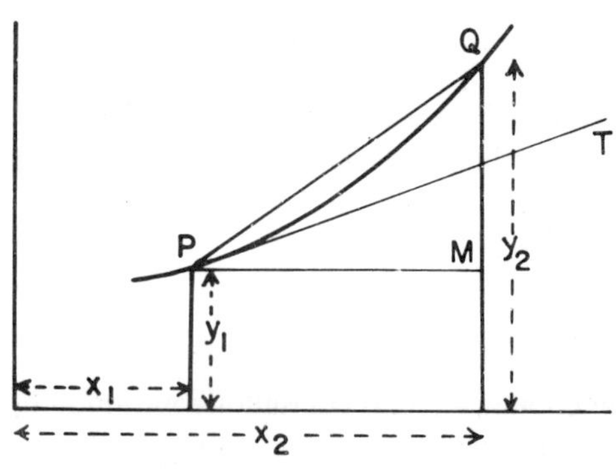

Fig. 9.7

This ratio may be regarded as a measure of the angle $M\hat{P}Q$, the angle which PQ makes with the x-axis. (Those familiar with trigonometry would recognise it as tan $M\hat{P}Q$). As x_2 gets closer to x_1, Q gets closer to P along the curve, and QM and PM both decrease in length. But the ratio QM/PM continues to fix the direction of PQ and be a measure of the angle $M\hat{P}Q$, except when PM and QM both become zero. This happens when Q merges in P. What happens to the direction of PQ then?

It is easy to see that as Q approaches P, the line PQ gets closer to PT, the tangent to the curve at P. Since the ratio QM/PM indicates the direction of PQ, and PQ gets closer to PT as PM and QM both get nearer to zero, it is reasonable to suppose that the ratio QM/PM gets closer to a definite number which indicates the direction of PT.

We thus arrive at the idea that the ratio $(y_2-y_1)/(x_2-x_1)$ may approach a definite number as x_2 approaches x_1. This number is called the limit of $(y_2-y_1)/(x_2-x_1)$ as x_2 tends to x_1, and is briefly written as

$$\lim_{x_2 \to x_1} \frac{y_2 - y_1}{x_2 - x_1}$$

Since (x_1, y_1) is any point on the curve, and (x_2, y_2) any other point on it, we make things look more general by writing x for x_1, y for y_1, $x + h$ for x_2, $y + k$ for y_2 (where $h = x_2 - x_1$, $k = y_2 - y_1$), and write the above expression as

$$\lim_{h \to 0} \frac{(y + k) - y}{(x + h) - x}$$

or, as

$$\lim_{h \to 0} \frac{f(x + h) - f(x)}{h}$$

because $y = f(x)$ and $y + k = f(x + h)$. An alternative notation is to denote by δx, a small change (positive denoting increase and negative decrease) in x and by δf the corresponding small change in f, thereby denoting h by δx and k by δf. The above expression then can be written as

$$\lim_{\delta x \to 0} \frac{\delta f}{\delta x}$$

This expression, as we have seen, is equal to a definite number which is a measure of the angle the tangent to the curve at any point (x, y) makes with the x-axis. It indicates the slope of the curve in relation to the x-axis at the point (x, y). In the example of the motion of the train, this number defines the speed of the train at time x. In general, it gives the rate of change of $f(x)$ with respect to x at the point x. The general name for this concept is the *derivative* or the *differential coefficient* of $f(x)$ with respect to x, and is symbolically written as

$f'(x)$ or $\dfrac{df(x)}{dx}$. The latter notation looks complicated, but is quite significant when we notice that

$$\frac{df(x)}{dx} = \lim_{\delta x \to 0} \frac{\delta f(x)}{\delta x}$$

To take an example of how the derivative can be actually calculated for a particular $f(x)$, let $f(x) = x^2$. Then $f(x + h) = (x + h)^2$, and so

$$\frac{f(x + h) - f(x)}{h} = \frac{(x + h)^2 - x^2}{h} = \frac{2xh + h^2}{h}$$

Now, so long as h is not zero we can divide the numerator and the denominator by h and get

$$\frac{f(x + h) - f(x)}{h} = 2x + h.$$

However small h may be, so long as it is not zero, the above statement is correct. As h gets closer and closer to zero, the right side of the above equation gets closer and closer to $2x$. Hence we say that for $f(x) = x^2$,

$$\lim_{h \to 0} \frac{f(x + h) - f(x)}{h} = 2x,$$

or

$$\frac{d(x^2)}{dx} = 2x.$$

Thus, the differential coefficient of x^2 is $2x$. The result can be interpreted as follows. If a particle moves such that its distance from a point at time x is x^2, then its speed at time x is $2x$. Thus at times 1, 2, 3 units, the distance of the particle is 1, 4, 9 units, and its speed is 1, 4, 6 units, respectively.

It is possible to obtain derivatives of functions (at points where the function is smooth) by evaluating the limit of the appropriate function as illustrated above. This is, however, not convenient except in the simplest of cases. Rules have been discovered which facilitate differentiation (meaning finding derivative) without having recourse to the basic definition every time.

It is not necessary that the derivative of a function must exist at every one of the points at which the function is defined. The geometrical interpretation of the derivative as a measure of slope of the curve at a point explains the different possibilities. The curve in Fig. 9.6 is discontinuous at $x = 1$, and we cannot draw a tangent to the curve at that point. Consequently, the notion of the slope of the curve at that point has no meaning. In Fig. 9.5 the function is continuous at $x = 1$ but the curve at that point changes direction abruptly. We still cannot draw a tangent at that point. We say that the derivative at such points does not exist.

Since the differential coefficient of a function is itself a function, it may be possible to differentiate it. Thus repeated or successive differentiation is possible. We can find not only the rate of change of $f(x)$ but also its rate of rate of change, and its rate of rate of rate of change, and so on. Such notions are of physical and geometrical significance. For example, rate of rate of change of distance with time is rate of change of velocity which is called acceleration.

The Importance of Neighbourhood

The development of the notion of differential coefficient near the end of the seventeenth century at the hands of Leibniz, and also independently at the hands of Newton, laid the foundation of the differential calculus. It was an epoch-making development. Its profound significance lay in the fact that a property of the function was defined at a point which reflected the situation in the immediate neighbourhood of that point. We define speed, or, to use a scientifically more correct term, velocity at a point or at an instant, though the concept of speed essentially involves a succession of points and passage of time. We define the direction of a curve at a point though direction involves at least two points. The apparent contradiction in describing change, which needs the existence of at least two states at two recognizably different points (of time or space), in terms of one point raised difficulties which bothered logicians for two centuries. Several mathematicians, including Leibniz's own teacher, the great Dutch mathematician and scientist Huygens, opposed the idea of differential coefficient. The famous Irish philosopher Berkeley also attacked the idea fiercely. The main plank of attack in all cases was that a quantity is either zero or not zero. If it is not zero to begin with, then it will amount to changing the hypothesis in the middle of the argument, if it is made zero finally. In the definition of the derivative, (page 167), h is not zero, for otherwise the expression becomes 0/0 which is meaningless. But it gets nearer to zero and finally becomes zero, which contradicts the original assumption. It was more than hundred years later that the concept of limit was satisfactorily clarified and calculus put on a sound basis. However, some logicians still feel that the lacuna remains, as the notion that a quantity can be as close to another as we can possibly imagine and yet not equal to it is not without difficulties.

But while mathematics has logic as its bedrock, mathematics is not logic. Mathematics advances through intuition, *ad hoc* assumptions and procedures whose initial justification is usually practical usefulness and seemingly dependable conclusions. Logical finesse is undoubtedly held in high esteem by mathematicians, but it is seldom a feature of new ideas in mathematics. Lack of logical perfection has never been a hindrance to development along a new line of thought. The blemishes in the method of calculus pointed out by logicians were no bar to the widespread use calculus found at the hands of scientists. At last a mathematical tool was available with which change, variation, motion, so characteristic of all phenomena, could be handled. So resounding was the success of calculus in the study of natural phenomena, particularly in astronomy and physics, that the feeble voice of its critics was completely drowned in the universal acclaim by which it was received by those who used it to discover patterns hidden under the apparently chaotic behaviour of nature.

Integration

The other basic idea in calculus is *integration*. It is the inverse of differentiation in the sense that if $f'(x)$ is the derivative of $f(x)$, then $f(x)$ is the integral of $f'(x)$. But the idea of integration grew independently of differentiation, and the relation between them was realized subsequently. The motivation for the development of integral calculus came from the necessity of calculating areas and volumes. We shall first see how the integral is defined as an area, and then establish its connection with the derivative.

Let $F(x)$ be a function whose graph is the curve AB, (Fig. 9.8), in the interval $x = a$ to $x = b$. Suppose we want to find the area enclosed by the curve AB, the x-axis and the vertical lines Aa and Bb (parallel to y-axis). We divide the interval (a, b) into a number of equal parts, say n in number, each of width h. Let the points of division be $x_1, x_2, x_3, \ldots x_{n-1}$, the two end points being x_o (which is the same as a) and x_n (which is the same as b). By drawing perpendiculars to the x-axis at these points, we divide the area $aABb$ into n thin strips. The sum of the areas of all these strips is equal to the required area. Each strip is as shown in Fig. 9.9 in a magnified form. The area of the shaded rectangle in this figure is $hF(x_r)$ which is less than the area of the strip. But it is easy to see that the thinner is the strip, the smaller is the difference between the area of the rectangle and the area of the strip.

The sum of all the rectangular strips of Fig. 9.8, each of the type shown shaded in Fig. 9.9, is

$$hF(x_0) + hF(x_1) + hF(x_2) + \ldots + hF(x_{n-1}).$$

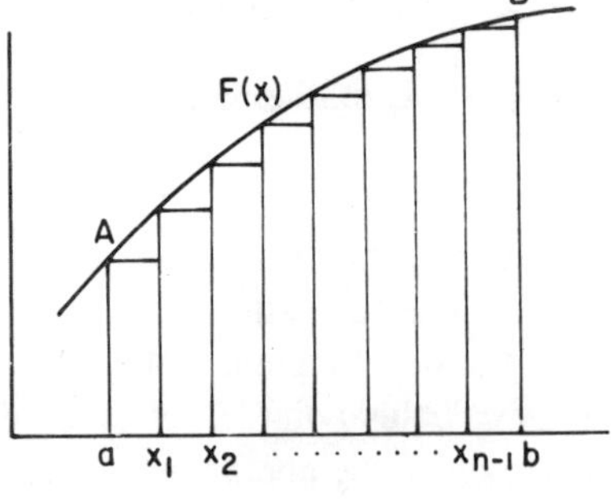

Fig. 9.8

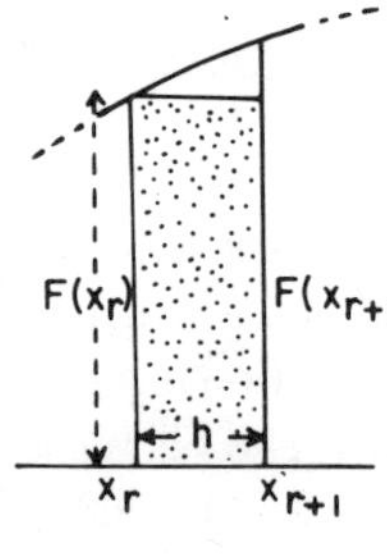

Fig. 9.9

The larger the number of subdivisions of the interval (a, b), the smaller is h, and then the nearer is the above expression to the required area. Imagine h to get nearer and nearer to zero, (n will then get larger and larger), the sum of the areas of the rectangular strips will then get nearer and nearer to the area $aABb$. This is expressed by writing

$$\text{area } aABb = \lim_{h \to 0} \left[hF(x_0) + hF(x_1) + hF(x_2) + \ldots + hf(x_{n-1}) \right]$$

$$= \int_a^b F(x)\, dx$$

The notation $\int_a^b F(x)\, dx$ stands for the limit of the sum of the areas of the rectangular strips, and therefore stands for the required area. It is called a *definite integral.* The symbol $\int$ is the 's' of the old English, and dx is to be regarded as a single symbol standing for a small increase in x, which is the thickness of a small strip. Therefore $\int F(x)\, dx$ came to mean the sum of the areas of the strips. Putting a and b at the lower and upper ends of $\int$ came to mean that the strips have to be summed up from $x = a$ to $x = b$. a and b are called the lower and upper limits of the integral.

Connection between integration and differentiation

Consider the area under the curve $F(x)$ from any fixed point $x = a$ to any general point x (Fig. 9.10). For different values of x we shall get different areas. The area is, therefore, a function of x. Let us denote it by $f(x)$. By the definition of an integral as an area, we may also express this area as

$$f(x) = \int_a^x F(x)\, dx$$

The area from a to $x + h$, by the same rule is

$$f(x + h) = \int_a^{x+h} F(x)\, dx$$

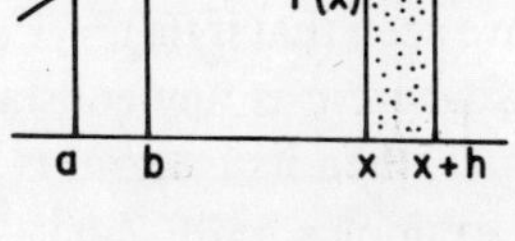

Fig. 9.10

The difference of the two areas is the thin strip of thickness h (shown shaded), whose area approximately is $hF(x)$. Therefore

$$f(x + h) - f(x) \approx hF(x)$$

or

$$\frac{f(x + h) - f(x)}{h} \approx F(x)$$

(The sign $\approx$ means 'approximately equal'). As the strip is made thinner and thinner, the two sides in the above approximate equation get closer and closer to each other. We may, therefore, say that

$$\lim_{h \to 0} \frac{f(x + h) - f(x)}{h} = F(x)$$

The left side is, by definition, the derivative of $f(x)$, and so we find that

$$f'(x) = F(x)$$

But, as noted before,

$$f(x) = \int_a^x F(x)\, dx$$

and so

$$f(x) = \int_a^x f'(x)\, dx$$

This means that if $f'(x)$ is the derivative of $f(x)$, then $f(x)$ is the integral of $f'(x)$. The operations of differentiation and integration are therefore inverse of each other.

It may be noticed that the lower limit $x = a$ of the integral was chosen quite arbitrarily. We could have chosen it differently, say $x = b$ (Fig. 9.10), and then we would have got

$$f(x) = \int_b^x f'(x)\, dx$$

But the area from b to x is not the same as from a to x, and therefore the $f(x)$ in one case is different from the $f(x)$ in the other. It means that, given $f'(x)$, $f(x)$ is not unique. It can be proved that the different functions, all integrals of the same function $f'(x)$, differ by constants (numbers independent of x) only.

To take an example, we have seen that if $f(x) = x^2$, $f'(x) = 2x$. But it can be shown that if $f(x) = x^2 + c$, where c is any constant, then also $f'(x) = 2x$. Therefore, if $f'(x)$ is given as $2x$, then its integral is not unique. It is $x^2 + c$, where c is any constant. As examples, $x^2 + 2$, $x^2 - 3$, $x^2 + \frac{1}{4}$, $x^2 - \sqrt{2}$ are all integrals of $2x$.

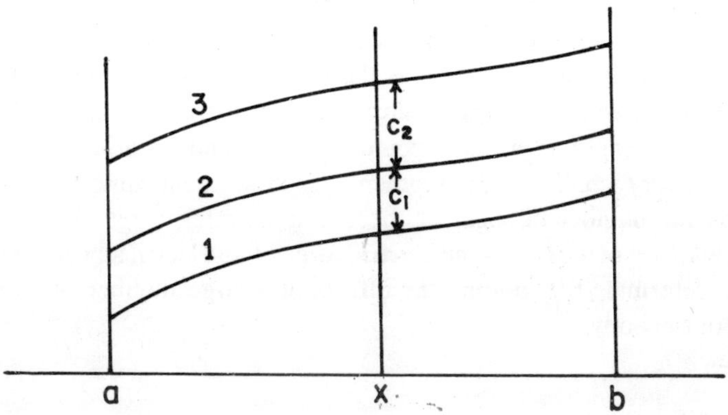

Fig. 9.11

How this ambiguity arises when $f(x)$ is evaluated from $f'(x)$ can be appreciated in another manner also. We had seen that $f'(x)$ indicates the direction of the tangent to the curve $y = f(x)$ at any point x. The problem of finding $f(x)$ from $f'(x)$ amounts to tracing the curve $y = f(x)$ when all that is known about it is its direction at every point in an interval. Can we trace the curve? It is like trying to make a road whose directions all along its course are given but not where it is situated. Any number of such roads can be made. Fig. 9.11 shows three curves which are parallel such that they have the same direction at any point x. For all these curves $f'(x)$ is the same, but one $f(x)$ differs from the other by some fixed number. If curve 1 is $y = f(x)$, then curve 2 is $y = f(x) + c_1$ and curve 3 is $y = f(x) + c_2$, where c_1 and c_2 are constants as shown in the figure.

Integral Calculus

In the definition of the integral also the same type of logical difficulty arises as in the definition of the derivative. So long as h is different from zero, that is, each strip is of finite thickness, however small, the sum of the areas of all the rectangular strips is not equal to the area $aABb$, (Fig. 9.8). If $h = 0$, then each strip shrinks into a line with area zero, and no matter how large the number of strips, they would only add up to zero. The difficulty was overcome only with the development of the idea of limit. Just as the ratio of two numbers, each getting nearer and nearer to zero, could approach a definite number, similarly the product of two numbers, one getting closer and closer to zero and the other getting larger and larger, could approach a definite number. In interpreting the integral as an area, the area of each strip approaches zero, but the number of strips increases without limitation, and so the product of the two approaches a definite number.

The invention of the integral calculus provided a tool for calculating the cumulative or additive effect of continuously varying quantities. To cite a few examples, an area could be calculated by dividing it up into a large number of thin strips, and a volume by dividing the body into a large number of thin slices, and in each case finding their sum as the number of strips or slices becomes indefinitely large with each strip or slice becoming extremely thin. By a similar procedure the length of a curve could be calculated by adding up a large number of very small straight segments, each segment almost becoming a point, and the number of segments becoming infinitely large. Likewise, the gravitational pull of a body or the electric force of an electrically charged body could be determined by adding the effects of a large number of very small portions of the body.

Applications

Ideas of differentiation and integration have been extended to functions of two, three or more variables also. This has made calculus a powerful and versatile tool of mathematical analysis in all branches of physical sciences and many areas of biological and social sciences. Very often, though not always, calculus enters a problem in the following manner.

Quantitative observations made through measuring devices and instruments form the basic check points in any scientific study of a phenomenon. As was emphasised in the beginning of this chapter, these observations are discrete, and are taken either at different points of space at the same time or at different times at the same point. The observations therefore, reflect some sort of variation of some quantity with space and time coordinates. (In measuring instruments like oscillographs discrete observations are replaced by continuous records which also reflect variation). The variations, or, in more accurate terminology, rates of change, often appear to be related to other quantities or their variations. This leads to the formulation of a *differential equation*, a mathematical relation connecting some functions and their derivatives. It may be the result of a hypothesis or based on some laws or principles already tested and believed to be valid. A differential equation is thus made to describe some characteristic of the phenomenon under study. Further characteristics of the phenomenon may be discovered by purely mathematical means by solving the equation, that is, by finding the function which satisfies the equation.

We illustrate by a very simple example. Suppose, observations are made on a small body, say a small spherical ball, falling freely vertically downwards. We assume that the air is still and offers little resistance to the motion of the ball. (To be doubly sure, the experiment can be performed in a vessel from which air has been sucked out). It is possible to monitor the fall of the ball very accurately by recording devices. Suppose the observations indicate that the body falls with increasing velocity, but the rate of increase of velocity seems to remain the same throughout the motion. We also measure accurately the height through which the ball falls and the time it takes to do so.

If x denotes the distance the ball falls through in time t, then $\frac{dx}{dt}$ is the velocity and $\frac{d}{dt}\left(\frac{dx}{dt}\right)$ is the rate of change of velocity (or acceleration) at time t. Let us postulate, on the strength of our observations, that the acceleration is a constant quantity, that is,

$$\frac{d}{dt}\left(\frac{dx}{dt}\right) = g$$

(g is some number which does not change with x or t). This is a differential equation. It is possible, through integration, to conclude from the above equation that the velocity v at time t is

$$v = \frac{dx}{dt} = gt$$

if we assume that the ball started falling at time $t = 0$ from a position of rest or zero velocity. On further integration, it follows that

$$x = \tfrac{1}{2}\, gt^2$$

if we assume that in the initial position of the ball $x = 0$ and $t = 0$.

These equations give a lot more information about the fall than the original differential equation, though, of course, much of the information was implied in the differential equation. For instance, from the last equation we can find what should be the value of the constant g by substituting the observed values of time and height of fall. Also for any given value of x, v or t, we can find the values of the other two.

Let us consider the same problem under different conditions. Suppose the ball is falling in water instead of air. It is observed that as the ball starts falling, its velocity first increases, but soon assumes a constant value. It seems reasonable, as a hypothesis, to suppose that the ball begins to fall for the same reason as in empty space, but water offers resistance. The faster the ball moves, the more is the resistance offered by water. There comes a stage when the resistance balances the downward pull, and subsequently the ball continues to move with the velocity acquired at that stage, there being no cause retarding or accelerating it.

The differential equation describing the first part of the motion may be written as

$$\frac{d}{dt}\left(\frac{dx}{dt}\right) = g - k\frac{dx}{dt},$$

$-k\dfrac{dx}{dt}$ being the retardation (or rate of decrease of velocity) which is assumed proportional to velocity, k being some constant factor of proportionality. As velocity increases, eventually there comes a time when velocity does not increase or decrease, that is, acceleration becomes zero. The differential equation describing this state is

$$\frac{d}{dt}\left(\frac{dx}{dt}\right) = 0$$

Obviously this happens when

$$g - k\frac{dx}{dt} = 0$$

This equation gives the constant velocity which the falling ball eventually acquires. These equations describe the fall of a small spherical ball through a resisting medium. Solution of these equations lead to more information about the phenomenon, and comparison with observations can lead to the determination of the constants g and k.

In the large, almost inexhaustible, list of differential equations formulated and used by various types of scientists, engineers, technologists, economists and others, the above two examples are like two trivial objects from a vast and ever increasing collection of objects in a very large museum. The motion of particles and bodies under various types of forces, of electrons and nuclei, of atoms and molecules, of billiard balls and gun shots, of rain drops and meteorites, of rockets, of planets and stars and galaxies, all are described and studied through differential equations. The vibrations of a ringing bell, of the strings of a piano or a violin, of the air column of a flute or the membrane of a drum, the swinging of a pendulum, the waves in the ocean or the currents in the atmosphere, the flow of liquid or gas though a pipe or of electric current in a cable, all have their respective differential equations. There are differential equations for the conduction of heat in a metal or the diffusion of gas through a diaphragm, the transmission of electromagnetic waves for radio or television, light waves and X-rays and sound waves. The models for the growth of population, for meteorological phenomena of winds and temperature changes, for flow of blood through veins and arteries, for business and trade, are all in the form of differential equations.

It would, however, be wrong to suppose that the collection of differential equations is chaotic. It is the purpose of science to discover order and relationships under confounding diversities. Differential equations have revealed basic similarities between apparently diverse phenomena. For example, all vibrations and wave motions, whether in solids, liquids or gases, – sound waves in air, water waves in rivers or oceans, electromagnetic waves in space, seismic waves in the earth, all are governed by the same type of differential equation, called the wave equation. Such basic mathematical similarities have played a vital role in the advance of scientific knowledge.

FROM THE GALLERY OF MATHEMATICIANS

Gottfried Wilhelm Leibniz

Unlike most great mathematicians, Leibniz (German, 1646-1716) was a philosopher, mathematician, scientist, engineer, diplomat, historian, all rolled into one. His greatest achievement was the invention of calculus. His dream and passion was to develop a generalized symbolic language, and an algebra to go with it, so that the truth of any proposition in any field of human enquiry could be determined by simple calculation. His quest was of course unsuccessful, but he did make an extended study of notation. He was responsible for introducing more signs and symbols than perhaps any other mathematician, and promoted the use of many more. Among the symbols he is credited with are: parentheses instead of the line above the terms in algebra, the dot to denote multiplication, the decimal point, the sign of equality, superscripts to denote power or repeated multiplication.

Isaac Newton

Sir Isaac Newton (British, 1642-1727), with humility characteristic of the truly great, seemed to himself 'only like a boy playing on the seashore... whilst the great ocean of truth lay all undiscovered before me', but he is rightly regarded as one of the very greatest scientists of all times, a supreme genius with rare intellect. Newton, as a child, did not show precocity in mathematics, but in his boyish amusements, which included making perfect mechanical toys, he gave ample evidence of his ingenuity.

The researches attributed to Newton in physics (heat, light, mechanics) and mathematics make a very long and varied list. He is credited with independently inventing calculus. He stood no doubt on the shoulders of giants like Kepler and Galileo, but to him goes the credit of formally postulating the law of gravitation, and connecting force and motion through his laws of motion. His system of mechanics still serves as a sound base for the analysis of natural phenomena on the terrestrial scale on which much of the technological advances of modern times are based. Only at the two extremes of material size, the atomic and the cosmic, have his ideas been superseded by other ideas in this century.

Controversy over Calculus

Newton and Leibniz were on cordial terms for most of their lives, but in their old age, after 1712, they got involved in a bitter and acrimonious controversy as to who invented calculus first. The controversy degenerated into a 'war' between England and Europe with the scientists and scholars on either side hurling accusations of plagiarism, dishonesty and thievery on the opponent. For many years the war of words raged fiercely with national pride rather than truth becoming the issue. The episode fouled the scientific atmosphere of Europe and England for many decades interfering with the exchange of scientific knowledge between the island and the continent.

It is now recognized on all hands that both Newton and Leibniz were independent inventors of calculus, though Leibniz published his work three years earlier than Newton. The modern notation in calculus is due to Leibniz which proved more convenient and powerful than Newton's.

Chapter 10

Curvature of Space

"How can it be that mathematics, being after all a product of human thought, independent of experience, is so admirably adapted to the objects of reality."

—Albert Einstein (1879–1955)

We have seen in Chapter 8 how algebraic methods enriched geometry. The invention of calculus gave a boost to further development of geometry. While the integral calculus provided methods to evaluate lengths of curves, areas of surfaces, volumes of different shapes, the differential calculus enabled the determination of slopes and curvatures of curves and surfaces. The application of differential calculus to geometry opened up an area of rich potentialities which came to be called differential geometry.

Differential Geometry

By the method of coordinate geometry it was possible to investigate and describe the properties of curves and surfaces with respect to chosen coordinate systems. However, geometrical figures also possess intrinsic properties which are not related to the coordinate system used to describe them. For example, the curvature or 'bendedness' of a circle, the 'straightness' of a line, the 'flatness' of a plane are properties which are intrinsic to them and are quite independent of where and how they are situated in relation to other geometrical figures. Differential geometry was particularly useful in describing such intrinsic properties.

Curves

Observe the three curves in Fig. 10.1, a line, an arc of a circle, and an irregular curve. The line does not bend anywhere, it goes all along in the same direction, it has no curvature. The circular arc is continuously bending. A person moving along the arc will be changing his direction of motion continuously to keep on the arc. The arc has a curvature. The third curve too has curvature but not like that of a circle. Its bent is not the same at every point. Seen from left, it first bends downwards, but less at A and more at B, and then it bends upwards as at C. Its curvature varies from point to point. But qualitative notions are not enough in mathematics. It is necessary to have an exact definition of the term 'curvature'.

Fig. 10.1

Consider two circular arcs of the same length but different radii, (Fig. 10.2). The one with the larger radius looks less curved than the one with the smaller radius. The larger the radius of a circular arc, the lesser is its curvature. *Curvature* is, therefore, defined as the *inverse of the radius*. The curvature of a circular arc of radius r is $1/r$. As its radius increases, a fixed length of the arc gets less and less curved, and ultimately as r becomes very large, $1/r$ gets very near to zero making the arc almost straight.

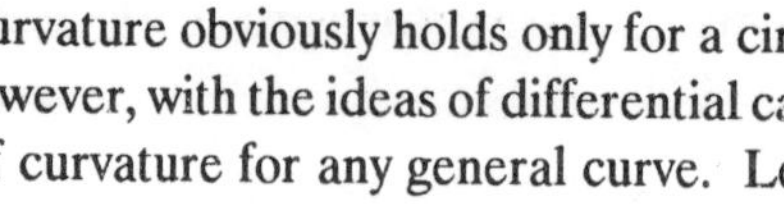

Fig. 10.2

This definition of curvature obviously holds only for a circle, because only a circle has a radius. However, with the ideas of differential calculus it is possible to define the radius of curvature for any general curve. Let P, Q, R be three distinct points on a curve AB (Fig. 10.3). Draw a circle through these three points. Since three points determine a circle, only one circle can be drawn through these three points. Let O be the centre of this circle. Now, imagine that the points Q and R both move along the curve AB to get closer and closer to P. The centre O may then get closer and closer to a definite point, say C. Then we say that C is the centre of curvature and PC the radius of curvature of the curve at P. The curvature at P is the inverse of this radius. We thus arrive at the definition of curvature of a curve at a point. We notice that curvature, like slope, is a local property of a curve determined by its behaviour in a small neighbourhood. We talk of curvature at a point though it depends upon how the curve goes on either side of the point.

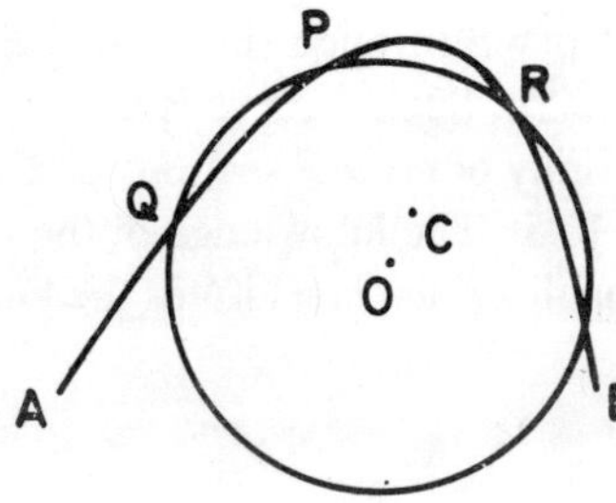

Fig. 10.3

Curvature of Surfaces

The property of curvature obviously extends to surfaces. A plane is a flat surface, while the surface of a sphere is curved. Curved surfaces may have different degrees of curvature at different points. For example, an egg is more curved at its narrow end than at the broad. In getting some measure of curvature of surfaces, there is, however, another complication also. The curvature of a surface may not only vary from point to point but also from direction to direction at the same point.

Consider, for example, a cylindrical surface, (Fig. 10.4). Through any point P on it and lying wholly on it, it is possible to draw a straight line AB and also a circle PD whose plane is normal to line AB. In the direction of AB the cylindrical surface is flat, but in the perpendicular tangential direction it is curved. In any direction in between these two also the surface is curved.

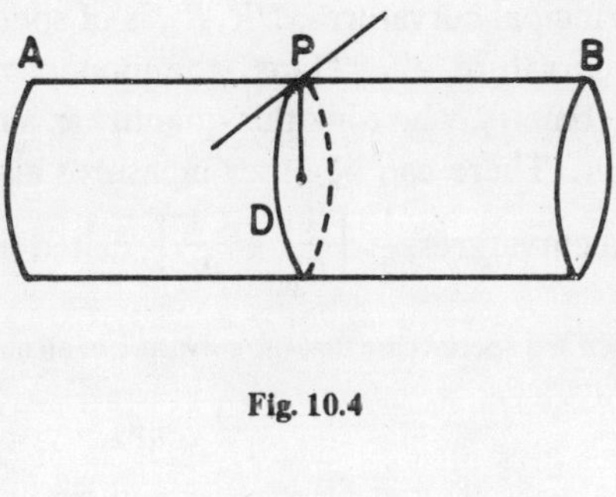

Fig. 10.4

Therefore to get a complete picture of curvature of a surface at a point, it is necessary to know the curvatures in all tangential directions to the surface through that point.

Let P be a point on a curved surface (Fig. 10.5). It is possible to draw (or determine) the tangent plane to the surface at the point. It is a plane passing through the point touching but not cutting the surface at that point. The line PN through P perpendicular to the tangent plane is called the normal to the surface at the point P. A plane through the normal PN cuts the surface in a curve (like APB in Fig. 10.5). Such a curve is called a normal section of the surface. There are infinity of normal sections of a surface through a point. Three are shown in Fig. 10.5. The knowledge of the curvatures of all normal sections of a surface through a point constitutes the knowledge of curvature of the surface at that point.

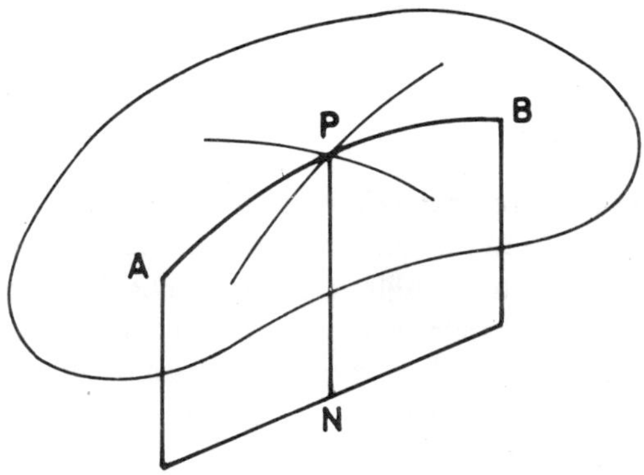

Fig. 10.5

It happens that, at every point of the surface, of all the normal sections, there is one with the largest curvature and another with the smallest.* These are called the *principal* normal sections. They always make a right angle between them. The largest and the smallest curvatures are called the *principal curvatures*. If R_1 and R_2 are the radii of curvatures of the principal sections of a surface at a point, then the principal curvatures at that point are $1/R_1$ and $1/R_2$.

The product of principal curvatures, $1/R_1 R_2$, is of special importance. It is called the Gaussian curvature, after Gauss, the pioneer mathematician in the field of differential geometry, who took this quantity as a measure of curvature of a surface at a point. There can be other measures also. For example, the mean of the principal curvatures, $\frac{1}{2}\left(\frac{1}{R_1} + \frac{1}{R_2}\right)$, called the mean curvature of

* Of course it may happen as a special case that the curvature of all normal sections is the same, as in a sphere.

the surface, is another measure. In generalization of differential geometry to higher dimensions, other measures of curvature also occur.

A Two-dimensional Being

We are naturally aware of a three-dimensional space, and any one- or two-dimensional objects are perceived by us as existing or, to use a mathematical term, embedded in our three-dimensional space. We see the curvature of a curve or a surface from outside it, and so have no difficulty in recognizing it. We can see the difference between a straight line and a circle, or a sphere and a cylinder, because we see these objects from outside. Imagine (it needs quite an effort) that there is a two-dimensional being living on a surface. He cannot possibly perceive or conceive anything outside his surface of existence. All his body organs are two-dimensional, his consciousness extends in two dimensions, and nothing whatever that exists outside his surface can ever touch his consciousness. The question is : can he know whether his surface is a plane, a sphere or an ellipsoid? Can he ever, in any way, grasp the idea of curvature of his space? He can, of course, perceive the curvature of a line in his surface, for the line is embedded in his world, and he can look at it from outside. But would the curvature of his surface, his whole world, be within his comprehension?

Geometry on the Sphere

To look into this question closely, let us take the simplest curved surface, a sphere. We assume that the two-dimensional creatures living on it are intelligent and have mathematicians among them who can discover the geometry of their world. Let us also imagine, for comparison, another two-dimensional world, a world in which entire space consists of a plane (extending infinitely in all directions in its own plane, as we understand it), and this world is also inhabited by the same type of creatures. We shall see how, if at all, the geometries discovered by the mathematicians of these two worlds differ.

The geometry of the plane discovered by the planar mathematicians would exactly be the same as our Euclidean plane geometry. The idea of the shortest distance leading to the definition of a line, the inclination of lines passing through the same point leading to the idea of an angle, the definition of a right angle, line capable of being extended infinitely in either direction, parallel lines as lines which do not meet however far they are produced, all triangles having the property that their angles add up to two right angles, properties of the circle and all other plane figures – all these can be discovered by the intelligent creatures of the plane world, for there is nothing in the Euclidean plane geometry which for postulation or proof needs a look from outside the plane.

The geometry discovered by the inhabitants of the spherical world would be similar in some respects but different in others. Let us assume that the sphere is not very large, and its inhabitants have the means to move all over it. It will be simple for them to define a line as the shortest distance between two points, and postulate that a line can be extended on either side without coming anywhere to the end of space. But they would also discover that, when sufficiently extended, a line turns on itself and arrives from where it started. They would postulate that the largest possible line is the one which connects a point to itself, which every line does eventually if continued to be extended in one direction. They would regard this postulate as a fundamental property of their space.

(From our superior point of view we know that the shortest distance between any two points *P*, *Q* on a sphere, (Fig. 10.6), is along the great circle passing through the points. It is the curve of intersection of the sphere made by the plane passing through the two points and the centre *O* of the sphere. There is only one great circle passing through two given points on the sphere, except when the two points are the ends of a diameter of the sphere, in which case there are any number of great circles. Equator and the circles of longitude are examples of great circles on the earth. Parallels of latitude are not great circles.)

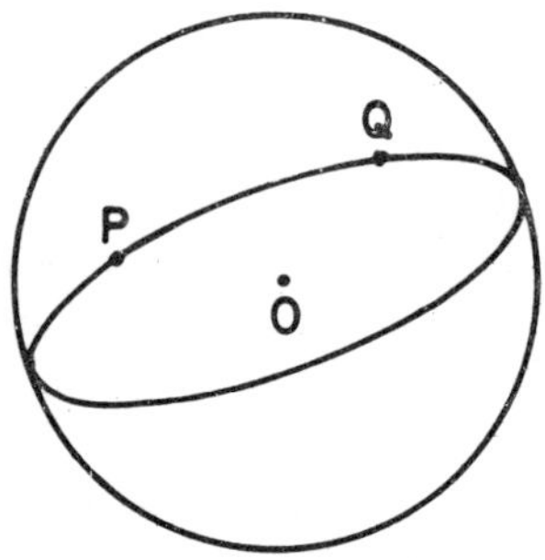

Fig. 10.6

Angle between two lines as a measure of their inclination would be comprehended by the geometers of the spherical world in exactly the same way as by us, except, of course, that what are lines to them are great circular arcs to us. A right angle would be easily defined as each of the four angles when two lines intersect to make all the four angles of intersection equal.

The idea of parallel lines, however, would be completely inconceivable to the people of the spherical world. On the spherical surface no two lines can be drawn which would not meet at all. Two lines, when extended sufficiently would always meet. The reason, from our point of view, is that two great circles on a sphere always intersect at two points which are the ends of a diameter. No such outside view is available to the two-dimensional creatures. To them it is a fundamental property of space that two lines always meet.

Figures like triangles, quadrilaterals and other polygons and circles would be defined in the same way as on a plane, (Fig. 10.7). But the sum of the three angles of their triangles would not always add up to two right angles. The sum of the angles of different triangles would be different. The theorem they would discover in this respect is that the sum of the three angles of a triangle is always greater than two right angles. Fig. 10.8 shows a triangle ABC all of whose angles are right angles, their sum being three right angles (270°), and another triangle $A\,B'C'$ the sum of whose angles is 210°.

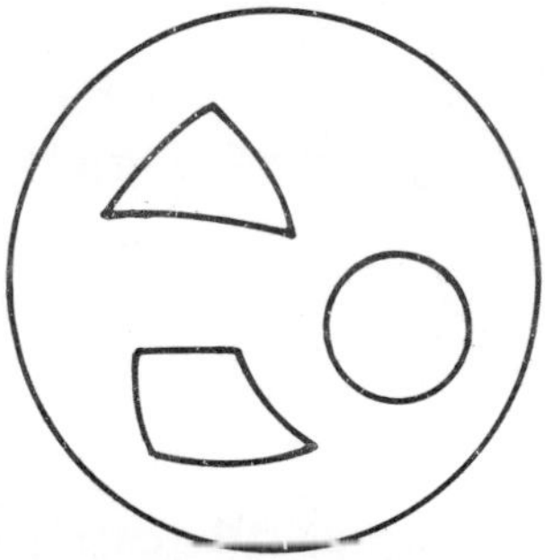

Fig. 10.7

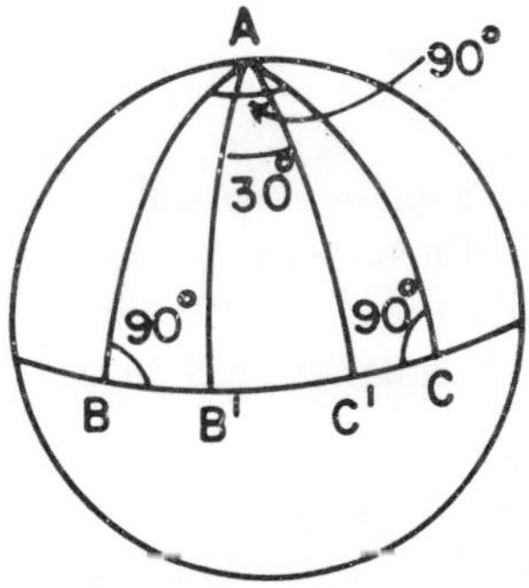

Fig. 10.8

If the flat creatures of the spherical world were somehow able to communicate with their fellow beings inhabiting the plane world, they would find that the geometrical truths of the two civilizations were different, but perhaps neither would know, why? To each their own geometry would be natural and comprehensible and the other crazy and inconceivable. The mathematicians of these worlds, however, would be able to explain the difference if they knew how to detect curvature from within.

Detecting Curvature

Curvature is an intrinsic property of a surface and can be detected by measurements confined to it. As has been mentioned, the sum of the angles of a triangle on a spherical surface exceeds two right angles. This is true of triangles on all surfaces with positive curvature. Curvature is said to be positive when all sections are bent in the same sense. There can be surfaces which are curved such that one section is concave towards one side and a perpendicular section is concave towards the opposite side. The surface of a saddle, (Fig. 10.9), is a typical example of such a surface. It is said to have a negative curvature. A triangle on such a surface has the sum of its angles less than two right angles.

Accordingly, by a careful measurement of the angles of triangles on it, the nature of curvature of a surface can be guessed.

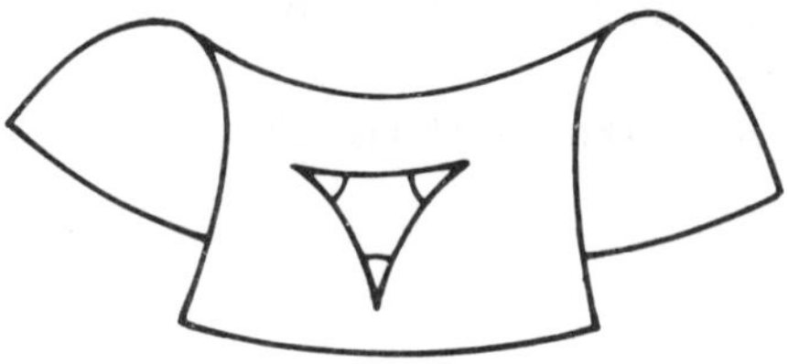

Fig. 10.9

Even a quantitative estimate of curvature is possible. The sum of the angles of a quadrilateral on a surface with positive curvature exceeds four right angles. According to a result in differential geometry, if E is this excess for a quadrilateral whose area is S, then

$$\lim_{S \to 0} \frac{E}{S} = \frac{1}{R_1 R_2}$$

where the expression on the right side is the Gaussian curvature of the surface at the point where the quadrilateral is situated as it is made smaller and smaller. An estimate of the limit of the ratio E/S will give a measure of the curvature.

The curvature of a surface also enters into a fundamental equation of differential geometry. The theorem of Pythagoras holds on a plane but not on a curved surface. On a plane it is possible to choose coordinate axes such that the distance s of the point (x, y) from the origin is given by $s^2 = x^2 + y^2$. By the same theorem, if ds denotes the distance between the point (x, y) and a neighbouring point $(x + dx, y + dy)$, then

$$ds^2 = dx^2 + dy^2$$

Putting the theorem in the notation of differential calculus, as has been done above, has special significance. It means that the distance ds between the points (x, y) and $(x + dx, y + dy)$ along any curve joining the two points, in the limit as the two points get closer along the curve, is related to dx and dy in the above manner.

This is the property of a plane surface. On a curved surface the expression for ds becomes more complicated. We can chose two sets or families of curves spreading like a net over the curved surface to serve as reference lines (Fig. 10.10). Choosing the point of intersection of any two curves, one of each family, as the origin, we may denote the coordinates of any point on the surface by (p, q), p being a measure of the distance along one curve and q along the

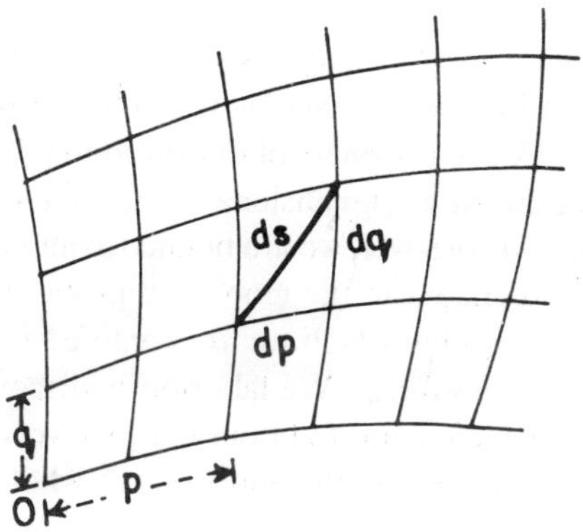

Fig. 10.10

other. Then the general formula for ds, the distance between the neighbouring points (p, q) and $(p + dp, q + dq)$, is given in the form

$$ds^2 = E\,dp^2 + F\,dpdq + G\,dq^2$$

where E, F, G are some functions of p, q. From the functions it is possible to deduce the curvature of the surface at the point (p, q). If by some transformation of axes, (that is, by choosing some other network as reference lines), it is possible to express ds^2 in the simpler form

$$ds^2 = dx^2 + dy^2,$$

then the curvature is zero, that is the surface is a plane. If this is not possible, the curvature is nonzero. It can be tested from the functions E, F, G whether such a transformation of axes is at all possible.

Thus, given the necessary mathematical skill, it is possible for the intelligent beings living in a two-dimensional world to detect any curvature in their space.

A Nagging Thought

Let us now consider a slightly different scenario. Suppose the spherical world is very large and that the two-dimensional creatures of our imagination are confined to a small region of it. They have no means to move out to distant regions of their space. A small area on the surface of a large sphere is almost flat, and therefore their geometry, which they have built on their experience of the small space in which they live, is the same as of the plane world. They imagine their lines to extend to infinity, they can draw parallel lines which never meet, and the angles of their triangles add to two right angles. The slight discrepancies in these assumptions are two small to be detected by their instruments. That something different might happen, if they could really follow their lines to 'infinity', they do not suspect.

This plight of the imaginary inhabitants of a nonexistent world would have bothered us the least but for the nagging thought that the ignorant creatures might really be we. We are prisoners of our three-dimensional consciousness. Can we be sure that our three-dimensional world is not embedded in a world of higher dimensions? Moreover, we are bound to our earth. Even taking into account our recent excursions to the moon and probes into other parts of the solar system, the space within which we are confined is but an infinitesimally small part of the entire universe. We laboriously discovered a geometry, the Euclidean geometry, which seems to fit our universe very well. Can we be sure that it gives the correct picture of the universe as a whole?

Curvature in Three Dimensions

In the three-dimensional Euclidean geometry the theorem of Pythagoras gives the distance between two points which, in the language of differential calculus, can be expressed as

$$ds^2 = dx^2 + dy^2 + dz^2$$

where ds is the distance between two neighbouring points (x, y, z) and $(x + dx, y + dy, z + dz)$ with respect to three mutually perpendicular axes of reference. Euclidean space is characterized by this formula. A similar formula in two dimensions characterizes the plane or the flat surface without curvature. We may, therefore, in analogy with this, call the three-dimensional Euclidean space as 'flat', that is, with no curvature. But this may only be a local picture. What if, in the large, our space is curved. A more correct version of the basic formula for the distance, in that case, would be

$$ds^2 = E_1dp^2 + E_2dq^2 + E_3dr^2 + F_1dqdr + F_2drdp + F_3dpdq$$

where $E_1, E_2, E_3, F_1, F_2, F_3$ are some functions of p, q, r, the coordinates of a point with respect to a three-dimensional network of curves. From these functions it is possible to get a measure of curvature of the space.

The question is – why should doubts about the flatness of our space arise? Till about the first two decades of this century the question was purely academic arising out of the discussion about the axioms of Euclidean geometry which had been going on among mathematicians almost ever since Euclid. In 1915 Albert Einstein based his famous Theory of Relativity on the assumption that our space is not three-dimensional but four, and moreover, not 'flat' but 'curved'. But let us first see what the situation was before Einstein's theory.

Parallel Postulate of Euclid

One of the postulates of Euclidean geometry had been baffling mathematicians for centuries. Euclid enunciated it in the following form.

> *If two coplanar lines intersect a third line such that the sum of the inner angles made by them with the latter on one side of it is less than two right angles, then the two lines meet on the side on which these angles are made*, (Fig. 10.11).

This postulate is not as self-evident as axioms are expected to be. For centuries it was believed that it need not be taken as an axiom but could be proved from the other axioms of Euclid. The history of mathematics is replete with attempts to prove it, but every proof was found to be wrong in the sense that in some form or the other the postulate was assumed. Many equivalent forms of this axiom thus came to be known. The form in which it is commonly introduced nowadays and which appears to be the simplest is due to John Playfair (1748-1819). It is as follows:

> *Given a line and a point outside it, it is possible to draw, in the plane determined by the point and the line, one and only one line which does not meet the given line, however far the two are produced*, (Fig. 10.12).

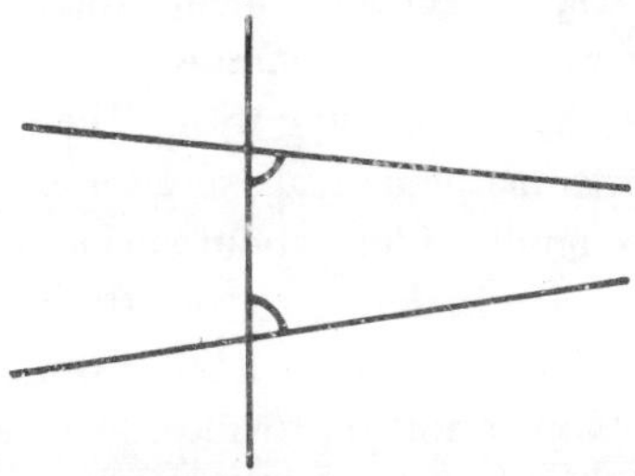

Fig. 10.11

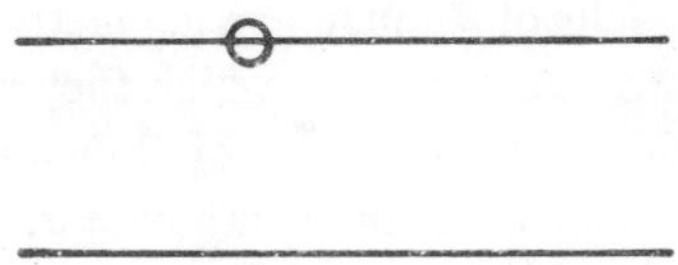

Fig. 10.12

The basic difficulty about this axiom is that it makes an assertion about what happens far out in space of which we have no experience. The form in which Euclid enunciated it did not have this difficulty, but logically the two forms are equivalent.

When all attempts to prove this postulate had failed, and there was no getting away from the fact that it was just an assumption, interest turned to the question whether the postulate could be done away with or modified. The result of enquiry on these lines was revolutionary.

Credit goes to the great German mathematician Gauss (1777–1855) to finally clarify that the parallel postulate or any of its equivalent forms is dispensable and replaceable by alternative axioms. For example, it was possible to assume that through a given point outside a given line, two or more lines could be drawn which would not meet the given line. A perfectly logical system of geometry could be built with this assumption, the other axioms of Euclidean geometry still holding. Of course, many theorems would turn out to be different from those of Euclid's. The new geometry would describe properties of a new type of space, different from the Euclidean space, but no less plausible. One could also assume that it is not possible to draw two parallel lines at all. The geometry on a spherical surface that was described earlier is of this type.

These discoveries opened up a new era of noneuclidean geometries. Interest in them was no longer academic when it was realized that other geometries also may possibly represent our space. Different geometries provide different models of space, and with our limited experience we could not reject outright models other than the Euclidean.

Riemannian Geometry

The generalization of geometry has been in two ways, first, in the direction of increasing dimensions, and secondly, by giving up the assumption of flat space and introducing the notion of curvature. Riemannian geometry, so called after its originator Riemann, combined the two effects and dealt with a general n-dimensional curved space. As the word space generally means the physical reality around us,Riemann introduced a new term, the *continuum,* as the name of the n-dimensional mathematical object he was dealing with. The general results of Riemannian geometry are abstract mathematical exercises except in two dimensions in which they reduce to familiar ideas about surfaces. The chief characteristic of Riemannian geometry is that it reveals the intrinsic properties of the continuum irrespective of the fact whether the continuum is embedded in a higher-dimensional continuum or not. It provides, so to say, the inside view of the continuum. We are so much accustomed to view two-dimensional surfaces as embedded in our three-dimensional space that we find it difficult to visualize a surface without the space around it. But unless we have means to do so, we shall not be able to make much progress in discovering the nature of our own space. We cannot get outside our dimensions to have an outside view of our space. Riemannian geometry enables us to discover its properties while looking from within.

Einstein's Theory of Relativity makes use of Riemannian geometry as its mathematical framework. It postulates the existence of a four-dimensional continuum, three dimensions of space and one of time, in which all physical phenomena occur. The concept of time as something flowing independently past us is discarded. Time is interwoven with space, and every phenomenon in the universe is an event in the space-time continuum. An event can be represented as a point in this continuum, the distance between two points giving the space-time interval between the two events.

The space-time continuum is assumed to be of a general type with curvature. The geometry of such a continuum is different from the Euclidean geometry, but the difference is significant only on the cosmic scale. In a small region of the universe, such as the one in which we are confined, the Euclidean geometry is a sufficiently good approximation.

The Cosmic Scale

Let us digress a little and be clear of the cosmic dimensions of space and time and the small region in which we are imprisoned. According to the present scientific beliefs, the universe is neither infinite in size nor eternal in time. It had a beginning and will have an end. This immediately raises a difficult question. What was there before the beginning and what would be after the end? This takes us to the realm of speculation. The scientists are talking of their present observable universe based on the physical laws discovered on the earth but holding far beyond. They believe that the universe began about 15 to 20 thousand million years ago with what astronomers call the 'big bang'. It has been expanding since then at an ever increasing rate. Eventually at some distant future it may exhaust its expansionist spirit and start contracting and finally come to an end. This may be only one cycle. There may be endless such cycles, who knows?

In the process of creation and condensation of matter forming galaxies, within them stars with accompanying planets, the earth is believed to have been formed about four to five thousand million years ago, about a quarter of the time since the big bang. It is in the last five thousand years that human kind has emerged from a primitive society to the modern complex civilization. An idea of the enormity of the cosmic time scale is obtained by considering that, if the age of the universe is reduced to an year, the age of the earth is about three months, and human civilization has appeared only in the last one second.

As for the size of the universe, the numbers defy human understanding all the more. The universe is a vast space with planets revolving round stars and stars clustering into galaxies. The number of galaxies is estimated to be of the order of hundred thousand million (10^{11}), the number of stars per galaxy also being of the same order. Astronomical distances are measured in light years; a light year is the distance travelled by light in one year. In one second light goes 300 thousand kilometers. It reaches us from our star, the sun, in eight minutes, and from the next nearest star, Proxima Centauri, in four years. Stars are mere points separated by large distances, a hundred thousand million of them forming a galaxy. Sizes of galaxies are of the order of hundreds of thousands of light years, and the inter-galactic distances are measured in millions of light years. The most distant astronomical bodies observed so far, the quasars, are about ten thousand million (10^{10}) light years away. This does not seem to be the end. The more penetrating the astronomical telescopes become, the further the frontiers of the universe are pushed. It perhaps has no borders.

Even with all the billions and billions of galaxies and billions of billions of stars, the universe is far from being a crowded place. In fact, on the contrary, it is a vast, empty, cold and dark expanse with galaxies drifting like innumerable small knotted threads of light floating on an unbounded ocean surface. If one were to be randomly thrown in the universe from somewhere outside, his chance of landing anywhere near a galaxy is extremely small, perhaps one in a million, while his chance of landing on a planet is less than one in 10^{33}. The universe is a little matter scattered very sparsely in a vast space over a long time.

Theory of Relativity

It is this gigantic universe that the space-time continuum of Einstein is designed to fit. It is a four-dimensional curved space and, like a two-dimensional spherical surface, has no boundaries, yet is finite. It has no centre and no preferential directions. A remarkable and fascinating part of Einstein's theory is that curvature explains the phenomenon of gravitation.

Gravitation, in classical mechanics, is postulated as a fundamental property of matter; it is a mutual force of attraction between two material bodies unaffected by any other intervening material or natural phenomenon, and is proportional to the masses of the two bodies and inversely proportional to the square of the distance between them. It is a very weak force as compared to other forces which dominate and regulate terrestrial life and technology such as the electromagnetic forces or the forces of pull or push exerted by bodies on each other through contact. But it is an all pervading force, keeping us bound to the earth, making our rivers flow, and producing innumerable other effects. It is an influence which we can neither control nor escape. On the astronomical scale, among planets, stars and galaxies, it is the most dominant regulating force.

In the Theory of Relativity gravitation is the property of the space-time continuum, its curvature causing what appears as a force of attraction. The presence of matter itself at a point in space is linked to its curvature there. The theory thus connects space, time, matter and gravitation in a single framework essentially geometrical in its structure.

The Theory of Relativity properly belongs to the area of theoretical physics and hardly falls within the scope of the present book. It has received this brief mention because it is a supreme example of abstract mathematical thought, unrelated to any human experience, providing a basis for a theory unifying some fundamental aspects of the physical world.

FROM THE GALLERY OF MATHEMATICIANS

Carl Friedrich Gauss

Born in a poor and unlettered family, Gauss (German, 1777-1855) was one of the most versatile and brilliant mathematical scientists the world has ever seen. He showed extraordinary precocity in childhood, and without any help learnt to calculate before he could talk. In school at the age of eight he astonished his teacher by instantly giving the sum of all integers from 1 to 100, a task which the teacher had set for the boisterous class as a punishment. At twelve he was already looking askance at the foundations of Euclidean geometry, and by sixteen he had caught his first glimpse of a geometry other than Euclid's. Beginning at fourteen with a stipend from a duke, he was able to concentrate on his intellectual pursuits for the next sixteen years. At twenty-five he was already a famous mathematician and astronomer. He was appointed director of the observatory at Gottingen at the age of thirty, where he stayed for forty-seven years.

Inspite of not a very happy personal life, Gauss maintained an amazingly rich scientific activity. An early passion for numbers and calculations extended first to algebra and then to analysis, geometry, probability and theory of errors. Concurrently he carried on intensive experimental and theoretical research in many branches of science including observational astronomy, celestial mechanics, surveying, geodesy, geomagnetism, electromagnetism, mechanics, optics, the design of scientific experiments and actuarial science. It is said of him that he was the last mathematician to be the master of all the branches of mathematics and its applications known in his time. After him there have been great mathematicians, but none who knew all mathematics, so vast had mathematics become.

Georg Friedrich Bernhard Riemann

One of the most original mathematicians of modern times, Riemann (German, 1826-66) unfortunately inherited a poor constitution and died before he could reap the rich harvests his mind was capable of producing. While still at the gymnasium (high school in German educational system) he had mastered many advanced works in mathematics through private study. He entered the University of Gottingen to study philology and theology, as his father desired, but could not keep away from mathematics, and soon changed his course to suit his talent. He left Gottingen for Berlin soon after.

At the age of twenty-five Riemann laid the foundation of the theory of functions of a complex variable in his doctoral thesis. His contributions in this area alone were sufficient to rank him among the greatest of mathematicians, but his genius flowered in many other directions.

Three years later, as a candidate for lecturership, he was advised by Gauss to choose 'the foundations of geometry' as the subject for his seminar. This was the subject Gauss had pondered over for over fifty years, and he was curious to know what the young and brilliant Riemann had to say on it. But it was not Riemann's first choice, still he came out with flying colours. Gauss was greatly impressed. Riemann's further work in the same area resulted in the development of Riemannian geometry.

Albert Einstein

The most celebrated scientist of the twentieth century and perhaps of all times, the man who became a legend in his own lifetime, Einstein (German-American, 1879–1955) was a slow child and disliked the regimentation of school. His scientific interests were awakened early at home. Graduating from the polytechnique at Zurich, Switzerland, and failing to get a teaching appointment, he did occasional tutoring and substitute teaching till he got a job as an examiner in the Swiss Patent Office at Berne. Far from being disappointed during the seven years at this job, Einstein concentrated in his spare hours on his chosen problems of physics and produced results which laid the foundations of large parts of twentieth century physics. After receiving his doctorate in 1905 from the University of Zurich, he moved through professorial appointments at Zurich, Prague and again at Zurich, to finally become the director of Kaiser Wilhelm Institute of Physics at Berlin in 1914.

His scientific work reached its culmination during World War I (1914-18) with the publication of the General Theory of Relativity. His personal life, however, suffered unhappiness. He was divorced from his first wife, and later married again. The theory of relativity was confirmed in a spectacular manner by the astronomical observations made during the total solar eclipse of 1919. The very abstruseness of his theory, demolishing the simpler notions propounded by Galileo (1564-1642) and Newton (1642-1727) about the nature of the physical world, made him and his theory household words round the world. He became a symbol of the highest intellectual attainment, held in awe and wonder even by the front rank intellectuals of his time. He was awarded Nobel Prize in 1921, not for his theory of relativity which was considered too abstruse to be properly judged but for his work in the quantum theory of light.

Einstein was no narrow scientist confining his activities to his specialized field. He had broad human sympathies with a deeply spiritual outlook. He was a pacifist opposed to all wars and always supported humanitarian causes. As a Jew he had to face the vicious attacks which were launched against the Jews in Germany with the rise of Hitler and anti- Jewish sentiment in 1933. Unable to bear humiliation, he moved to the Institute of Advanced Study in Princeton, U. S. A., and became an American citizen in 1940.

Because of his immense prestige some young physicists requested him to use his weight to impress upon President Roosevelt during World War II (1939-45) the potentialities of nuclear fission as a weapon of destruction, and the danger of Germany being able to lay hands on it before America. This started the atomic bomb project in America culminating in the manufacture of the atomic bomb. Einstein, otherwise, was in no way connected with it, and was shocked and pained when the two bombs were dropped in Japan. In postwar years he became actively engaged with the movement initiated by Bertrand Russell for the renunciation of nuclear weapons and abolition of war.

Subrahmanyan Chandrasekhar

Born in India, educated at Madras and Cambridge, living in Chicago (U.S.A.) since 1937, Chandrasekhar (1910–) will go down in history as one of the most outstanding theoretical astronomers of the twentieth century. He applied his extraordinary mathematical ability to theoretical investigations concerning the structure of stars, the dynamics of galaxies, the blue of the sky, the magnetic fields of heavenly bodies, and many other astrophysical topics. Every topic that he took up, he investigated relentlessly for a decade or so, until he attained a mature perspective culminating in an epoch-making book. In the words of another eminent contemporary astronomer, "He just batters his way through problems no one else could do. His concentration is unbelievable – a mixture of sheer mathematical intelligence and phenomenal persistence. There is not one field that he has worked in where we are not now daily using some of his results."

As a young scientist at Cambridge in 1935, Chandrasekhar concluded that a star more than 1.4 times as massive as the Sun will continue to radiate and collapse finally attaining the size of a few kilometres diameter with such a strong gravitational pull that not even its own radiation can escape it. At that time he was ridiculed for this theoretical result. Four decades later, with the discovery of black holes – the extraordinarily massive bodies which emit no radiation – Chandrasekhar's theory was confirmed, for which he was awarded Nobel prize in 1984. It is remarkable that only once before, about fifty-five years back, the Nobel prize in physics was awarded to an Indian – that time the recipient was Chandrasekhar's uncle, C. V. Raman.

Chapter 11

Mathematics of Chance

"Each discipline couched in mathematical symbols is ultimately susceptible of independent mathematical existence."

—*C. Truesdell, American (1919–)*

We live in a world of chance. All the time events are happening by chance, so at least we say. We talk of the chances of rain tomorrow or the chances of nuclear war in the next decade, the chance of winning a lottery or the chance of meeting an accident. When we try our luck at the races or run the risk of losing money in the stock market, we are taking chances. Birth of a boy or a girl is a matter of chance, so is health or sickness.

Events, by and large, are the effects of causes. So do the scientists believe at least so far as the gross physical world is concerned. It is the cause-and-effect chain that science usually investigates. The more human knowledge advances, the more one is able to explain events and phenomena in terms of causes producing effects according to principles. To the extent the various factors constituting the cause can be known, the effect can be determined. The meteorologist today knows more about the factors that cause rain than he did a decade ago, and so his forecast is more likely to be correct today than before. But there are chances that he may prove to be wrong. The factors determining any event are so many and so rapidly changing that their complete determination is beyond human capability. Moreover, even a slight variation in cause may produce a large variation in effect. However detailed and precise human knowledge about anything may be, it will always be incomplete, and therefore, from our point of view, events will be happening never with certainty but always with some element of chance. Moreover, knowledge of a thing does not necessarily mean the power to control it. We can only hope or wish or pray in circumstances beyond our control, and whatever the outcome, it is for us a matter of chance. In this sense, chance is merely another name for one's failure to predetermine an event.

Are events predetermined? This is one of those fundamental questions which have been asked ever since people began asking questions, and would never be fully answered. Indeterminacy involves lack of power to control. In the face of their own ignorance and helplessness, people had to seek succour in an all-knowing, all powerful deity. God had to be free from all human inadequacies, otherwise He was no use. From His side there could be no indeterminacy, for that would imply lack of power or knowledge. Theists therefore cannot afford to accept indeterminacy as the basic principle of nature.*

That leaves the agnostics and the atheists to carry on the debate. Till the end of the nineteenth century the scientists were, so far as this question was concerned, on the side of the theists. Without bringing in God** explicitly, they believed in the law of causation as a basic tenet of their faith. To them the universe was a big machine, everything moved according to fixed principles and laws, and events happened compulsively in a cause-and-effect chain.

This belief received a jolt with the quantum theory in physics. It knocked the bottom out of the deterministic view of nature. Things seemed to happen at the level of electrons, atoms and molecules just by chance. Considerations of probability started replacing search for certainty in the basic outlook of scientists. Chance seemed to be the operative principle of nature. With some scientists the pendulum swung to the other extreme with the entire universe with all the happenings in it, – the birth of stars and planets, the evolution of life on earth, the brain, the mind, consciousness, the extinction of dinosaurs, wars and epidemics, – attributed to chance alone without any preconceived design. There are on the other hand people to whom such 'mindlessness' in creation is unacceptable. Albert Einstein, acclaimed as the greatest scientist of all times and enjoying enormous prestige in his lifetime, was totally unreconciled to chance being a governing principle of Nature. "God does not play dice", he exclaimed. But people play. And that was what brought the study of chance within the realm of mathematics.

Throughout the ages gambling has been a pastime with many and a passion with some. Games of chance provide amusement to all. What are one's chances of winning, was a natural question. Observations indicated that in games of chance, whereas the outcome of a single trial was entirely unpredictable, in large number of trials some events appeared to occur more often

* The law of karma in Indian philosophy is determinacy with a vengeance. It does not leave even God to act arbitrarily, eliminating the concept of chance completely. Other philosophies and religions at least give power to God to act as He likes and thereby admit chance by backdoor.

** The French mathematician Laplace, (1749-1827), was the first to banish God from scientific books. On being asked by Napolean why he had not once mentioned the author of the universe in his huge book on the system of the world, Celestial Mechanics, Laplace replied, "Sire, I had no need of that hypothesis." Scientists do not, as a rule, bring in God in their writings because they work on the principle of 'minimum hypothesis'. It in no way reflects their religious belief.

than others. In everyday life also, while we are not certain, we still say that one thing is more likely to happen than the other. There are obviously degrees of uncertainty. Can we measure chance? If a measure of chance could be devised, then the probability of occurrence of an event could be quantitatively described and subjected to some mathematical considerations.

Tossing a Coin

Let us begin with the simplest of the games of chance – tossing a coin. It results either in head (H) or tail (T). These are the only two possible outcomes of a trial, but by no means it is possible to predict which of the two would occur in any trial. Also we have no reason to believe that one outcome is more likely than the other. Both have an equal chance. Of the two possible outcomes, one is H. Another way of saying this is that the probability of H is 1 in 2, or 1/2. Similarly we say that the probability of T is 1/2. This measure of probability conveys nothing more nor nothing less than what has been said just now in so many words. It makes no claim to predict the happening.

Suppose we toss the coin twice. The second toss is quite independent of the first, and the outcome in the second is in no way dependent on the outcome in the first. Every time the probability of getting a head is 1/2. If the first toss results in H, the second toss still has an equal chance of resulting in H. If we make 100 tosses, and 70 of them happen to be H (as it might well be), then in the 101st toss the probability of H is still 1/2. It is not diminished at all, nor does the probability of T go up. The statement that the probability of H is the same as of T, and is 1/2, does not imply that successive trials tend to bring the number of H's closer to the number of T's. What then is the point in making the statement? What does the number 1/2 signify? What is its use? We shall answer these questions a little later. Just now let us take some more examples of defining probability.

It will be convenient to use a notation for probability, a word too cumbersome to write repeatedly in full. We denote by $P(x)$ the probability of the event x. With this notation $P(H) = P(T) = 1/2$.

Suppose we toss two coins, or toss the same coin twice. The two operations are equivalent as the two tosses are independent. There are four possible outcomes of the two tosses considered jointly: both heads; first head, second tail; first tail, second head; both tails. We indicate them as

$$HH \qquad HT \qquad TH \qquad TT$$

Any of these four situations can turn up with equal chance. We therefore, say that the probability of getting HH (or any of the other three) is 1 in 4, or 1/4:

$$P(HH) = P(TT) = P(HT) = P(TH) = 1/4.$$

Suppose we are not interested in the order in which T and H occur, and want to know the probability of one T and one H, no matter in what order. We notice that one T and one H constitute two of the four possible outcomes. Therefore

$$P\,(HT \text{ or } TH) = 2/4 = 1/2.$$

Let us consider three tosses. The joint outcome of three tosses can be any of the following eight situations, each having an equal chance.

$$HHH \quad HHT \quad HTH \quad HTT$$
$$THH \quad THT \quad TTH \quad TTT$$

Three heads is one of the eight situations, so is three tails. Hence $P(HHH) = P(TTT) = 1/8$.

In three of the situations H occur twice and T once, so

$$P\,(2\,H, 1\,T, \text{ in whatever order})$$
$$= P(HHT \text{ or } HTH \text{ or } THH) = 3/8.$$

On the same principle it can be easily seen that

$$P(TTH \text{ or } THT \text{ or } HTT) = 3/8,$$
$$P(HHH \text{ or } TTT) = 2/8,$$
$$P(\text{at least one } H) = 7/8,$$
$$P(\text{no } H) = P(TTT) = 1/8.$$

The above are examples of how probability of an event is defined mathematically. Let us consider a few more illustrations.

Rolling Dice

Rolling a die (plural dice) is a familiar way of deciding moves in games of chance. A die is a small perfect cube with its six faces marked 1,2,3...6 by dots, (Fig. 11.1)

Fig. 11.1

Since the cube is perfect, there is no reason why one face should have greater chance of showing up than any other. There are six possible outcomes of a throw. Therefore, by definition, the probability of any one particular face showing up is 1 in 6, or 1/6:

$$P(1) = P(2) = P(3) = P(4) = P(5) = P(6) = 1/6.$$

As the odd-numbered faces are three, the probability of an odd number turning up is

$$P(1 \text{ or } 3 \text{ or } 5) = 3/6 = 1/2,$$

and similarly of an even number

$$P(2 \text{ or } 4 \text{ or } 6) = 3/6 = 1/2.$$

Suppose we roll a pair of dice, one white with black marks, the other black with white marks. There are 36 possible outcomes of this operation, (Fig. 11.2), since each face of one die can combine with any of the six faces of the other die.

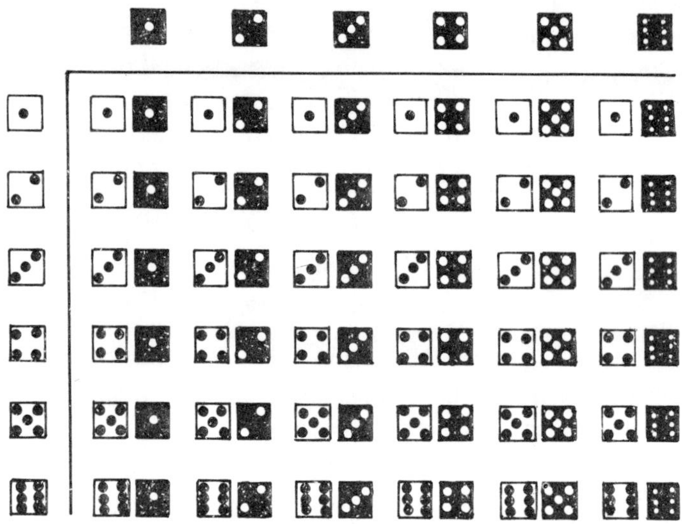

Fig. 11.2 36 ways of throwing a pair of dice.

The probability of any one particular combination is 1/36. Out of the 36 there are two outcomes in which one die shows 1 and the other die 2. Hence

$$P(1{,}2 \text{ or } 2{,}1) = 2/36 = 1/18.$$

By similar reasoning the following probabilities can be easily worked out.

$$P(2{,}3 \text{ or } 3{,}2) = 2/36 = 1/18,$$

$$P(\text{sum} = 6) = P(1{,}5 \text{ or } 5{,}1 \text{ or } 2{,}4 \text{ or } 4{,}2 \text{ or } 3{,}3) = 5/36,$$

$$P(\text{sum} = 4) = P(1{,}3 \text{ or } 3{,}1 \text{ or } 2{,}2) = 3/36 = 1/12,$$

$$P(\text{sum} = 12) = P(6{,}6) = 1/36,$$

$$P(\text{sum} = 1) = 0/36 = 0,$$

$$P(\text{sum} \geq 2) = 36/36 = 1,$$

$$P(\text{at least one face odd}) = 27/36.$$

Drawing Cards

Any number of examples of defining probability in the above manner can be given from other situations. Drawing cards from a well-shuffled deck of playing cards presents interesting examples. There are in all 52 different cards, and so the probability of drawing any particular card is 1 in 52, or 1/52. The following are some other cases.

$$P(\text{an ace}) = 4/52 = 1/13,$$

$$P(\text{a diamond}) = 13/52 = 1/4,$$

$$P(\text{a picture}) = 12/52 = 3/13,$$

$$P(\text{a Jack or higher}) = 16/52 = 4/13,$$

$$P(\text{a spade or an ace}) = 16/52 = 4/13.$$

The last case is slightly different from the others. There are 13 spades and 4 aces, but the ace of spade is common, so there are 16 cards in all which are either a spade or an ace. Hence the probability of drawing a spade or an ace is 16/52.

Algebra of Probability

We are now in a position to introduce a few standard terms which are commonly used in the theory of probability, and give a general definition of probability of which the preceding cases are examples. An activity like drawing cards or rolling dice or picking samples from a collection of objects is called an *experiment.* An experiment results in an *outcome*. For example, getting a six on a die is an outcome of the experiment of rolling a die, and getting an ace and a king is an outcome of the experiment of drawing two cards from a deck. The set of all the outcomes of an experiment is called the *sample space* of the experiment. For example, Fig. 11.2 indicates the sample space of the experiment of rolling a pair of dice, and the set of 52 playing cards is the sample space of the experiment of drawing a card from the deck. A subset of the sample space is called an *event.* Thus one or more outcomes of an experiment constitute an event.

The probability of an event E in the sample space S is defined as the ratio of $n(E)$, the number of elements (outcomes) in the set E, to $n(S)$, the number of outcomes in the set S,

$$P(E) = \frac{n(E)}{n(S)}$$

This is just a mathematical definition. The examples cited in the preceding sections are all in conformity with it, as can be easily verified. The number of elements in S and E are necessarily non-negative integers, and since E is a subset of S, $n(E) \leq n(S)$. Hence always $P(E) \leq 1$. The possibility of E being empty may not be ruled out, and so, if $n(E) = 0$ and $n(S) \neq 0$, then $P(E) = 0$.

Thus, the probability of an event is a real non-negative number less than or equal to 1:

$$0 \leq P(E) \leq 1.$$

Zero probability means impossibility and 1 means certainty. For example, in a throw of a pair of dice, the sum will always be greater than 1, and so P(sum $> 1) = 1$, and $P(\text{sum} \leq 1) = 0$, the former indicating certainty and the latter impossibility.

This definition of probability is axiomatic. It is a mathematical fiction, but like most mathematical fictions it is useful, as we shall see presently. Also one can define operations and formulate rules for manipulations, thus inventing an algebra of probability which gives to the subject a separate mathematical existence. Of course, rules of operations have to be plausible and make sense in the real situations to which probability considerations apply, but in the abstract sense they are axioms on which the theory of probability is based.

To take one example of such a rule, since events are defined as sets, we can have unions and intersections of events. If E_1 and E_2 are two events of the same sample space, then $E_1 \cup E_2$ and $E_1 \cap E_2$ are also events. A rule connecting their probabilities is

$$P(E_1 \cup E_2) = P(E_1) + P(E_2) - P(E_1 \cap E_2).$$

Let us verify this with an example. Let S be the sample space of drawing a card from a well-shuffled deck of playing cards, and let E_1 be the event of drawing an honour (Jack or higher), and E_2 the event of drawing a spade, so that $n(S) = 52$, $n(E_1) = 16$, $n(E_2) = 13$. Then, $E_1 \cup E_2$ is the event of drawing either an honour or a spade; there are 25 such cards (4 being common to spades and honours), so $n(E_1 \cup E_2) = 25$. Also, $E_1 \cap E_2$ is the event of drawing a card which is a spade as well as an honour. There are 4 such cards and so $n(E_1 \cap E_2) = 4$. Hence the following probabilities:

$$P(E_1) = \frac{n(E_1)}{n(S)} = \frac{16}{52}, \quad P(E_2) = \frac{n(E_2)}{n(S)} = \frac{13}{52},$$

$$P(E_1 \cup E_2) = \frac{n(E_1 \cup E_2)}{n(S)} = \frac{25}{52},$$

$$P(E_1 \cap E_2) = \frac{n(E_1 \cap E_2)}{n(S)} = \frac{4}{52}.$$

These verify the rule

$$P(E_1 \cup E_2) = P(E_1) + P(E_2) - P(E_1 \cap E_2).$$

Cumulative Effect of Chance

We can now turn to the question we have been postponing so far. What is the use of this definition of probability? When we say that the probability of rolling a six on a die is 1/6, what is it we are trying to express? Do we mean that out of six trials, one will result in a six? Definitely not. Absolutely no prediction is made about the result of a trial. It is possible that six, twelve or even twenty consecutive trials fail to show up a six, but it would in no way increase the chance of a six in the subsequent throw. Every throw is independent of the other, and, if the die is true, no face is more likely to come up than the other in any one throw. Yet, it is an experimental fact that as the number of trials increases, some pattern seems to emerge out of all the results taken together. The outcome of any one trial is erratic, but the cumulative effect of a large number of trials shows some order. Therein lies the significance of the definition of probability.

Table 11.1 shows the outcomes of actually rolling a die 3000 times. The outcome of every trial was noted. The first column gives the number of trials, and the second column the number of times six appeared in those trials. For example, six appeared 6 times in the first 20 trials, 19 times in the first 100, 193 times in the first 1000, and so on. In the third column the corresponding hypothetical number, $\frac{1}{6}$ × (number of trials), is written. It is the number of times six is expected to appear on the hypothetical assumption that it should appear once in six times. This number, as we have already remarked, is a mathematical fiction based not on experiment but on *apriori* reasoning. The fourth column tabulates the difference between the observed and the expected frequencies, while in the last column is entered this difference expressed as a percentage of trials.

Table 11.1
Frequency of occurrence of six on a die in an experiment

Number of trials	Observed frequency	Expected frequency	Difference	% difference
20	6	3.3	2.7	13.50
40	9	6.7	2.3	5.75
60	13	10.0	3.0	5.00
80	17	13.3	3.7	4.63
100	19	16.7	2.3	2.30
200	44	33.3	10.7	5.35
400	81	66.7	14.3	3.57
600	126	100.0	26.0	4.33
800	161	133.3	27.7	3.46
1000	193	166.7	26.3	2.63
1200	241	200.0	41.0	3.42
1400	279	133.3	45.7	3.26

(*contd.*)

Table 11.1 (*contd.*)

Number of trials	Observed frequency	Expected frequency	Difference	% difference
1600	317	266.7	50.3	3.14
1800	350	300.0	50.0	2.78
2000	383	333.3	49.7	2.49
3000	555	500.0	55.0	1.83

It will be noticed that the difference between the observed and the expected frequencies increases with the number of trials. In 20 trials the difference is 2.7, in 3000 it is 55. This increase is not very regular, for example, it drops down from 3.7 to 2.3 as the trials go up from 80 to 100. But the overall trend is unmistakable. The percentage difference shows the reverse trend. From 13.5% for 20 trials, it has dropped to 1.83% for 3000 trials. This decrease too is unmistakable, though not regular. Indeed, regularity is not expected, for every trial is independent, and its result is erratic.

The entries in Table 11.1 are the result of an actual experiment performed by the author. Every time such an experiment is done, these numbers will be different (except in column three), there may be great variations, but while the absolute difference between the observed and the expected frequencies will increase with the number of trials, this difference expressed as a fraction (or percentage, which is the same thing essentially) of the number of trials will decrease. In other words, as the number of trials increases the ratio of the observed frequency of an event to the total number of trials approaches the axiomatic definition of the probability of that event.

Table 11.1 has another feature also which should be noticed. How is it that the difference is always positive? Why are the actual frequencies always greater than the expected? This is perhaps just a chance. In another experiment they could be less, or sometimes less and sometimes more. If, by chance, in the beginning a lead is taken by the face six over other faces, that lead becomes easier to maintain, because it does not put the other faces to any more advantage or the face six to any less in the subsequent trials. However, suppose with a particular die this difference is always positive even when the experiment is performed not only hundreds but thousands, tens of thousands and millions of times. Then there begins to arise doubt about the perfectness of the die. It is quite possible that the die is not a perfect cube, and there is something in its shape that favours six. The mathematical definition of probability thus helps to check the hypothesis that the cube is perfect.

The Gambling House Trick

Gamblers, in a short time, win or lose, but, in the long run, while most gamblers are ruined, the gambling houses make profits. The theory of probability is nowhere better vindicated than in the inexorable fate of gamblers.

Take, for instance, the roulette wheel, a popular game in the fashionable casinos of America and Europe. The American roulette wheel has 38 compartments around its rim. The even-numbered, 2,4,6...36, are coloured black, the odd-numbered, 1,3,5...35, are coloured red, and the remaining two, marked 0 and 00, are green. The wheel is spun and a small ivory ball is rolled in the opposite sense. As the wheel slows down the ball drops into one of the slots. The wheel is true in the sense that the ball has an equal chance of falling in any slot.

The simplest betting game is that if you bet a dollar on red, then if the ball drops in a red slot, you get your dollar back plus one more dollar, otherwise you lose your dollar. Similarly, you may bet on black. There are 18 red slots, 18 black and 2 green. So the mathematical probability of winning is 18/38 and of losing 20/38. The slight edge towards loss is sufficient to ensure the ultimate ruin of the persistent player and high profits to the gambling house. All other types of permissible bets are also similarly weighted against the player.

Each spin of the wheel is independent of the other and can repeatedly end in favour of the player, but as the number of spins increases, the ratio of gain to loss gets closer to 18/20. Out of 38 spins, 30 might favour the lucky player, but out of 38,000 spins, roughly around 20,000 will go against him. In millions of spins the ratio 18/20 is very closely approached. The lesson is: in organized gambling, play a few times and run with whatever gains or losses you have, do not persist. Of course the best is not to play at all, but that is a moral, not mathematical, advice.

Frequency Distribution

The theory of probability, based upon the definitions and axioms of probability, enables the determination of probabilities of events more complicated than the simple examples discussed so far. Let us consider the following problem. A die is rolled a number of times, say, 20. It is possible that the face six (or any other particular face on which we choose to fix our attention) may not turn up even once in the 20 trials; it is also possible that it may turn up all the 20 times. In between these two extreme cases, there are nineteen other possibilities, namely, the face may show up once, twice, thrice.... nineteen times. What is the probability of any one of these events? In other words, what is the probability that the same face will come up r times in the total number of n consecutive trials, $0 \leq r \leq n$. Without going into the mathematics of this problem, we shall remark that these probabilities can be calculated. They are tabulated in the second column of Table 11.2, not as fractions but as percentages. For example, the theoretical probability that the face six will show up exactly 5 times in a sample of 20 throws is 12.9% or .129. The sum of this column is 99.6 and not 100 because the probabilities for more than 9 times have not been entered. Actually the table would be complete with entries in the first column going up to 20, but since the corresponding entries in the second column would be very small and in the third and fourth columns they are exactly zeros, we have not completed the table.

Table 11.2
Outcomes of 150 samples, each of 20 trials of rolling a die

Number of times face six showed up	Theoretical probability in %	Number of samples	Frequency of samples per hundred samples
0	2.6	4	2.7
1	10.4	7	4.7
2	19.8	30	20.0
3	23.7	35	23.3
4	20.2	29	19.3
5	12.9	20	13.3
6	6.4	15	10.0
7	2.6	6	4.0
8	0.8	1	0.7
9	0.2	3	2.0
	99.6	150	100.0

The experiment consisted of repeating a package of 20 throws 150 times. The third column of Table 11.2 shows the number of packages (or samples) against the number of times the face six showed up in them. For example, in 4 samples the face did not come up at all, and in 7 samples it came up once. The last column gives this frequency as a percentage of the total number of samples, so as to bring it to the same scale as the second column. The entries in the second column compare favourably with those in the last, except against the times 1,6,7,9. In fact the agreement is surprisingly good for 150 samples which is not a very large number. If larger number of samples, say 1000, had been observed, the agreement would have been still better.

The principle emerging out of Table 11.2 is essentially the same as of Table 11.1. A few repetitions of an experiment, the outcomes of which are governed by chance, will not generally show any pattern; they may be totally erratic. But as the number of repetitions increases, the results, proportionately, start falling in line with the theoretical probabilities. There begins to appear a law out of lawlessness, some order out of chaos.

Fig. 11.3 is a graphical representation of the data of Table 11.2. It is what statisticians call a histogram. It gives the frequency distribution of the occurrence under discussion. The area of a vertical rectangular strip gives the frequency of occurrence of the number at which the rectangle stands. A continuous curve is also drawn in the figure passing through the middle points of the tops of the vertical strips. Strictly speaking the continuous curve does not make much sense in the context of the present problem in which the data are discrete*. The occurrences are integral numbers 0,1,.....20 and not all the real numbers going from 0 to 20, and so the continuous curve is not justified. Imagine, however, that each sample, instead of 20 throws, consists of 100 throws. Then the discrete occurrences will range from integers 0 to 100, and on the same base length thickness of the vertical rectangular strips will be one-fifth of what it is now. As the sample size increases, the strips will get thinner and thinner, and the continuous curve would begin to make sense. Such a curve is called a probability curve.

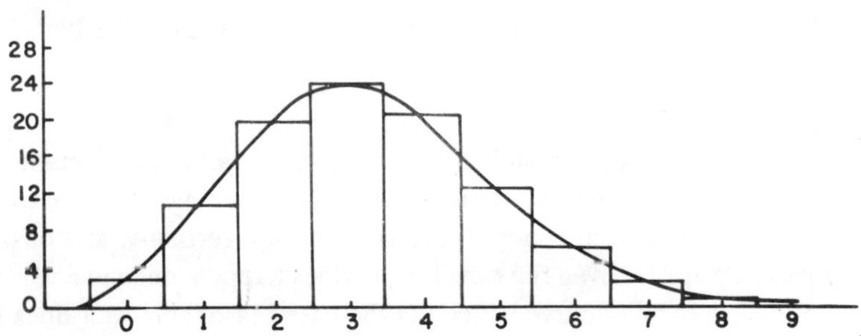

Fig. 11.3

Normal Curve

Fig. 11.4 shows the probability curve that the histogram of the last example would approximate to, if the sample size and the number of samples both become very large. The curve, like the definition of probability itself, represents a purely mathematical idea. It represents a hypothetical distribution of probabilities. It is the graph of a complicated function.** With respect to the axes of x and y as shown in the figure, the curve is symmetrical about the y-axis and theoretically extends endlessly on both sides, but beyond $x = 3$ on the right side and $x = -3$ on the left, it comes so close to the x-axis that its height beyond these points can be practically taken to be zero. Interpreted as a probability distribution curve, the probability that the variable x lies between two numbers, x_1 and x_2, is given by the area of the strip under the curve and between x_1, x_2 (shown shaded). The total area under the curve is 1. The area between $x = 0$

* See chapter 9, page 170, for appreciation of this point.

** The function is $\frac{1}{\sqrt{\pi}} e^{-x^2/2}$. The area under the curve of the function can be proved to be equal to 1.

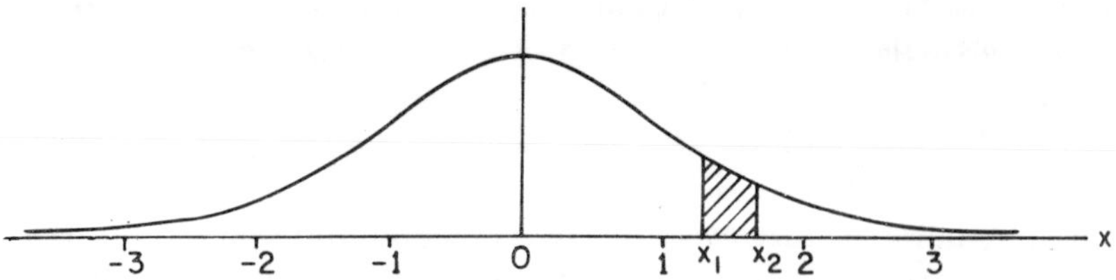

Fig. 11.4

and $x = 1$ is about .34, and between $x = 1$ and $x = 2$ is about .14. Thus about 95% of the area lies between $x = -2$ and $x = 2$. If the different values of x, theoretically varying from $-\infty$ to $+\infty$, constitute events the probabilities of whose occurrence are given by this probability curve, then the probability of x lying between -2 and 2 is about 95%, and the chances that it lies beyond $x = 3$ or before $x = -3$ are very small (about .26%).

This curve, known as the normal curve, is the most famous and popular curve in probability theory and statistics. It is, like all abstract mathematical ideas, a mathematical fiction, yet many chance happenings conform to it more or less. In chance occurrences there is never any certainty, any of the possibilities can happen, even the rarest event does happen once in a while, but a theoretical probability curve which fits the case reasonably well does help to estimate quantitatively the chance of an occurrence.

We have already mentioned how the probability distribution in the example of the last section approximates to the normal curve. To cite another similar example, suppose we want to estimate the average per capita income of inhabitants of a state. The state has a large population and it is not possible to approach every individual. So we take samples of, say, 50 persons each. For each group of 50 persons we calculate the average income by dividing their total income by 50. We take a few hundred, or, to get better results, a few thousand of such groups, and find the average income for each group. The graph of the frequency distribution of average incomes would be the normal curve. The point of symmetry of this curve would be an accurate estimate of the average income of the people of the state. There is, however, one important condition. The samples should be collected randomly. The persons who are approached to tell their income should not be selected on any social, educational, economic, age, sex or any other basis. There should be no bias for or against any person or group of persons. Every person should have an equal chance of being included in a sample; whether he is actually included or not is immaterial. This is often a difficult condition to satisfy. A mechanism of random selection from a heterogeneous and scattered population is not easy to evolve.

The statisticians tell us that in the above two examples it can be theoretically proved that the distribution is normal. There can be many other examples of this type. Many numerical data are symmetrically distributed about a mean position with deviations from the mean getting less and less in number as the magnitude of the deviation increases. The distribution looks more or less like normal, and a normal curve fits in fairly well. The errors in scientific measurements, for example, follow the normal distribution. It is an experimental fact that in precision measurements with sensitive instruments the repeated measurements of the same item yield never the same number but slightly different numbers. Why such a thing happens, nobody really knows. The continuous changes on the minutest scale in the observer's subjective reactions as well as in the objective reality are perhaps the cause of the variations. Since they are beyond control, they are regarded as chance variations, and the theory of probability applies to their distribution.

But all frequency distributions are not normal. Sometimes their graph may look like a normal curve, a bell-shaped curve symmetrical about a point, but may not exactly be so, for the normal curve is a very definite curve representing a mathematical function. Just as all oval-shaped curves are not ellipses, all bell-shaped curves are not normal. There are other frequency distributions which do not resemble the normal at all. The interesting thing, however, is that the normal curve has captured the imagination of the people to an extent which is hardly justified. Everybody who handles numerical data seems to have almost a subconscious faith in the normal curve. The mathematician thinks it is an experimental fact, the experimenter thinks it is a mathematical theorem. In reality it is neither. The temptation to fit a normal curve to a statistical distribution and to assume that all outliers are vagrants to be smoothed out may generally do no harm but at times may be very unfair. The learned professor who draws a normal curve through the examination scores of a class of students, and grades the top 10% as *A*, the next 40% as *B*, the lower 40% as *C*, and gives the failing grade of *D* to the remaining 10%, may be grossly unfair in his evaluation. Even a class of hundred students is not a sufficiently large sample to conform to this pattern. None may deserve to fail, or none may deserve an *A*.

Pollster's Problem

A national election in a democratic society where each citizen votes freely and fearlessly is an exciting event. Who will be the next president or prime minister is a question everybody asks and volunteers to answer. The pollsters get into business and make forecasts, not on the basis of their personal predilections, not through astrology, but through getting to know the minds of the people.

The pollsters really do not predict, they estimate. They select a small sample of the entire electorate, a few thousand voters out of millions, and find out how they would vote. The presumption is that the percentage of like-minded voters in the population is, within specifiable limits, nearly the same as in the sample. The reason for this presumption and the conditions under which it will be justified will be clear from the following model.

Suppose there is a large number of balls in an urn. They are similar in all respects except that some of them are white, others black. We want to estimate the proportion of white and black balls in the urn. We shake the urn well so that all the balls are thoroughly mixed, and draw out a ball blindly. If the ratio of the number of white balls to that of black is x/y, then, by the mathematical definition, the probability of drawing a white ball is $x/(x + y)$ and a black ball $y/(x + y)$. Let us suppose that the total number of balls in the urn is so large that drawing a few balls does not appreciably change the ratio x/y. If we draw a hundred balls, then we expect that $100x/(x + y)$ of them would be white and $100y/(x + y)$ black. Of course, our expectation is not likely to be fulfilled accurately, but by what we have been discussing, the larger the number of balls we draw, the closer we shall be to this ratio. For a given number of balls drawn out, let the actual ratio be a/b. Then we can estimate what percent chance is there for a/b to differ from x/y by as much as it does. The sample size (that is, the number of balls drawn) can be suitably chosen to make this chance small, and thereby the ratio x/y can be estimated within known limits of error.

In 1948 Harry Truman and Thomas Dewey were the presidential contestants in U.S.A. The pre-election scene was covered by three pollsters, and all of them, after independent surveys, declared Dewey the winner with 5% lead. The result was just the opposite. Truman won by 5% lead. What went wrong?

The crucial condition in the model is that the sample should be randomly chosen. The chance of any one particular ball being drawn should be the same as of any other. The pollsters must therefore ensure that there is no bias against any voter in the entire electorate. It is not easy to devise such a method of conducting opinion poll. It is easier to contact people of one type than the other, urban dwellers rather than village folks, the educated with definite work rather than the illiterate and the unemployed, the rich with telephone connections rather than the poor with no homes. Pollsters in U.S.A. in 1948 failed to survey random samples. Since then, however, they have not erred and their forecasts in all subsequent elections have turned out to be true. It is because the methods of selecting random samples too have been the subject of careful study, and the reliability of sample surveys has increased.

Heredity and Chance

Perhaps the most spectacular breakthroughs in science in the second half of the present century have been in biology where the chemical nature of life at the molecular level has been revealed more and more. Particularly significant have been the researches into the nature of genetic material and the mechanism of heredity. It is in the latter that chance seems to play a large part. Without going into the biochemical details, the modern theory of heredity is somewhat as follows.

The cell of a living organism is the smallest unit of life characteristic of the species to which the organism belongs. The nucleus of the cell contains thin elongated strands called chromosomes. These are ultra-microscopic bodies made of large molecules of protein and DNA (deoxyribonucleic acid). The DNA molecule is the genetic material, the carrier of all information and instructions about how the individual will grow and function. The cell of a human being contains forty six chromosomes, that of the fruitfly *Drosophila melanogaster* contains eight, that of the onion sixteen. These occur in homologous pairs. (A homologous pair of chromosomes consists of two chromosomes carrying the same genetic information, duplicate of each other, very largely but not exactly identical). The human chromosomes are twenty-three homologous pairs.

The individual organism starts its life as a single cell and grows through multiplication of cells by continuing duplication. The DNA molecule is in the shape of a double helix, a double chain of organic molecules coiled as if round a long cylinder. The way a cell duplicates itself is explained satisfactorily by this structure. Each resulting cell contains an exact copy of the chromosomes of the original parent cell. Every cell of a living body thus carries within itself the information about what the whole body is and going to be, including, of course, the part it itself has to play. It is as if each player in a musical orchestra has the complete musical script before him so that, while he plays his own part, he remains in tune with the rest.

The cells used in reproduction, the male sperms and the female eggs, the gametes, as they are called, are of a different type. Each gamete contains only half the number of chromosomes of the cell, one of each homologous pair. The human gamete thus contains twenty-three chromosomes. The gametes are produced by the division of ordinary cells. When the male gametes, the sperms, come close to the female gametes, the eggs, a sperm combines with an egg to produce a complete cell with the normal number of chromosomes, forty-six for the human cell, each chromosome in the egg finding its homologous partner from the sperm. This forms the nucleus for a new individual.

What genetic material from the parents has combined to give the offspring its genetic characteristics is a matter of chance. Let us see how the process works in a simple hypothetical case of an organism whose cell contains three pairs, six in all, of chromosomes. Fig. 11.5 shows in how many ways a complete cell can divide to produce two gametes. Each complete cell contains three pairs of homologous chromosomes marked $A_1 A_2$, $B_1 B_2$, $C_1 C_2$ in the cell from the male parent and $A_3 A_4$, $B_3 B_4$, $C_3 C_4$ in the cell from the female, (Fig. 11.5).

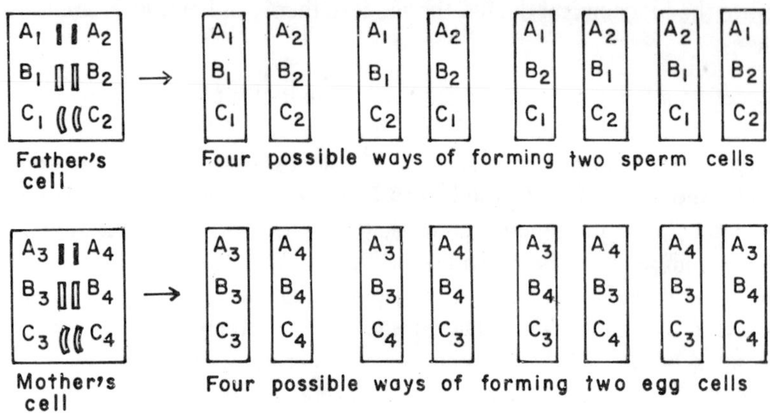

Fig. 11.5

There are four possible ways in which the complete cell can divide to produce two sex cells (gametes), such that each gamete contains one chromosome from each of the three pairs. Thus a resulting gamete can be any one of the eight types. Each type of gamete from the male can combine with each type from the female, the total number of different possible types of genetic combinations in the offspring being $8 \times 8 = 64$. Any one of these sixty-four combinations is equally possible. With thousands of cells dividing into sex cells with random distribution of chromosomes, 12.5% of the sperms are expected to be of any one of the eight types, and similarly 12.5% of the eggs. Any one of the sperms, by chance, would combine with any one of the eggs to fertilize it. The other thousands or perhaps millions of sperms and eggs never get a chance to meet and are wasted.

The above hypothetical example is of a living organism with only three pairs of chromosomes in its cell. A human cell has twenty three pairs, so that there are 2^{23} types of sperms, each somewhat different from the other in its genetic content, which a single man carries within him, and the same number of different types of eggs a woman carries. The union of a particular couple can result in any one of the $2^{23} \times 2^{23} = 2^{46} \approx 7.0369 \times 10^{13} \approx$ seventy thousand million (seventy thousand American billion) different genetic combinations. This does not take into account the immense element of chance in crossing over of chromosomes before gamete formation, the sexual union of individuals and of the female conceiving. No wonder no two humans, no two insects, no two leaves are exactly alike.

There is overwhelming evidence in science that in the reproduction of life chance plays an important role. Nothing seems to be predetermined. Starting from the sexual union of two adults of the same species and upto the birth of a new individual, at every stage there are chance happenings. Add to it the chance of mutations that are believed to occur in genetic material causing biological evolution of species. Out of almost unlimited possibilities one event happens, and there is no evidence that that particular event was predetermined. A handicapped child or a genius, nature seems to leave it to chance.

Conclusion

Coming back to where we started, is chance the operative principle of nature? Yes, perhaps at the individual level of an atom, a molecule, a living organism, a planet or a star, but at each level the law of large numbers also operates mysteriously producing a direction, an order, a principle, a seemingly cause-and-effect chain. God does seem to play dice, despite Einstein's angry protest, but the apparently chance moves weave out beautiful patterns building into functionally efficient and purposeful designs which could hardly be the product of pure chance.

FROM THE GALLERY OF MATHEMATICIANS

Pierre de Fermat

A lawyer by profession and enjoying a high status and financial security all his life, Fermat (French, 1601-1665) has been called the greatest among the amateur mathematicians. He shares with his contemporary Pascal (French, 1623-62), the credit for laying the foundation of the theory of probability. In a brief exchange of correspondence with Pascal in 1654, Fermat discussed the solution of a problem posed by a gambler. The solution was based on the principle of evaluating the expectation of a player as the ratio of outcomes favourable to him to the total number of possible outcomes.

By advancing algebra as a formal analytical tool and using it in geometry, Fermat gave a system of analytical geometry almost identical with but independent of Descartes, and was the first to apply it to three-dimensional space. Descartes had confined himself to two dimensions.

Fermat is also credited with having conceived and applied the leading ideas of calculus prior to Newton and Leibniz. His greatest contributions, however, were in the theory of numbers, a subject called by some as the 'Queen of Mathematics', but which has found no place in this introductory book because, like all queens, it has little practical use.

R. A. Fisher

It is difficult to find in the modern world an area of human activity or branch of knowledge where statistics based on the theory of probability does not find application. None of its applications is, however, more profound than in probing the mystery of heredity in the biological world. In fact much of modern statistics has grown hand in hand with biometry (application of mathematical methods to biology) and genetics (the science of evolution of species and heredity). R.A. Fisher (British, 1890-1962) was the pioneer in this field.

After studying physics and mathematics at Cambridge, and a few years of varied life, Fisher joined in 1919 the Rothamsted Experimental Station in England as a one-man statistics department. Within fifteen years he had established himself as the leading statistician and genetist of the era. In 1933 he became Galton professor of eugenics at University College, London, and ten years later moved to Cambridge as professor of genetics. Modern statistics bears indelible marks of his achievements.

EXERCISES

1. Two coins, a rupee and a half-rupee, are tossed. What is the probability that
   (i) the rupee shows head and a half-rupee shows tail?
   (ii) neither of the coins shows a head?
   (iii) at least one coin shows a head?
2. Three identical coins are tossed. What is the probability of the following events?
   (i) Exactly two heads.
   (ii) One head and two tails.
   (iii) Not all tails.
3. Two coins are tossed together a thousand times. How many times do you expect both of them showing heads? Will your expectation be fulfilled? What result do you expect if the coins are tossed 10,000 times?
4. A die is rolled. What is the probability of each of the following events?
   (i) An odd number.
   (ii) A number greater than 4.
   (iii) The number 5 not showing up.
5. Two dice are rolled. What is the probability of the following events?
   (i) The sum of numbers is 8.
   (ii) Both dice show the same number.
   (iii) A six shows on one die and a three on the other.
   (iv) The sum of numbers is greater than 8.
   (v) The sum of numbers is less than 9.

6. A card is drawn at random from a well-shuffled deck of 52 playing cards. What is the probability that

   (i) a king is drawn, (ii) a spade is drawn?

7. Two cards are drawn one after another at random from a well-shuffled deck of 52 playing cards. What is the probability of the first being a king and the second a queen if

   (i) the first card is put back in the deck before the second is drawn,

   (ii) the first card is not replaced in the deck?

8. There are 6 blue, 4 yellow and 3 red balls of the same size and material in a box. One ball is picked up at random. What is the probability of picking

   (i) a blue ball, (ii) a black ball, (iii) a yellow or a red ball, (iv) a yellow, a red or a blue ball?

9. A pollster takes up the telephone directories of Bombay, Calcutta, Delhi and Madras and calls 10, 000 numbers at random to find out which party, *A* or *B*, they are supporting in a national election. He finds 80% support for *A*, and therefore predicts that *A* is going to win. He is proved wrong. What was wrong with his method?

10. It is required to estimate the average height of 10 year-old boys (age between $9\frac{1}{2}$ and $10\frac{1}{2}$ years) in a city where all children are required by law to attend school. What procedure would you suggest?

ANSWERS

1. (i) 1/4, (ii) 1/4, (iii) 3/4.
2. (i) 3/8, (ii) 3/8, (iii)7/8.
3. x times where x is close to 250; y times where y is close to 2,500; but y/10,000 will be closer to 1/4 than x/1,000.
4. (i) 1/2, (ii) 1/3, (iii) 5/6.
5. (i) 5/36, (ii) 1/6, (iii) 1/18, (iv) 5/18, (v) 13/18.
6. (i) 1/13, (ii) 1/4.
7. (i) $(4/52)^2$, (ii) $(4/52) \times (4/51)$.
8. (i) 6/13, (ii) 0, (iii) 7/13, (iv) 1.
9. The sample was not random. Only telephone holders were considered.
10. Select at random a few, say 10, boys of age 10 from each school and find their average height; then find the average of all the averages.

Chapter 12

Queen or Servant

"As far as the laws of mathematics refer to reality, they are not certain; as far as they are certain, they do not refer to reality."

—Albert Einstein (1879–1955)

The above quotation pithily describes the nature of mathematics in relation to its applications. Within its own realm of symbols precisely defined and rules of operations axiomatically accepted, mathematics makes exact statements about relationships among sets of defined symbols. It proceeds from statement to statement through ruthless application of deductive logic producing propositions which are valid and certain within their own premises. But when they are applied to describe real situations they become fuzzy and are valid only within limits.

The Ideal and the Real

Take, for example, the following mathematical proposition: *If L is the circumference of a great circle of a sphere, then the surface area of the sphere is* L^2/π. (Proof: If r is the radius of the sphere, the circumference L of its great circle is $2\pi r$, and its surface area S is $4\pi r^2$. Hence $S = L^2/\pi$.) This is an absolutely certain and exact statement. The terms sphere, surface area, great circle are precisely defined in Euclidean geometry which is itself based on a few definitions and axioms. Given a number L, L^2/π is a definite number. There is no inexactness in the statement anywhere. Now consider the following statement: *If L is the length of the equator, then the surface area of the earth is* L^2/π.The statement refers to reality, but obviously is highly inexact. A less inexact relationship between the two may be obtained by taking into account the deviation of the earth's shape from a sphere. Still it will be inexact. Corrections due to many more factors may be incorporated in the equation connecting the length of the equator with the earth's total surface, but still it will represent an ideal situation different from the real, for reality is always too complicated to be described precisely.

Mathematics deals with the ideal, the ideal of its own making, and its statements are strictly true within that ideal. The moment it steps out into reality, it loses its grip on certainty. In its own ivory tower mathematics is beautifully perfect, in the rough and tumble of actualities its image gets blurred. But what is lost in beauty is gained in utility, for a civilization without mathematics is inconceivable.

Beauty versus Utility

The two faces of mathematics, one perfect but of no use, the other imperfect but highly serviceable, have their devotees among the world's great mathematicians. To some mathematics is a queen, a paragon of beauty and perfection, sitting on a high pedestal, commanding awe and adoration, serving no mundane ends, fulfilling no purpose except to satisfy the emotional needs of her subjects. Their motives in pursuing the study of and research in mathematics is to discover more treasures of beautiful forms for purely aesthetic reasons. They are no party to dragging mathematics down to the level of human endeavours in science, engineering, commerce, etc. to serve social and material ends. On the other hand there are mathematicians to whom mathematics is an indispensable servant, an efficient aid, a resourceful companion, a dependable guide, giving and taking, helping to understand the mysteries of nature or to solve worldly problems.

The distinction between these two aspects of mathematics has existed from the earliest times, but it is only in the last about hundred fifty years that it has become sharply defined. Till about the middle of the last century most top-ranking mathematicians who gave mathematics a beauty of form with aesthetic appeal were, perhaps primarily, sharpening it as a tool, for investigating nature and advancing engineering and technology. Descartes, Leibniz, Newton, Euler, Lagrange, and many others who are remembered as mathematicians today were in their lifetimes physicists, astronomers and engineers too. They were interested in physical problems and practised mathematics as a practical art. Because of their superior intellectual capabilities for abstraction, they could also see the tool separate from its function, and gave it a shape which made it more versatile and a finish which made it more appealing.

Pure Mathematics

There has been a phenomenal growth of knowledge in mathematics, as in all other sciences, in the last hundred years or so. The growth has been exponential, that is, the more it has grown, the more rapidly it grows. The process is continuing unabated. This has naturally resulted in the decline of the universalists and the rise of specialists. More and more people, even at the highest levels of intelligence, are able to cope, in their individual capacity, with narrower and narrower areas of knowledge. In mathematics, inspite of the continuous assertion by all its devotees that all mathematics is one, the philosophy and motivations of the worshippers of the queen have come to differ sharply from the admirers of the serviceable maid.

Pure mathematics, as the queenly subject shorn of all metaphors is called, has been defined by Bertrand Russell as follows:

> "Pure mathematics is the class of all propositions of the form '*p* implies *q*', where *p* and *q* are propositions containing one or more variables, the same in the two propositions, and neither *p* nor *q* containing any constants except logical constants."

Less pedantic in words but identical in sense is the definition given by C.I. Lewis:

> "A mathematical system is any set of strings of recognizable marks in which some of the strings are taken initially and the remainder derived from these by operations performed according to rules which are independent of any meanings assigned to the marks."

More briefly, in A.N. Whitehead's words, "mathematics in its widest sense is the development of all types of formal deductive reasoning."

Marshall Stone (American, 1903–   ) puts forth the same view when he says,

> "The fact is that mathematics can equally well be treated as a game which has to be played with meaningless pieces according to formal and essentially arbitrary rules, but which becomes intrinsically interesting because there is such a great fascination in discovering and exploiting the complex patterns of play permitted by the rules. Mathematicians increasingly tend to approach their subject in a spirit which reflects this point of view."

This approach has produced a mass of pure mathematics in the present century which makes sense only within its own domain of reasoning and only to those who laboriously seek initiation into it. It is the new esoteric knowledge, more cabalistic than any occult and mysterious practices of ancient cultures or primitive tribes. It seeks no points of contact with experience or reality. The practitioners of this art boastfully proclaim, (to paraphrase Bertrand Russell), that they do not know what they are talking about, and drink to their queen the toast proposed by G.H. Hardy (British, 1887-1947) – "Here is to pure mathematics; may it never have any use."

Art for Art's Sake

Splitting hairs in an ivory tower is not everybody's meat. There have been vigorous protests against this 'logic for logic's sake' mentality taking hold of mathematics. Richard Courant expressed his dissent forcefully as follows:

> "A serious threat to the very life of science is implied in the assertion that mathematics is nothing but a system of conclusions drawn from the

> definitions and postulates that must be consistent but otherwise created by the freewill of the mathematician. If this description were accurate, mathematics would not attract any intelligent person. It would be a game with definitions, rules and syllogisms without motive or goal. The notion that the intellect can create meaningful postulational systems at its whim is a deceptive half- truth. Only under the discipline of responsibility to the organic whole, only guided by intrinsic necessity, can the free mind achieve results of scientific value."

According to John von Neumann (Hungarian – American, 1903-57), mathematical ideas are empirical in origin, although the genealogy is long and obscure. But once they are so conceived, they begin to live a peculiar life of their own governed by almost aesthetical motives. It is the latter development that appeals to the pure mathematician, and it is good that it does, for the abstract generalizations in mathematics have produced the true weapons with which to probe the nature of the real world. There is no disagreement about the usefulness of pure mathematics, but only up to the point the pure mathematician does not disclaim the original source of mathematical ideas, and does not cut himself away from them like a kite cut loose. To carry the simile a little further, the kite soars to great heights and glides gracefully among the clouds only so long as there is the string to pull it up whenever it loses its balance. Neumann warns of the danger of decline of mathematics if it cuts itself away from its original moorings and drifts aimlessly in the realm of pure logic unrelated to realistic thought:

> "As a mathematical discipline travels far from its empirical source, or still more, if it is second or third generation only indirectly inspired by ideas coming from reality, it is beset with very grave dangers. It becomes more and more purely *l'art pour l'art*. This need not be bad, if the field is surrounded by correlated subjects which still have closer empirical connections, or if the discipline is under the influence of men with an exceptionally well-developed taste. But at great distance from its empirical source, or after much abstract inbreeding, a mathematical subject is in danger of degeneration. In any event when this stage is reached the only remedy seems to be the rejuvenating return to the source, the reinjection of more or less directly empirical ideas."

There are, however, the extremists of the other school who are not convinced. Jean Dieudonne, a leading French mathematician of the Bourbaki group (page 227) does not share Neumann's fears:

> "I would like to express how little history has been willing to conform to the pious platitudes of the prophets of doom, who regularly warn us of the dire consequences mathematics is bound to incur by cutting itself off from the application to other sciences. I do not intend to say that close contact with other fields is not beneficial to all parties concerned, but

even if mathematics were to be forcibly separated from all other channels of human endeavour, there would remain food for centuries of thought in big problems we still have to solve within our science."

The Challenge of Natural Numbers

In this book it is the utilitarian view of mathematics that has been emphasized. In every chapter the usefulness of a new idea or the need for extension or generalization of an old one has been sought to be brought out. The need may be purely logical, as in the extensions of geometry, or severely practical, as in the development of calculus. The usefulness may be immediately apparent, as in probability theory, or may appear much after the germination and the growth of the idea, as in Boolean algebra, matrices or Riemannian geometry. No glimpse of the 'useless' part of mathematics has been given in this book, much of it being too abstract to be introduced to nontechnical readers. There is, however, one subject which is without any use but is easy to appreciate. It deals with the properties of natural numbers, and is called the theory of numbers. A glimpse of it may not be out of place.

The natural numbers, 1, 2, 3, 4,..........., have fascinated people since the earliest of times. Accomplished mathematicians as well as ordinary people have been tempted to formulate problems and attempt solutions concerning them. It is because the problems are often deceptively simple in their appearance but not easy to solve. The problems can usually be stated in simple terms, free from the usual jargon of mathematics, and can be understood by everybody. In some cases solutions are also simple and free from the esoteric language of mathematics, in other cases solutions have defied mathematicians for centuries. For the last over two thousand years the theory of numbers has been a favourite subject of research by leading mathematicians and thousands of amateurs. It is the oldest part of mathematics, but contains some of the most challenging problems still awaiting solution. And with all its fascination, it is practically useless to science, engineering or technology.

The Riddle of Primes

Among the natural numbers some are primes and others are composite. A prime number is one whose only divisors are 1 and itself. For example 2, 3, 5, 7, 11, 13, 17, 19, 23, 29, 31, 37 are the first twelve prime numbers. A fairly simple proof that there are infinitely many primes has been known since long, and is attributed to Euclid. There are some pairs of primes which differ from each other by two. For example, 3,5; 5,7; 11,13; 29,31; 41,43. These are called twin primes. It is still not proved or disproved that there are infinity of such twins.

A Russian mathematician, Goldbach, in 1742 made a conjecture that every even number greater than 2 can be expressed as the sum of two primes. For example, $4 = 2 + 2$, $8 = 5 + 3$, $12 = 7 + 5$. There may be more ways than one of doing so. For instance, $48 = 5 + 43 = 7 + 41 = 17 + 31$. Nobody has been able to prove or disprove this conjecture.

For very large numbers it is not easy to know whether a number is prime or not. There is no mathematical formula which will produce all the primes. Even the attempt to find a formula which will yield only primes has not succeeded. Fermat (page 213) gave the formula

$$F_n = 2^{2^n} + 1, \quad n = 1, 2, 3, 4, \ldots\ldots,$$

thinking that this always gives a prime number. $F_1 = 5, F_2 = 17, F_3 = 257, F_4 = 65537$ are all known to be primes. $F_5 = 4,294,967,297$ was believed to be prime until Euler (page 225) gave its factors:

$$4,294,967,297 = 641 \times 6,700,417$$

It is obvious that for large n, F_n becomes very large indeed. For $n = 73$, F_n is so large that it is absolutely impossible to write it in full, and so nobody knows what that number exactly is. Yet, such is the nature and power of mathematical reasoning, it has been proved that it is not a prime.

These are just a few examples of how challenging and at the same time how useless questions about primes can be.

Quaint Properties

There are various types of strange properties that crazy amateurs discover in particular numbers which become teasers for mathematicians. There are, for instance, numbers which have been called perfect. A perfect number is one which is equal to the sum of all its divisors, including 1 but excluding itself. For example, the divisors of 6 are 1, 2, 3 (excluding 6), and $6 = 1 + 2 + 3$. Also the divisors of 28 are 1, 2, 4, 7, 14 (excluding 28), and $28 = 1 + 2 + 4 + 7 + 14$. It has been proved that an even number is perfect if, and only if, it is of the form $2^n(2^{n+1} - 1)$ where $2^{n+1} - 1$ is prime*. What about odd perfect numbers? Are there any? The question is unanswered.

Then there is the theorem which has become famous in history as Fermat's last theorem. Consider the equation

$$x^2 + y^2 = z^2$$

This is only the algebraic statement of the theorem of Pythagoras in geometry. There are many triplets of natural numbers which satisfy this equation, such as

$$3^2 + 4^2 = 5^2, \quad 5^2 + 12^2 = 13^2, \quad 8^2 + 15^2 = 17^2.$$

---

* The curious reader may test this formula by locating some other perfect numbers. The next one is for $n = 4$.

Are there any natural numbers which would satisfy the equation

$$x^3 + y^3 = z^3, \text{ or } x^4 + y^4 = z^4,$$

or, in general, $x^n + y^n = z^n$, where n is a positive integer?

No such numbers have been found, nor the attempt to prove that no such numbers exist has yet met with success. Fermat in the margin of his notebook noted that he had assuredly found an admirable proof of this, but did not write out the proof. Since all efforts to prove the theorem have failed so far, it is now suspected that Fermat might have been wrong in thinking that he had a proof.

What are popularly known as magic squares are another example of problems involving natural numbers. The 5×5 square given below has numbers 1 to 25 arranged such that the sum of every row, every column and every diagonal is the same, 65. Many such arrangements are possible. There are many variations of magic squares, extending to magic cubes and other regular geometrical figures, and a large amount of literature exists on the subject.

19	23	2	6	15
22	1	10	14	18
5	9	13	17	21
8	12	16	25	4
11	20	24	3	7

There is a story about Ramanujan (page 226) who had a peculiar mastery over strange properties of numbers. Once Hardy visited him in a hospital where he was lying ill. Ramanujan asked Hardy the number of the taxi he travelled in. "1729, a very uninteresting number," Hardy said. "Oh no, on the contrary it is an extremely interesting number; it is the smallest number which can be expressed as the sum of two cubes: $1729 = 1^3 + 12^3 = 9^3 + 10^3$," replied Ramanujan to an astonished Hardy.

Though much of research in the theory of numbers is without use, it would be wrong to think that it is irrelevant. In the words of G.D. Birkhoff (American, 1884-1944), "the simple conundrums about integers have been a source of revitalization of mathematics over the centuries." Theory of numbers has an impact on many branches of mathematics. Some parts of mathematics may be less useful to science, engineering or daily life than others, some may even be totally inapplicable so far, but all mathematics is intrinsically one and no part

Ramanujan returned to India in 1919, a sick man, and died of tuberculosis the following year.

"Nicolas Bourbaki"

In distant future the most famous and versatile mathematician of the present times would perhaps be a Frenchman with a Greek name who never existed. Bourbaki is the author of an ambitious work, Elements de Mathematique, which beginning in 1939 has already run into over three dozen volumes with many more still to come. Merging their individual identities under a common pseudonym, (a gesture so uncommon in a highly egotistical society), a group of very distinguished French mathematicians have joined in a cooperative effort to present the whole of mathematics in an axiomatic, abstract and general form. Andre Weil, regarded by some as the greatest living mathematician of the world, and Jean Dieudonne were among the founding fathers of this group, whose membership, generally between ten and twenty at a time, goes on changing. The emphasis is on youth, and both Weil and Dieudonne retired from the group on attaining the age of fifty. In a playful vein and jest with posterity, Bourbaki has been given a hometown, Nancy, a place in France which is the birthplace of a number of celebrated mathematicians of this century, and is supposed to be a Professor at the University of Nancago, a nonexistent place made out of Nancy and Chicago.

Some Books on Related Topics

Bell, E.T.: *Men of Mathematics*, Simon and Schuster, New York, 1937.

Bell, E.T.: *Mathematics, Queen and Servant of Science*, McGraw Hill, 1951.

Bergamini, David and the Editors of Life: *Mathematics*, Life Science Library, Time Inc., New York, 1963.

Carter, L.R. and Huzan, E.: *Computers and their Use - An Introduction*, Hodder and Stroughton, 1984.

Hogben, Lancelot: *The Wonderful World of Mathematics*; Doubleday and Company, New York, 1968.

Jain, V.K.: *Basic Programming with Applications*; Tata Mcgraw Hill, 1986.

Klein, Morris: *Introduction to Mathematics* - A Survey of Mathematical Ideas and their Relations to other Fields of Knowledge.

Klein, Morris: *Mathematics, The Loss of Certainty*; Oxford University Press, New York, 1980.

Mathematics: An Introduction to its Spirit and Use—Readings from Scientific American, 1979.

Mathematics in the Modern World: Readings from Scientific American, W.H. Freeman and Company, San Francisco, 1968.

Newman, J.R.: *The World of Mathematics,* Volumes I and II; Simon and Schauster, New York, 1956.

Rajaraman, V.: *Principles of Computer Programming,* Prentice Hall of India Limited, 1986.

Satya Prakash: *Founders of Sciences in Ancient India*; Research Institute of Ancient Scientific Studies, New Delhi, 1965.

Turnbull, H.W: *The Great Mathematicians,* New York University Press.

Index

Many terms occur repeatedly in this book. This index indicates where the term is defined or explained.

RELATED BOOKS

THE C LANGUAGE TRAINER WITH C++

Jayasri, J.

This book covers the basic concepts of languages, the syntax of languages, the graphics features of C and introduces the Object Oriented Programming in language C++. All programs are tried in Turbo C compiler and the corrected programs are presented in the book. More than 100 programs are included in this book to exercise the brains of the reader. Programming solutions are also given in the last chapter for the reader's benefit.

Contents: Introduction to Computer Languages. Introduction to 'C', Lexical Elements of 'C' Language. Entering and Executing A 'C' Program. Input/output in 'C'. Operation and Expressions. Control Structures. 'C' Functions. Arrays and Strings. Pointers, Structures and Unions. 'C' Files 'C' Preprocessors and Command Line Arguments. Graphics Features in 'C'.

81-224-0551-7 **1993** **284 pp** **In press**

UNIX OPERATING SYSTEMS

Azam, M.

A comprehensive guide to learning UNIX, this book gradually moves from the elementary principles of the subject to the more complex concepts. Adopts an integrated approach in treatment of commands and concepts. The lucidity of the text accompanied by the numerous exercises provide a theoretical and practical knowledge of UNIX.

Contents: The Operating System. Structure of UNIX. Getting Started with UNIX-1. Getting Started with UNIX-IIvi Editor. Shell Programming. Special Utilities. System Administration. Program Development Aids. Hello 'C' Shelt. UNIX Internals. Fast Track.

81-224-0552-5 **1993** **248 pp** **In press**

INTRODUCTION TO COMPUTER SCIENCE

Govindaraju, S., M. Chandrasekaran, A. Abdul Haq & T.R. Narayanan

The overwhelming demand for computer professionals has led the authors to write an introductory text initiating readers to the theory and applications of Computer Science. The progress from fundamental concepts to advance programmes is in tune with the prescribed syllaby for the +1 and +2 students of Computer Science. Also recommend for college students for their subsidiary course and other non-computer professionals as an introductory text.

Contents: Overview of Computers. Information Representation. Algorithm and Flow-charting. Theoretical Models of a Computer. An Operating System for Personal Computer. Software Packages. Programming in BASIC. Information Processing Computer Graphics. Pascal from BASIC. Artificial intelligence.

81-224-0425-1 **1992** **239 pp** **Paper** **Rs. 70.00**